THE LIBRARY OF CONGRESS

The west front of the 1897 Thomas Jefferson Building of the Library of Congress.

Westview Library of Federal Departments, Agencies, and Systems

The National Park Service, William C. Everhart

The Forest Service, Michael Frome

The Smithsonian Institution, Paul H. Oehser

The Bureau of Indian Affairs, Theodore W. Taylor

THE LIBRARY OF CONGRESS

Charles A. Goodrum and
Helen W. Dalrymple

OXFORD & IBH PUBLISHING CO. PVT. LTD.

Westview Library of Federal Departments, Agencies, and Systems

All photographs courteously provided by the Library of Congress.

Published in 1982 in the United States of America by
    Westview Press, Inc.
    5500 Central Avenue
    Boulder, Colorado 80301
    Frederick A. Praeger, President and Publisher

First Indian Edition 1987
Second printing 1987
ISBN 81-204-0197-2

Rs. 96.00

Published in India by Mohan Primlani for Oxford & IBH Publishing Co. Pvt. Ltd., 66 Janpath, New Delhi-110 001 and printed at Rekha Printers Private Limited, A-102/1, Okhla Industrial Area, Phase II, New Delhi-110 020   2-T7-10

CONTENTS

PREFACE

This book, an attempt to describe how the world's largest library works, was first written at the beginning of the seventies. At that time the Library of Congress was struggling to cope with four recent shocks that had jarred the even tenor of its ways. The intellectual community was reacting to the challenges of Sputnik and Soviet technology, the social community was building the Great Society, Congress was expanding under a series of structural reforms, and the Library's traditional role of the keeper of all knowledge placed it at ground zero in the information explosion. It was an interesting time to write about.

A decade has passed since then, and, assuming that enough progress must have occurred to require at least an updating of the statistics, the publisher asked us to make the text current. We started the task routinely enough, but soon learned to our chagrin that there had been more dramatic changes in the Library's life in the seventies than in the previous fifty years.

Under the Legislative Reorganization Act of 1970, the Legislative Reference Service had gone from 306 employees when the Act was passed to become the Congressional Research Service with a staff of 868 in 1980. More important, both its purpose and its way of doing business had changed. The Copyright Office had undergone a revolution as the result of the first statutory revision of the copyright law in 64 years, and the Copyright Law of 1976 had turned a book-oriented register into a cable television, videodisc, phonograph franchise factory. The Division for the Blind, with a budget of $7 million in 1970, had become the National Library Service for the Blind and Physically Handicapped, with a 1980 appropriation of $34.5 million (larger than the total budget of many major universities). And so on, through dozens of departments and divisions.

We found that the questions for (and about) the Library had changed too. In 1970 we were asking, Should the Library be moved to the Executive Branch? For the moment, that question is moot. By 1980, the question had become, What do you use a national library for? or even, Do we need a national library at all? In 1971 Library officials were worried about providing printed catalog cards at the rate of 74 million a year to 25,000 "outside" libraries. By 1981 the Library had closed down its own card catalogs completely, was totally reliant on its computer to control and retrieve its current and future holdings, and had turned to printing cards a single copy at a time as outside libraries requested an entry for their traditional catalogs. We found that revisionism had even overtaken the history of the Library, and two of its hoariest legends required modification.

Ultimately almost every page of the original book had to be rewritten. New programs and vastly new and larger problems required the creation of four completely new chapters just to get the story caught up to the necessarily brisk account of the original volume, and once more we are in debt to everyone who helped us. We returned to the organizational units and asked not, What are the figures now? as we had expected, but, What's new? What are you doing now? What will you be doing in 2001? What we learned is the book before you.

This book is in no way an official statement of the Library management. Between us, the authors have spent over fifty years on the Library staff, but neither of us is presently employed by the Library, and the perceptions of the institution are neither ours nor the Library leadership's as such. Although the reader is always at the mercy of what the authors decided to talk about, what is reported here is (if our intent has been successful) what the concerned people throughout the Library's middle and upper management are thinking. The thoughts include some by "the administration," but the administration made no attempt whatever to suggest what we should say. By the same token, staff members throughout the Library gave us great amounts of time, with great civility and candor, for which we are most grateful.

Although we tried to keep the statistics to a minimum throughout the book, one of the aspects of the Library that is clearly news is its scale. Thus, we tried to provide figures when they would give a basis for comparison with other institutions with which the reader would be familiar. Whenever a year date is given, it is a federal government fiscal year, which runs from October 1 to September 30. The year date refers to the year of the final date, so a sentence reading, "In 1980, the Library discarded 8.5 million volumes," means "in fiscal year 1980," or literally, "from October 1979 through September 1980, the Library . . ."

Enough. This is an exciting time at the Library of Congress. Not since the institution moved out of the Capitol to start its new life as the national library in the great gray building across the street has there been such a feeling of "the end of one book, the beginning of another." We hope we have been able to capture a little of that excitement for you in the volume that follows.

Charles A. Goodrum
Helen W. Dalrymple

Washington, D.C.

INTRODUCTION

The Library of Congress is the largest center for information storage in the world. Although its 19 million volumes make it the greatest library in the West, books represent less than one-fourth of its collections. The other 58 million pieces of stored data are on phonograph records, motion picture reels, computer tapes or in the form of manuscripts, maps, prints, and photographs. Less than one-fourth of the collections are in English—we could go on with such anomalies for pages, but we will stop right here for this book is not about what is *in* the Library at all. We are concerned instead with *how* what is in the Library got there, what the Library does when it is working properly, and where the cracks are appearing as the Library is put under pressure.

Telling such a story would seem to be a fairly straightforward challenge, but it is not as simple as it appears. To begin with, the Library is much more like a great university than it is like a government agency. It operates with a staff of almost 6,000 employees, of whom only a comparative few know where their fellow librarians work, much less what their peers do to earn their pay. Only a scattering of the Congressional Research staff knows where the 1,500-person Processing Services is even located; even fewer in the Copyright Office know where the American Folklife Center is; and almost no one in any of these units has ever seen the National Library Service for the Blind and Physically Handicapped.

The primary building of the Library is the largest library building in the world, and of all the buildings owned by the federal government, only the Pentagon and the FBI have more floor space than the James Madison Memorial Library. Yet the Madison is but one of seven multistoried buildings filled with Library staff in Washington, and that

1

count ignores the Library of Congress offices in Nairobi, New Delhi, Buenos Aires, Jakarta, et cetera. In short, the Library is made up of well over a hundred self-sufficient duchies, each quite complete in itself, which—like a typical medical school, law school, or French Department on a campus—share little more than a letterhead and a central disbursing office.

A similar problem exists in describing whom the Library works for. It serves five very different audiences. Each is quite discrete, and each is convinced that it should receive the first attention of the staff and be the principal focus of the Library's purpose. There is the Congress, whose library it is. There is the professional library world, which is dependent on the Library's bibliographic services, looks to the Library as a "mother church," and perpetually pleads for "leadership." There is the government world of all the executive agencies whose own oversight committees have repeatedly said they must rely on the Library for information resources "to avoid duplication and redundancy of effort and appropriations." There is the scholarly world, which thought the Library was building its great collections so they might be used to further knowledge, and there is the creative world, which relies on the copyright to protect its product, backed by the great musical, theatrical, and literary collections to preserve its traditions. With hard-edged limits to time, money, and staff, whom *do* you satisfy first, and how far do you go?

Very few of the people we are watching here are passive caretakers. A full 65 to 70 percent of the LC staff is doing something new, *creating* something. Staff members are staging concerts for the Library's Stradivarii, they are analyzing legislative options for congressional committees, they are making audio cassettes, editing film, publishing research tools, translating foreign texts, repairing vellum manuscripts, loading computer tapes for sale to other libraries.

The Library is indeed a highly complex but vibrantly active institution, and we will try to examine it in four steps.

First, we will take a hurried, informal look at its history to see how it got to be what it is. This will take us at a brisk pace from Jefferson's gift of his Monticello collection to the closing of the catalogs in 1981 and the Library's total commitment to the computer. At that point we will look just long enough at the organization of the institution to give us a road map of its bureaucratic elements.

Second, we will look at the Library when it is working well—the day-to-day work of acquiring the collections, selecting what it will keep (it receives 10 million pieces a year and promptly throws 8.5 away), how the remaining 1.5 million is controlled so that the librarians can find it when they need it. We will watch how the accumulated collections are being used in quite different ways by the Congressional Research Service; the Law Library; the Asian, Hispanic, and Cyrillic divisions; the Map Division; and by the Rare Books and Manuscript divisions. We will examine the services to the blind and scan the spectrum of the Library and the performing arts.

In Part 3, we will discuss the programs of the Library under stress. Many are in trouble. Some of the problems arise from conflicts inherent in any mature government agency. Some of the problems come from programs that have outlived their time and their original purpose (recall, many of the things being done have been done in much the same manner for nearly 200 years now!). But most of the Library's troubles come from new technology, which is having a severe effect on the Library's traditional means of information storage.

The national library is an institution at the end of its beginning. It has the space it needs, it has the staff it needs, and it has the materials it needs to serve the nation. But techniques and services that have worked for nearly two centuries are no longer appropriate; audiences that have been served for 100 years are turning to other sources for their working data. And, indeed—a final frustration—hundreds of thousands of the Library's materials are literally crumbling to dust at the very time when image processing, satellite transmission, computer control, and facsimile transport are challenging the roles of and needs for libraries as institutions everywhere.

We will therefore conclude with an exploration of the challenges and the options available for meeting them. With *what* the library does changing, and with *whom* it does it for in flux, we will reflect together on the question, Do we really need a national library at all?—and if so, for whom to do what?

Part One

AN INFORMAL HISTORY: HOW THE LIBRARY GOT WHERE IT IS

1

THE HISTORY THROUGH SPOFFORD

What do we have here? Without doubt the greatest collection of knowledge, memory, and experience ever assembled in one space since the beginning of man. The ancients tried to achieve such a collection in their library at Alexandria and (given a somewhat shorter memory and not so much knowledge and experience) almost brought it off. Strangely enough, we are probably as near totality today as they were then. Like the Greeks and Egyptians, we have assembled as much as the world knows about *all* the cultures of the world, not just our own. Do you want a fact? a song? a formula? a philosophy? Nowhere in the world can it be found more efficiently. One-stop knowledge. For whom? Gathered why?

We owe this monumental pile of facts to the work habits of the Founding Fathers. They were book oriented from the very first. Most of them were lawyers and shared their profession's traditional respect for the printed word in codes and precedents; most of the few who were not lawyers were philosophers and pamphleteers, nourished on the literature of the Enlightenment. For them, thinking meant first reading—and then, as a rule, writing more themselves.

It started with the first Continental Congress in 1774. As unlikely as it might seem, almost the first action taken by that body was to secure borrowing privileges from the Library Company of Philadelphia. That book collection was already one of the largest in the colonies, and it was housed with rare good fortune at the other end of Carpenters' Hall where the delegates were meeting. The Library Company graciously resolved "to furnish the Gentlemen . . . with the use of such Books as they may have occasion for during their sitting, taking a Receipt for them."

Thirteen years and a revolution later, when many of the same

7

SCENE IN THE OLD CONGRESSIONAL LIBRARY, WASHINGTON, D.C., SHOWING PRESENT CONGESTED CONDITION.—Drawn by W. Bengough

By 1876 Librarian Ainsworth Spofford reported that there was no space left in the Library proper and that "books are now, from sheer force of necessity, being piled upon the floor in all directions." The situation had reached impossible proportions by 1897, as depicted in this drawing by W. Bengough, which appeared in *Harper's Weekly* on February 27, 1897. Spofford is seen on the far right, emerging from his desk area with papers in his hand; David Hutcheson, Assistant Librarian, is on the left holding a lamp.

delegates met again in that incredible summer of 1787, they relied on the same Library Company collection, and when they assembled in 1789 as the First Congress of the United States, they found themselves in the same building as the New York Society Library. The legislators promptly secured access to that library's 4,000 volumes, but there followed a minor argument that came to nothing at the time but that presaged endless debates from that time to this.

The discussion was precipitated by Elbridge Gerry, distinguished signer of the Declaration of Independence and delegate to the Constitutional Convention. On August 16, 1789, he urged that a Committee be appointed to select "a catalogue of books" for Congress to use and to estimate the cost of and the best way to come by them. Acting with precedential dispatch, such a committee was indeed formed eight months later, and in only seven weeks it delivered a report to the House. It noted that the delegates were "obliged at every session to transport to

the seat of the general government a considerable part of their libraries,"
and "having due regard to the state of the treasury," it recommended
that $1,000 worth of books be bought at the outset and that $500 a
year be spent to purchase books thereafter.

The motion generated vast apathy on the part of the Congress but
splendid outrage from the taxpayers. A typical demur is the following
from the *Independent Chronicle* of Boston, May 13, 1790:

> The late motion respecting the "Library" for Congress is truly novel—
> could it be supposed that a measure so distant from any thing which can
> effect the general purposes of government, could be introduced at this
> important period? . . . How absurd to squander away money for a parcel
> of Books, when every shilling of the Revenue is wanted for supporting
> our government and paying our debts?
>   . . . It is supposed that the Members of Congress are acquainted with
> history; the laws of nations; and possess such political information as is
> necessary for the management of the affairs of the government. If they
> are *not*, we have been unfortunate in our choice. . . . It is supposed that
> the members are fully competent for these purposes, without being at the
> expence of furnishing them with Books for their improvement.
>   . . . The people look for *practical politicks*, as they presume the *Theory*
> is obtained previous to the members taking their seats in Congress.

That was the last anyone ever heard of the committee or its recommendations, but "the people's" position was to reappear.

By 1791, the government had returned to Philadelphia, and although
the Library Company had moved into its own quarters, Congress
recovered access to the Company's volumes. In this manner, for nearly
twenty years, the Founding Fathers managed to keep a broad information
base easily accessible, and it was used daily as an integral part of their
legislative activities—without having to "squander away money" or to
further distress the treasury.

With the spring of 1800, we come to the formal founding of the
Library and the first attempts to decide whose library it was and what
kind of a library it was to be. The decision was forced on the members
of Congress by Hamilton and Jefferson's Great Compromise, which
placed the new capital in a marshy area just south of the Great Falls
of the Potomac. The time had come to fix a permanent seat of government,
and funds were appropriated to move the personnel of all three branches
of government from Philadelphia to the new District of Columbia.

On April 24, 1800, President John Adams signed the transfer bill,
the fifth section of which legislated the Library of Congress into being.
It called for the purchase of $5,000 worth of books and the "fitting up
of a suitable apartment for containing them." The purchase was to be
made by the secretary of the Senate and the clerk of the House; the

books were to be used by both houses of Congress. A Joint Committee on the Library was established to assist in the selection of volumes and the establishment of rules. Neither the executive branch nor the judiciary was to be given access. It was strictly Congress's library.

The Library's first home was in an upper room of the new Capitol Building, and it soon received its second (and almost its last) legal underpinning. In January 1802, Congress passed a law that has been called the "charter of governance" for the new library. It called for the appointment of a Librarian to be made "by the President of the United States solely," note, *not* by the legislature whose books they were. Possibly because this step had already created a breach in the separation of powers, the President and the Vice-President were granted borrowing privileges. The Librarian was to be paid at a rate not to exceed 2 dollars a day, and all moneys spent on the Library were to be under the review of the joint committee, which now consisted of three members from the Senate and three from the House.

President Thomas Jefferson promptly appointed a close personal friend, one John James Beckley, as the first Librarian of Congress. The new Librarian and his committee began by querying bibliophiles throughout Washington for suggested purchases, and among those asked was Jefferson himself. Jefferson sent an extensive list "in conformity with your ideas that books of entertainment are not within the scope of it, and that books in other languages, where there are no translations of them, are not to be admitted freely." He avoided "those classical books, ancient and modern, which gentlemen generally have in their private libraries, but which can not properly claim a place in a collection made merely for the purpose of reference."

The President did soften his reference-only rule in one area:

> The travels, histories [and] accounts of America previous to the Revolution should be obtained. It is already become all but impossible to make a collection of these things. Standing orders should be lodged with our ministers in Spain, France and England and our Consul at Amsterdam to procure everything within that description which can be hunted up in those countries.

That suggestion, in fact, appears to have been a corollary to the numerous recommendations for maps suggested by almost everyone. The thirst for maps, it turns out, was not for finding tools with which to deal with an empty continent, but for proof against expected litigation when "the new countries" began to fill up. It is clear that everyone expected the space to be Balkanized (France, England, and Spain still held great portions of it), and the Founders wanted proof of contemporary settlements, boundaries, and "presence." Every recommended map was pursued, and most of them were acquired.

One of the more colorful recommenders at the time was the chairman of the Joint Committee, Senator Samuel Latham Mitchill. Mitchill was a medical doctor from New York, who was referred to by his colleagues as a "veritable chaos of knowledge," and he is remembered for providing one of the better justifications for the Library: He urged the acquisition of "such materials as will enable statesmen to be correct in their investigations and, by a becoming display of erudition and research, give a higher dignity and a brighter luster to truth."

If that was Mitchill's justification, what did the committee think it was trying to accomplish? It would appear that the first Joint Committee believed it had three options. First, and obviously, it could build a small collection of working tools similar to what the legislators knew back in their homes and law offices: ready-reference, statutes, and books on the philosophy of the law. Second, the new collection could be a "public library" for the members. The concept of a public library at that time meant a private, usually subscription, collection, which was available to the mercantile community in a city, to the social elite, or to a college community. In terms of the legislators' experience in the towns they came from, such a library would have a broader, more balanced collection, which would be used by the members of the legislature or even all the government leaders, and it would include cultural and recreational volumes as well as working books. And finally, the committee could have begun what would in fact be a national library. This would serve the federal government in Washington, but it would also act as a cultural and historical archive for the young country. Several of the European nations had such a national library, and the early leaders of the nation were both proud of the new government's achievements and eager to take on the ornaments of the older, established nations.

So which option did the committee choose? The "public library." That answer will come as news to the present-day library community, because for the last 100 years, we have been taught that the Library of Congress started as a reference collection. We now know that the early historians were misled by their study of the book *purchase orders* for the first decade. (Among them, incidentally, they found such intriguing lists as that of June 1800, in which 152 titles in 740 volumes were ordered from England and were rather quickly delivered to the United States in eleven hair trunks. The London bookseller noted that he "judged it best to send trunks instead of boxes, which after their arrival would have been of little or no value." Taking the dealer's sensitivity to the needs of an underdeveloped country at face value, Congress instructed the secretary of the Senate "to make sale of the trunks in which the books lately purchased were imported." The 152 titles were rigorously limited to law, political science, economics, and history, and there was a special case filled with rolled maps.)

But recent scholars have concentrated on an *inventory* of the Library as it looked in 1812 instead of what was ordered—and we now know precisely what was in the collection as opposed to what was purchased. The difference is the result of a carefully selected acceptance of gift volumes, which were presumably begged from members of the government. All of the volumes "which gentlemen generally have in their private libraries," as Jefferson had said, were indeed in that first collection, apparently given by the Library's patrons. The result was a well-balanced "public library." From its very beginning the Library of Congress collections had run the full spectrum of factual *and* creative writing.

By 1812, the Library had 905 titles in 3,000 volumes, and almost every volume had been printed in England. The books were arranged by general subjects, and history and biography was the largest group with 248 titles. Law, as might be expected, was next with 204, but less expected was the rest of the span. There were 105 titles in geography and topography—including Jeffrey's *American Atlas* (London, 1800), Jedidiah Morse's *American Geography* (London, 1794), and Welde's *Travels Through the States of North America* (London, 1800)—16 titles on natural history; 24 titles on medicine, surgery, and chemistry; and 42 on poetry and the drama and works of fiction. The titles in the last group sound as appealing as a good browsing collection should: Mrs. Elizabeth Inchbald's *British Theatre* in 25 volumes, Burns's poems, Shakespeare's plays, four volumes of Rabelais, the complete works of "Nichola Machiavel," 12 volumes of Samuel Johnson, 14 volumes of Henry Fielding, Pope, Virgil, Aeschylus, Cicero, Scott's *Marmion*, and 7 volumes of Mrs. Inchbald's *Collection of Farces*. There were 33 dictionaries and one set of Diderot's *Encyclopédie* in 35 volumes (Paris, 1751), which had cost the Librarian $216 and was the most expensive title in the collection. By 1812, the Joint Committee had spent $15,000 total and had acquired a tight, well-balanced library that would have been a credit to any institution.

Then, in the spring of 1813, an event occurred that had a profound effect on the Library. An American force fought its way into the capital of Upper Canada (then called York, now Toronto) and set fire to the Parliament Buildings. The troops destroyed the archives, stole the plate from the church, and burned the parliamentary library. The British sought revenge, firmly targeting the Capitol and its Library, but here our otherwise straightforward history of the Library stumbles onto an overgrown part of the path. The fact is that, from this distance in time, we are just not sure what happened next.

We do know that on August 18, 1814, a fairly substantial British force sailed up the Chesapeake Bay, eager to get even for the burning of York. The War Department in Washington, having a fair idea of what was in the invading commander's mind, called out all the ablebodied men in the city and on August 19 (a Friday), put them into the Maryland fields.

On Saturday and Sunday, the working archives of the State and Treasury Departments were evacuated from the city. On Sunday afternoon, someone remembered the congressional papers and files, and one of the clerks of the House was instructed to find transportation to evacuate the legislative materials. The executive branch had already appropriated all the local wagons, so the clerk had to go outside the city, where he ultimately found a cart and four oxen at the farm of one John Wilson, who lived six miles out of town. The cart arrived at the Capitol after dark on Monday, and the clerk and Assistant Librarian (too old to be caught in the militia draft) began to load it, first with the manuscript papers of the clerk's office and then with books from the Library. These materials were taken "on the same night, nine miles, to a safe and secret place in the country," according to the Assistant Librarian and the clerk writing on September 15.

The cart was loaded and moved, loaded and moved, back and forth, throughout Tuesday and until Wednesday morning (August 24), when the British appeared in Washington and promptly set fire to the Capitol. The two men admitted with sorrow that "the last volumes of the manuscript records of the Committees of Ways and Means, Claims and Pensions, and Revolutionary Claims" were lost, and "a number of the printed books were also consumed, but they were all duplicates of those which have been preserved." There is no question but that the Capitol itself was gutted.

On September 21, barely four weeks later, Thomas Jefferson wrote a letter to his friend Harrison Smith, a newspaper publisher in private life and, in public life, commissioner of the revenue. Writing from Monticello, Jefferson opened his letter, "I learn from the newspapers that the vandalism of our enemy has triumphed at Washington over science as well as the arts, by the destruction of the public library, with the noble edifice in which it was deposited." Jefferson noted that it was going to be exceedingly difficult to replace the Library "while the war continues, and intercourse with Europe is attended with so much risk." He described his own collection of "between nine and ten thousand volumes," which he had acquired while living in Europe and subsequently when he was President. The contents, he noted, mainly "related to the duties of those in the high concerns of the nation."

He explained that it had been his intention to give the Congress "first refusal" of his library at its own price on his death, but in view of the present difficulties, this might be "the proper moment for its accommodation." He offered to sell the library in annual installments but was ready to make it available at once. "Eighteen or twenty wagons could place it in Washington in a single trip of a fortnight." He appended a detailed catalog of its contents and declared, "I do not know that it contains any branch of science which Congress would wish to exclude from their collection; there is, in fact, no subject to which a Member of Congress may not have occasion to refer."

On October 3, Smith told Congress of the offer. On October 7, the Joint Committee on the Library offered a resolution authorizing and empowering it to "purchase . . . the library of Mr. Jefferson." The committee sent a delegation to Monticello, where the collection was counted and found to contain 6,487 volumes. Appraisers costed the volumes at $3 each for the common-sized books, $1 for the very small ones, and $10 for the full-scale folios. The total came to $23,950, and the Senate promptly passed a bill to buy the collection. But the House balked. The bill's supporters pointed out what an appropriate, economic, and almost providential solution was available to them to acquire an entire library in one sweep. The critics objected to "the cost of the purchase, the nature of the selection, embracing too many works in foreign languages, some of too philosophical character, and some otherwise objectionable." Note was taken of "books of an atheistical, irreligious, and immoral tendency."

The final vote (on November 8) was very close. The library was acquired by the narrow margin of ten votes, and the roll call followed party lines. Federalist New England was against it (the roll call included a nay from Representative Daniel Webster); the Middle Atlantic was for it by two votes; the West, by eight; and the South produced the rest of the votes needed for passage. On November 28, a bill was presented to the Congress to make payment to Mr. Jefferson.

On December 12, a committee looking into the loss of the Capitol reported "that they have satisfactory evidence that the library of Congress, consisting of volumes agreeably to the catalogue herewith submitted was destroyed by the enemy on the 24th of August last; and, also, the manuscript records, papers, and secret journal of Congress." The committee chided the clerk of the House and his staff for their failure to properly care for the materials in their custody. On December 17, two clerks expressed their resentment of the admonition and stated, "the several loads which were saved, were taken from the shelves on which they were placed, and deposited in the carts by which they were taken away; they have suffered no injury, and, to have procured boxes or trunks to pack them in, if that plan had been preferred, would have been utterly impossible."

And that is the extent of our knowledge of *why* the Congress thought it needed Jefferson's library. We cannot seem to establish whether all, most, or merely some of the books went up in smoke. Jefferson was then seventy-one years old and deeply in debt. We do know that two-thirds of the $23,950 paid him went directly to his creditors (among whom was the Polish patriot, Thaddeus Kosciuszko, who had loaned him $4,870). Why the Congress bought the library is blurred, but it is clear that Congress *did* buy it and, with it, suddenly became the owner of the finest library in America.

Jefferson had kept the books in separate modules, which had been stacked to form instantly portable bookcases along the walls at Monticello. Each shelf/box was taken down, had a face-board nailed across it, and was placed in one of ten horse-drawn wagons. The wagons were limited to 3,000 pounds a load, and the drivers were paid $4 a day for the job. It took six days for the wagons to reach Washington.

When the face-boards were pried off, the Library of Congress was a reality again, now doubled in size with a broad-ranging collection that reflected the interests of one of the leading humanists of the age— a philosopher, historian, scientist, and practical politician. As Jefferson wrote to Smith when the collection started north, "It is the choicest collection of books in the United States, and I hope it will not be without some general effect on the literature of our country." The Librarian of Congress and the Joint Committee realized that they had become custodian of a national treasure and proceeded to expand and care for it as Jefferson would have done had it remained his own.

Mr. Jefferson had one more impact on the ultimate personality of the Library before he and his books merged into the helical stream of the institution. He had organized his collection around a rather phil-osophical division of the world's knowledge devised by Sir Francis Bacon. Bacon identified three kinds of science—memory, reason, and imagination. Jefferson developed those three categories into forty-four subject divisions and arranged his books within those clusters. The Librarian refined the forty-four somewhat, locked them into a printed book catalog, and froze the Library of Congress's classification scheme for 100 years. As late as Theodore Roosevelt's time, the Library's catalogers were dutifully sorting hundreds of thousands of volumes into the same forty-four compartments in which the earliest titles had sat on the shelves at Monticello.

From 1815, we can move fairly quickly through fifty years to the close of the Civil War. We are searching here only for those precedents that explain the Library of Congress as we find it today, and through those antebellum decades, only a half-dozen events need be noted for our purpose.

Librarian of Congress (and clerk of the House) Patrick Magruder never recovered from the loss of the Capitol, and he had resigned under pressure before Jefferson's books arrived. President Madison then appointed George Watterston, a "local man of letters," to take his place. Three things happened to Mr. Watterston that interest us. First, in 1816, the use of the Library was extended to the Attorney General of the United States, the justices of the Supreme Court, and the members of the diplomatic corps.

Second, just before Christmas in 1825, Watterston suffered a traumatic night when a menacing glow was observed in the windows of the Library in the Capitol. The guards broke down the door and sounded the alarm, and the occupants of the neighborhood rooming houses rushed in to extinguish the blaze. (Daniel Webster carried a bucket in the melee and made amends for his earlier vote against the purchase of Jefferson's library.) The fire was quickly controlled, and only a few sets of duplicate government documents were lost, but it was a close call and should have made the custodians more careful than it did.

Finally, in terms of the long view, Watterston's most telling contribution to his post was the manner of his leaving it. He was fired. President Andrew Jackson was inaugurated on March 4, 1829, and Watterston was relieved on May 28. His sin had been too overt a commitment to the Whig party. He had been active in political affairs and was known to be a supporter of Henry Clay, but most of all, as David Mearns, a leading historian of today's institution, has gracefully put it, "He had been Librarian of one side of the aisle rather than Librarian of Congress." His experience was not lost on his successors, and without exception, the Librarians of Congress since that time have been as dispassionate and detached in their political careers as the Speaker of the House of Commons.

Jackson appointed John Silva Meehan to the position, and he proceeded to hold it for thirty-two years. His contributions were unspectacular, but he has come down to us as a conscientious, able administrator. Like his predecessor, Meehan, in one of his first acts, liberalized access to the collections: Under him, ex-Presidents, the secretaries of State, Treasury, War, and Navy, and the Postmaster General were permitted to use the books. The real point of interest here is how literally the rules were applied. Only those half-dozen individuals were to be admitted to the Library—not their staffs or representatives of their departments. It was still a legislative library, not an executive one (much less a public or national library).

However, in 1832, Congress passed a law that began to open the collections, genuinely, for the first time. The statute instructed the Librarian to remove all the law books from the shelves and set them apart as an independent law library to be housed in a "nearby apartment." The justices of the Supreme Court were to recommend continuing purchases to the Librarian, who was to buy the books with congressional funds, but the new Law Library was to be open to the use of the Justices "and the attorneys and counsellors, during the sittings of the said Court." Members of the two houses were still to have unrestricted access, but the "congressional" library was broadening its statutory clientele.

By 1836, the Library of Congress had grown to 24,000 volumes. At that time the British Museum had 180,000 volumes; the Imperial Library at St. Petersburg, 300,000; the Vatican Library, 400,000; and the Royal Library in Paris almost half a million.

The Library of Congress was about to start its plunge into mass acquisition. In 1840, under Meehan, it became the first agency of the federal government to participate in a program of "international intellectual cooperation." Congress passed a law that permitted the Librarian to exchange duplicate books and documents for other needed works and, more importantly, decreed that "hereafter 50 additional copies of each volume of documents printed by order of either House be printed and bound, for the purpose of exchange in foreign countries." With this law began the broad programs of international exchange that have brought to the Library the government publications of the major nations of the world and, of nearly equal importance, have placed the records of our own government in the collections of the world's libraries. Acquisitions began to increase not by hundreds but by thousands of volumes. Most appropriately, too, the law made the first area of subject strength the holdings on *government* itself.

Early in the morning of December 24, 1851, a passerby noticed another threatening glow through a window of the Library, and once again the guards broke down the door to find one end of the room in flames. Fire companies, neighbors, and sailors and marines from nearby barracks rushed to the scene, but by the time this blaze was put out, 35.000 volumes had been destroyed. With them went almost all of the Library's map collection; Gilbert Stuart portraits of Washington, Adams, and Jefferson; and many lesser works of art. The Library had never had an open fire in its rooms; in fact, no light had ever been lit in the Library (it was locked when Congress met at night to prevent anyone carrying in a lamp or candle). But the flues from committee rooms on the floor below ran under the Library's floor and through its walls, and one of those chimney flues had caught fire. The result was the destruction of almost two-thirds of the collection.

This loss was a bitter one, and about the only positive note that could be struck was rejoicing over the safety of the Law Library, saved by its move to an adjacent room. Congress promptly passed substantial sums for the replacement of the book collection and the repair of the quarters. A minor footnote appeared in the floor debate over one of these restorative pieces of legislation. The chairman of the Public Buildings and Grounds Committee, in reading the bill, referred to "the fire by which the National Library was consumed"; he later apologized and asked that those words be changed to "the Congressional Library" or "the Library of Congress."

President Lincoln relieved Librarian Meehan from office in May 1861 so he could install in his place a physician from Terre Haute, Indiana, John G. Stephenson. By 1863, the Library held 79,214 volumes and was the fourth largest in the country. Near the end of 1864, Dr. Stephenson was forced to resign because of "speculations created by war," among which was a sum of $1,480, which a later law directed be paid an English bookseller who had been "unjustly defrauded by the conduct of the librarian in the year 1863." And thus ended the first portion of the Library's history.

During the first sixty-five years, three things had been established: (1) The Library was to be a broad, comprehensive collection, not a simple legislative one; (2) to survive, the Librarian must be firmly nonpartisan; and (3) the executive's power to remove a legislative employee had been repeatedly demonstrated.

The First Giant: Ainsworth Rand Spofford

The Library as we know it today began with Lincoln's appointment of Stephenson's successor. Ainsworth Rand Spofford, sixth Librarian of Congress, was the Cecil Rhodes of the institution, an empire builder in the finest Victorian tradition.

Before we examine Spofford's impact on the Library, let us recall again the major issue he represents. What was the Library of Congress to be: Congress's library? or the nation's library? Since we have lived with it for more than 180 years, it seems self-evident that it was always "our" government's library; it quickly became one of the largest libraries in the country—naturally it was the nation's library! Not so. This was not evident at the time and could easily have been otherwise. Recall, there is still no national university. There was no national art gallery until 1941, no national opera house or concert hall until 1971. There was no conspicuous need for a central, federal library for the people and no self-evident truth proclaiming that there must be one. The only obvious and immediate need was for a reference collection to support the legislative work of the two houses.

There was a European tradition for a national collection, but here again, the institution should have developed down a different path. The European libraries had each started as the sovereign's library. The American analogy would then have been the President's library, and the first copyright law of 1790 had indeed decreed that the record copy of all copyrighted works be deposited in the library of the Department of State. From the first, State's library was the President's reference collection, and for many years, it was the central collection for the whole executive branch.

When the first attempt was made to refine the copyright law in 1846, the new version contained an even more likely candidate for the "national library"—the newly founded Smithsonian Institution. It was a tax-supported center, dedicated to scholarship and the advancement of research, and ideal for housing a central collection. The Copyright Act of 1846 was therefore broadened to require deposit of three copies: one to go to the State Department, one to the Smithsonian, and one to the Library of Congress. Thus, an accumulation of any one of the three might well have become the national collection, if there was to be one, but the one that did was the copyright collection of the Library of Congress, and the reason was probably Ainsworth Rand Spofford. There was never a question in his mind. The Library of Congress was to be the national library, and he dedicated forty-four years to bringing this about.

He began as the very model of a proper librarian. He had two rooms, a staff of seven, and 80,000 books. In 1864, he produced the first catalog of the Library of Congress to be arranged alphabetically by author. Previous catalogs, as he explained, had had titles "distributed through a series of 179 distinct alphabets, arranged in an arbitrary sequence, and without an index." He quickly secured the confidence and active support of the Joint Committee on the Library. And then he began to build.

He started with the copyright law. When he became Librarian, that law was in a state of near paralysis, at the exhausted end of a long, confused, and disheartening struggle. Ignoring its corrosive effect on authors, publishers, and the literary world in general, from the Library's point of view alone, it was enough to make a bureaucrat despair.

There had been copyright legislation in 1790, 1846, 1859, 1865, and 1867, during which years the place of deposit was shifted from one agency to another, the method of securing protection was repeatedly changed, and what was copyrightable at all had been constantly amended. Throughout the years, compliance had been mainly an act of faith, and penalties for failure nonexistent. From the close of the Civil War, the situation had been as follows.

In order to get a work copyrighted, an author went to the clerk of his nearest district court, filed a copy of the title page of his work, and gave the clerk a dollar. Once the book was actually published, the author sent a printed volume to the same clerk, who then forwarded it to the Patent Office in the Department of the Interior. (The books had previously gone to the Department of State, but the material was taking up so much room, State had gotten the law changed to read Interior. There the Patent Office was putting the deposits in its basement—uncataloged and unarranged—and by 1870, had 30,000 to 40,000 volumes in dark storage and was as repelled by the whole thing as State had been.) The district clerks were supposed to send the dollars they had collected to the Treasury, but most district judges let the clerks keep the money for their trouble. There were still no penalties for noncompliance, so vast quantities of books were printed with "Deposited for copyright" on the backs of title pages that had never been registered, paid for, or deposited anywhere. Everyone was dissatisfied, but nobody wanted to take over the mess—except Spofford, who saw the copyright collection as the base for a national library.

To skip all the lobbying, successive amendments, and general legislative exercises, when "the great copyright law of 1870" was finally passed, it declared that "all records and other things relating to copyrights and required by law to be preserved, shall be under the control of the librarian of Congress" and that anyone claiming a copyright on any book, map, chart, dramatic or musical composition, engraving, cut, print, or photograph or negative thereof must send two copies to the Librarian within ten days of its publication. Penalties for failure to comply were spelled out, and the Librarian was given authority to demand the receipt of anything that carried the copyright statement but had not been filed.

The new arrangement worked beyond Spofford's wildest hopes. In the next twenty-five years, the Library received 371,636 books, 257,153 magazines, 289,617 pieces of music, 73,817 photographs, 95,249 prints, and 48,048 maps. Each one had to be acknowledged, recorded, and preserved somehow and somewhere, but the Librarian was at least consistent. In the midst of the deluge, he turned to the Departments of State and Interior and carried off their previous deposits, so the Library of Congress recovered most of what had slipped away before Spofford's time. State and Interior thus abandoned, without apparent regret, their chance to be the national library. The Smithsonian Institution yielded its opportunity with like eagerness.

The founders of the Smithsonian had almost certainly pictured it as becoming *a* if not *the* national library. The Smithsonian dialogue, charter, and laws contain phrases like "for the purchase of a great national library," "for the gradual formation of a library composed of valuable works pertaining to all departments of human knowledge," and "a great national library, worthy of the country and the donor," but when the first Secretary of the Smithsonian was hired, he had a different image in mind. Joseph Henry came from Princeton with an international reputation as a physicist. He had accepted the new responsibility reluctantly, but once aboard, he had very clear ideas of how the Smithsonian was to act: It was to pour its energies into scientific research and pursue a vigorous publication program to disseminate the results of that research. The charter required him to operate a museum and a library, but these distractions were to be suppressed as much as he dared.

The law did direct Henry to spend $25,000 a year on a library, so he hired Charles Coffin Jewett from Brown University to run it. In spite of the fact that Jewett was probably the leading librarian in the nation at the time, he was relieved of his duties six years later. He had been determined to build a great reference library, and Henry resented the money Jewett spent and the space the library absorbed. (Jewett went on to become the director of the Boston Public Library, where he made a major impact on both that institution and librarianship in general.)

What interests us in respect to the Library of Congress is not so much the Smithsonian's library as its publications, which were eminently successful. The Smithsonian's *Contributions to Knowledge* began publication in 1848; its *Reports*, in 1850; and its *Miscellaneous Collections*, in 1862. Literally tens of thousands of volumes from all parts of the world were received in exchange for these widely distributed series. By 1865, Henry was becoming engulfed and repelled by the sheer bulk of the exchange publications—which Spofford saw and coveted, picturing them as filling the scientific gaps in his own collections. An exchange, satisfactory to both parties, was worked out, and by the end of 1866, Spofford was able to report the transfer of "this large accession . . . especially valuable in the range of scientific books, comprising by far the largest collection of the journals and transactions of learned societies, foreign and domestic, which exists in America."

The collection itself was spectacular, but the precedent it set was more so. First, from this point on, the Library of Congress was to be the recipient of the exchange material generated by the Smithsonian's publications and agreements, and the Library of Congress has since received over 2 million pieces in the Smithsonian Deposit. Second, the law that made the exchange possible provided that "the Smithsonian

Institution shall have the use thereof, in like manner as it is now used, and the public shall have access thereto for purposes of consultation." The legislature's library, first opened to cabinet officers, then to lawyers using the Supreme Court, was now to be available to the public in general. Amusingly, not only did the law permit access to the Library, it required that the Library remain open nights and weekends to keep faith with the scholars who had enjoyed such privileges when the books were in Mr. Henry's care.

Spofford thus had the copyright law and the Smithsonian exchange working for him, automatically funneling into the Library of Congress almost limitless quantities of free, generalized material. Simultaneously, he was pursuing specific collections.

The most embarrassing gap in the Library's catalogs lay in the one area that should have been the strongest: the history of the United States. Sixty years before, Jefferson had said that a national library should be the repository of the nation's traditions, but two-thirds of Jefferson's contributions had been lost in the ensuing fires. Spofford solved this challenge as he had solved the problem of his scientific lacuna—by buying a library complete. The finest collection of Americana had been privately assembled by the publisher of the *American Archives,* one Peter Force. The historian Francis Parkman had been trying to raise money to secure the collection for the New York Historical Society, but Spofford swept in, convinced the Joint Committee that the expense was justified, and in 1867, the Congress voted $100,000 to purchase all of Force's holdings. When they were moved to the Library of Congress, they proved to contain 22,529 volumes of Americana, nearly 1,000 volumes of bound newspapers (a fourth of them dated from the 1700s), 40,000 pamphlets, 1,000 early maps, and 429 volumes of manuscripts, many from the Revolutionary period. Similar collections (the great Toner library of medical history and American biography is a preeminent example) were sought and acquired, and Spofford was increasingly able to get what he wanted as outright gifts to the nation.

The outcome of all these labors was not hard to predict. In no time at all, Spofford ran out of room. He was inundated with paper and the printed word. Bulk. Sheer, remorseless mass. The struggle for space began to dominate his life and all his energies. He had barely taken his job when the room on the original shelves had been exhausted. He persuaded Congress to convert two nearby "wings" to stacks, and he filled those. He put up wooden shelves in the corridors and filled them. He filled the Capitol attics. He filled the crypt under the Capitol dome. Material was piled in the halls between committee rooms and through the working space of both houses.

As early as 1872, Spofford admitted that the reading room was "an

A total of twenty-seven architects entered designs in an 1873 competition to plan a new Library building, and the winning design, submitted by the firm of Smithmeyer and Pelz of Washington, D.C., was announced in December 1873. But much to Librarian Spofford's frustration the new Library building was not authorized by the Congress until 1886, and it was 1889 before the final design was approved. Between 1874 and 1886, at the request of the Joint Library Committee, Smithmeyer and Pelz submitted drawings in several architectural styles, each appropriate to a different site. This Victorian Gothic design was, according to Smithmeyer, "calculated to be erected solitarily on the grand Judiciary Square" at the foot of Capitol Hill.

unfit place for students" and complained that "masses of books, pamphlets, newspapers, engravings, &c., in the course of collation, cataloguing, labeling, and stamping, in preparation for their proper location in the Library, are necessarily always under the eye and almost under the feet of members of Congress and other visitors." Pictures from *Harper's Weekly* of the time show the reading room with books stacked on tables and chairs in piles six and eight feet high.

By 1880, the Joint Committee on the Library was beginning to worry about fire again. Although the Library rooms were fireproof, the collection was spread so widely through the Capitol "that a fire once communicated would sweep shelving, periodicals, maps, and all before it." "Fire may break out at any moment in that dark upper loft, where gas has to be lit. . . . The very dust of decomposing paper, and of the friction induced by constant handling may become inflammable."

The usual obligations of librarianship were abandoned one by one. Periodicals could no longer be stored in series. Printed catalogs fell further and further behind and were ultimately abandoned. Complaints were increasingly heard about the outmoded classification scheme, about the absence of updating of the manuscript catalog books, about the refusal to consider interfilable cards. As the century neared its close, the energies of the Librarian and all his staff were devoted desperately to copyright matters, acquisitions, legislative reference—and getting themselves out of the Capitol's walls.

We need not go into the details of Spofford's struggles to create the great, gray building that we now think of as *the* Library of Congress. It took him a full fifteen years to get a law passed and an appropriation for its construction, and eleven more to build it. In many respects, however, it is some kind of a wonder the work went as quickly as it did. Although Spofford promised to leave a "legislative library" behind in the Capitol, the members of Congress understood that they were now abandoning even the appearance of an in-house, at-hand congressional library and, instead, housing a library for the nation.

Spofford's library clearly became a personal monument to his singleness of purpose, and, as it happened, it became a greater monument to its time—the end of the Gilded Age in which the United States had become rich and artistically sensitive.

Two city blocks were cleared of homes and churches, and then granite began to rise across the park from the Capitol. The building was magnificent (and eclectic) Italian Renaissance, but the floor plan was Spofford, who had given it long thought. (In 1872: The building must hold at least 3 million volumes. "The Library will reach 700,000 volumes by the year 1900; one million and a quarter by 1925; 1,750,000 by 1950; and 2,500,000 by the year 1975, or about a century hence." What design? It should be circular so that books could easily flow to and from the center for use and service, and as collections are added to be inserted in the middle of present arrangements, "only a single spoke need be shifted, rather than great masses of books as is required if books are in rectangular ranks"—and so forth through masses of detail.)

The building was immense for its day and decorated beyond anything the Medici had ever dreamed of. Marble was brought from Verona and Siena, from France, and from Tennessee. Details from a hundred European buildings were incorporated, but each was reexpressed in American terms. Every wall, mural, fresco, and mosaic is drenched in allegory. The frieze above the Visitors' Gallery is typical: Twelve figures symbolize the Evolution of Civilization. Starting with Egypt, typifying Written Records, it circles around to the United States as Science—represented by a picture of Abraham Lincoln seated by an electric motor and dressed "as an engineer, in the garb of the machineshop." The tenth figure gives us England as Literature with the actress Ellen Terry in an

The molding of the figures on the staircase in the Great Hall of the Jefferson Building is incredibly detailed and realistic. Each figure depicts a different occupation; shown here is the hunter.

Elizabethan costume, and the eighth is Germany and Printing. The Reformation figure standing by his printing press is that of General Thomas Casey, chief of the Army Corps of Engineers, who built the building for Mr. Spofford.

No one knows how many craftsmen were involved, but a rather casual examination of the more obvious walls, ceilings, and fireplace mantels reveals the signatures of thirty artists and twenty-three sculptors, not including the creators of literally hundreds of square yards of scrolls and birds and plants and cupids. Although in detail much of the building's decoration no longer speaks to us, in the mass the building, even after eighty-five years, is a splendid success. It is still graceful, inspiring, and efficient, bearing with ease the almost monthly shifts of this department or that collection. The present occupants are as much in debt to Spofford for having the foresight to provide them with a working library as is the nation for his having provided it with its national library.

By the spring of 1897—after more than thirty years of dedicated labor—Ainsworth Spofford had led his library to the heights overlooking the promised land. The long wooden trays were being readied to move the books. The last fresco was drying. On March 4, 1897, William McKinley was inaugurated as President, and on June 30, he replaced Mr. Spofford with a new Librarian of Congress.

On July 31, the "old library" in the Capitol closed, and on November 1, Mr. John Russell Young reopened the Library of Congress in its own building, with a new life and a new role before it.

2

THE HISTORY:
YOUNG TO BOORSTIN

John Russell Young

Although the injustice to Mr. Spofford was outrageous, it was also understandable. He had indeed stayed too long. His error in retrospect was an overpreoccupation with a single facet of a librarian's three-sided responsibility. Librarians are expected to acquire materials, organize them for use, and then use them—acquisition, cataloging, and reference. Mr. Spofford had fulfilled the requirements of acquisition beyond possibility of cavil, but his cataloging was in an unforgivable shape, and since he had such limited knowledge of what was in the collections, his reference service was equally impaired.

Mr. Spofford's misfortunes, moreover, were as much those of poor timing as poor judgment. He had lived beyond the age of the amateur bookman into the time of the professional. By the close of his career, a librarians' association had been organized, standards of techniques and skills had been established, and the science of organizing material for use (nowadays we call it retrieval) had come to pass.

Librarianship had come into its own as the result of a confluence of forces. The nineteenth century closed with a surge of professionalism in education, the proliferation of free public libraries, the establishment and growth of colleges and universities throughout the country, and the simple combination of affluence plus popular, cheap publishing. The resultant creation of libraries in every town and on every campus called for organization and agreement on the science of librarianship. The result was the establishment of the American Library Association (ALA) in 1876 and the coming to prominence of the great names of librarianship: Melvil Dewey of the Dewey Decimal System, George H. Baker of Columbia University, John Cotton Dana from Newark, William I. Fletcher of Amherst, Herbert Putnam from Boston. Those men were

The John Adams Building (for many years known simply as "The Annex"), located directly behind the Library's 1897 Jefferson Building, opened to the public in April 1939. Intended primarily as a giant bookstack, the building has a capacity of some 10 million volumes and holds approximately two-thirds of the Library's collections.

the very antithesis of the popular image of the timid bookman. They were zealots, dogmatic and doctrinaire, for whom all bibliothecal matters were either jet black or lily white.

Poor Mr. Spofford symbolized all the things that distressed the new men most. They believed in rational order so that any scholar or any person in the street could enter their libraries and quickly find precisely what was sought and take it with him or her. Mr. Spofford was so casual about order that when his 740,000 volumes were moved into the new building, barely one-third had been cataloged.

The new librarians believed in uniformity. They were trying to work out a basic set of rules by which all books would be identified and all classified in a similar way. Mr. Spofford felt no such obligation, and as he shuffled his volumes into the forty-four classifications he had inherited, literally floors of volumes were mixed together in whatever organization he found most congenial at the time.

The new professionals were outraged at the duplication within their trade. A new book would be published. A thousand libraries would each buy a copy. A thousand librarians would each spend time reading the same volume to discover its subject, and each would prepare cards to describe it. Each would identify it in his catalogs by appropriate subjects and on his shelves by an appropriate call number. The new men could see no reason why a single superlibrary should not do all this once, do it well, and then let everyone else copy the result. They felt, of course, that the Library of Congress was the appropriate place for such activity, but Mr. Spofford was so preoccupied with getting and housing that he had no time for the niceties of shared or centralized cataloging.

Finally, these men felt the need for a system of interlibrary loans by which all their book collections could be mutually shared through a network of records and holdings so the sum would be vastly greater than the parts. Poor Mr. Spofford was having enough trouble finding the books he needed to keep Congress happy without concerning himself with the waiting world without.

For all these reasons, the American Library Association was not sorry to see him go and assumed that his successor would be one of the professionals. The *Library Journal,* the official organ of the ALA, declared in January 1897: "Mr. Spofford has been so busy with the mass of detail which he has undertaken to handle that he has not trained himself as an executive for this kind of work, nor been able to keep in touch with the modern developments of library organization and practice." It assumed that his successor would be properly qualified, for "that this library will ultimately become in name as it is in fact the national library is beyond doubt, and the failure to recognize now this manifest destiny and to provide now on the large scale which this implies will be nothing short of a national misfortune."

So President McKinley appointed John Russell Young, a newspaperman, Librarian of Congress. Young had been the managing editor of Horace Greeley's *Tribune,* had gone around the world with President Grant in 1877, and in the course of the trip so impressed the former President that Grant persuaded his successor to appoint Young minister to China in 1882. In 1885, Young returned to join the *New York Herald* and shuttled back and forth between Paris and London until the 1890s. He was in Philadelphia when McKinley called upon him to take over the Library of Congress.

The outrage of the professional librarians could scarcely be contained. In no time, the outcry became so acrimonious, so personal, and so virulent that Melvil Dewey himself felt compelled to write the new appointee to try to smooth things over. Whenever Dewey picked up a pen, he wrote as the director of the New York State Library, the president of the Library Department of the National Education Asso-

ciation, and the secretary and executive officer of the American Library
Association. After the usual amenities, he declared:

> Many librarians have expressed themselves strongly against any appointment
> except of an experienced technical librarian. I have said from the first that
> I could easily conceive of a strong administrative man being put at the
> head, who might be better for the country than any of the professional
> librarians. I profoundly hope that you are the man needed for the wonderful
> work that is possible.

Dewey elaborated this theme at some length (the letter was written on
board an ocean liner and sent back by pilot boat, while Dewey proceeded
to an international congress) and closed by saying: "You can understand
how deeply I am interested in having the whole body of librarians in
cordial sympathy with the national library. I am sure that a cable from
you, followed by a letter which would reach me before we separate,
if sent at once, would do much good."

John Russell Young was an unusually able man, so it is impossible
to know whether he was intimidated by the initial torrent of criticism,
but the fact is that in the next two years, he initiated some of the most
progressive programs of any comparable period in the Library's history.

He opened the new building on November 1, 1897. When the
Library had closed in the Capitol, Congress had supported 42 positions.
When it reopened, Congress permitted 108 for initial staffing, and Young
decided to organize them according to a plan Spofford had recommended
several years before. The personnel were therefore divided among the
Reading Room, Periodical Department, the Law Library, and a Copyright
Office, the last to be presided over by a "register." In addition, there
was to be an art gallery, a hall of maps and charts, a Manuscripts
Department, a Music Department, and a Cataloging Department that
would serve all the units, regardless of the purpose or format of their
materials.

The wide publicity about the new building, which appeared in
almost all the popular magazines of the time, generated literally thousands
of applicants. From those, Young took the best for the junior positions
(at $720 a year), but he personally sought out the men he wanted for
the administrative roles. His first appointment, to the continued distress
of the profession, was Ainsworth Rand Spofford as Chief Assistant
Librarian. Spofford accepted the position without apparent resentment
and worked diligently to make the public services a success. Young
proceeded to fill the other roles with some of the leading figures in
bookmanship. He brought in James Christian Hanson, then in charge
of cataloging at the University of Wisconsin Library, to head the new

Cataloging Department. Arthur R. Kimball, state librarian of New Hampshire, was placed in charge of the Order Unit. Appleton P. C. Griffin of the Boston Public Library and the Boston Atheneum was made principal assistant in the Reading Room. Dr. Herbert Friedenwald, specialist in the records of the Continental Congress and Revolutionary War archives, became head of the Manuscripts Department. There were many others. The *Library Journal* relented and declared, "the new librarian of Congress continues to give the best of evidence of his intention to make the library worthy of its opportunities, by appointing skilled and fit men in the leading positions."

While Young built up his staff, he continued to build the collections. His ambassadorial experience had convinced him of the importance of foreign learning, and he planned to employ the worldwide network of foreign service officers as acquisition agents. With the help of the Secretary of State, he sent out 500 instruction circulars to U.S. embassies and consulates, describing what the Library needed and how it was to be sent. His one-sentence list of specifics was imaginative.

> Public documents, newspapers, serials, pamphlets, manuscripts, broadsides, chapbooks, ballads, records of original research, publications illustrative of the manners, customs, resources and traditions of communities to which our foreign representatives are accredited, the proceedings of learned, scientific or religious bodies, the reports of corporations such as railways, canals, or industrial companies, legislative records and debates, public decrees, church registers, genealogy, family and local histories, chronicles of county and parish life, folklore, fashions, domestic annals, documents illustrative of the history of those various nationalities now coming to our shores, to blend into our national life, and which as a part of our library archives would be inestimable to their descendants—whatever, in a word, would add to the sum of human knowledge, would be gratefully received and have due and permanent acknowledgement.

Shades of Jefferson.

In October 1898, Young extended the Library's Reading Room hours from nine o'clock in the morning until ten at night, adding an hour to his predecessors' most generous service. He requested Congress's permission to lend books from the Library's collection to adult borrowers in the District of Columbia and explored the possibilities of an inter-library loan system to support scholarship throughout the nation. He developed the details of a system of trust funds with which to secure rare or large holdings inappropriate for tax-supported, congressionally appropriated book budgets.

While organizing, acquiring, and extending services, he was struggling to overtake the enormous cataloging arrearage he had inherited. A half-million unprocessed volumes would tax the resources of a present-day librarian. Young was bravely trying to pull his shelved collections into a usable whole, pick up his past receipts, create a "scientific classification scheme," and cope with daily acquisitions arriving in every mail when his health began to fail. In 1898, he suffered a fall on Christmas Eve, and on January 17, 1899, he died. He had been Librarian of Congress only nineteen months, but his impact on the Library was many times greater than the span would imply.

Young's passing was followed by a rush of interest in who his successor would be. The new Library building and the role the institution was assuming in the national intellectual scene had, in a very brief time, made the position widely known and fashionably desirable. Candidates from the political world, publishers, educators, and Civil War heroes were suggested to President McKinley by various groups representing either a man or an interested elite. Contemporary news reports identified over fifty leading candidates for the job. Nicholas Murray Butler of Columbia was lobbying for James H. Canfield, president of Ohio State. Henry Adams and Secretary of State Hay were pressing for William Woodville Rockhill, the minister to Greece. William Coolidge Lane, president of the American Library Association and librarian of Harvard, worked the White House and Capitol Hill in support of Herbert Putnam, then head of the Boston Public Library.

Apparently McKinley was leaning toward Putnam when McKinley became caught in a political crossfire over a Boston churchman who had been a congressman but who had just been retired by his constituents. The pressures built swiftly, and McKinley nominated the Reverend Representative Samuel June Barrows to be the eighth Librarian of Congress, February 15, 1899. On February 28, the Joint Committee on the Library recommended against the nomination. On March 4, Congress adjourned without having considered the matter, so McKinley offered Barrows a recess appointment. Barrows refused, and on March 13, McKinley appointed Herbert Putnam, the library profession's candidate, as Librarian. Congress confirmed the appointment with apparent enthusiasm when it reconvened.

The Second Giant: Herbert Putnam

With Herbert Putnam, we come to the second great figure in the development of the Library, and like Spofford, he swung the entire institution in the direction which he, personally, felt appropriate. Putnam ruled for forty years, and again as with Spofford, when the power was transferred to his successor, the Library was in many ways vastly different from the form in which he found it. Spofford built it, Young housed it, and Putnam *used* it.

Putnam was the son of the founder of the publishing house that still bears the family name. He had been graduated from Harvard *magna cum laude*, had made Phi Beta Kappa, had studied law at Columbia, and had been admitted to the Minnesota and Massachusetts bars. He had served as librarian of the Minneapolis Public Library from 1884 to 1891, had returned to Massachusetts for reasons relating to his wife's family, and had practiced law there until 1895. In that year, at the age of thirty-three, he had been made librarian of Boston Public Library on the strength of his nationally recognized innovations in Minneapolis. He was in the process of innovating at the Boston Library when the American Library Association selected him as its prime candidate for the newly available position at the Library of Congress.

Putnam was a small, vital, red-haired man, with a bristling mustache, who was repeatedly referred to by his contemporaries as a patrician. His personality seems to have significance to our understanding of the Library because it appeared to have been the agent with which he steamrollered his way through staff, Congress, and his intellectual peers. He was rarely blocked or even resisted, and, on the few occasions when this occurred, his ability to outflank the opposition was impressive. We are asked to picture a man who was "aloof, remote, detached, [with] impenetrable dignity." His associates describe him as "formal" (no one could ever recall his having been addressed by his first name, and no subordinate was permitted to sit or take notes in his presence— orders were to be memorized as they were delivered).

His relations with his staff were particularly intriguing. On the occasion of his retirement—having taken the Library from the Gay Nineties, through World War I, the Roaring Twenties, and the Depression, to the threshold of World War II—he was repeatedly lauded as "venerated." This in spite of the fact that for much of his career, he paid his employees less than a dollar a day, that his employees' salaries were dramatically lower than those for similar employees in Washington or in the library profession, and that he had resisted any form of civil service, job classification, or merit increases for years. Instead, we hear how he was able to infuse his staff "with a sense of mission, dedication, and their almost limitless opportunities for patriotic endeavor." Throughout his forty years as Librarian of Congress, professionals begged to work for him for nothing in exchange for training and experience.

He was a thoroughgoing bureaucrat but of a peculiarly perverse variety. On the one hand, he hired, fired, and paid each individual as he saw fit; on the other, he was passionately fond of formal organization. He would create departments and divisions and units endlessly. When he arrived, he inherited nine administrative elements. In the first year, he increased that number to eighteen: an Executive Department, a Mail and Supply Department, a Packing and Stamping Department, an Order Department, a Catalog and Shelf Department, a Binding Department, a Bibliography Department, a Reading Room Department, a Periodical Department, a Documents and Exchanges Department, a Manuscript Department, a Maps and Charts Department, a Music Department, a Prints Department, a Smithsonian Department, a Congressional Reference Library at the Capitol, a Law Library, and a Copyright Department. By the time he retired, he had increased the number of departments to thirty-four, all directly responsible to himself alone.

Putnam had the good bureaucrat's ability to paint a proposed program in the most dramatic and appealing terms and an even greater ability to implement it beyond the limits of the original proposal. He drove the institution into a frenzy of activity and seemed to be personally distressed at the sight of any parts of the collection simply sitting there.

He started with the cataloging arrearage. Young had managed to sort it according to a rational program of attack, and Putnam promptly requested funds from Congress to carry out Young's program. Putnam pointed out that in addition to working on the unprocessed materials (hundreds of thousands of untouched volumes in storage, 59,589 prints to be classified, over 50,000 government documents, 50,000 maps, 230,000 pieces of music, and "many tons of periodicals and newspapers"), he had decided to recatalog every volume that was already on the shelves. Simultaneously, it was his intention to pursue Young's program of converting the book catalogs to cards and of applying new subject headings and a "scientific format" to each revised entry. Until those tasks were carried out, he complained, normal service would be impossible.

Faced with such righteous demands, Congress gave Putnam what he asked for, whereupon he instructed his staff that

> it would not do to be enthusiastic as to the amount of the Appropriation, as if it were a matter of surprise. The Committee must not be made to feel that they have been lavish. They have only done what an expert would say, I think, was necessary; but they have done no more, and ought not to be made to feel that they have done more, for it is their duty not to be lavish. So that the gratification should not be that Congress has been generous to the Library, but only that Congress has been able to take an intelligent view of the real needs, and to grant what was reasonable and necessary to meet them.

While Putnam was getting control of the processing problems within the Library, he threw himself into the task of resolving those of the profession at large. For thirty years, the professionals had talked about a single-point preparation and distribution of catalog cards. In October

Neptune, god of the sea, dominates the fountain designed by Roland Hinton Perry that is located in front of the Jefferson Building.

1901, Putnam circularized 400 libraries and seventeen state library commissions to find out what their responses would be if the Library of Congress were not only to catalog and print cards for its own use for the books it received, but were also to make additional copies of those cards and sell them for the cost of printing plus 10 percent. The question, of course, was rhetorical, and the response was immediate and as predicted. Within two years, the Library of Congress was producing cards at the rate of 225 titles a day, and in a short time, it could be said that "libraries the country over have come to depend absolutely on the Library of Congress for the greater part of their cataloguing." (By our own time, the printed LC card has become so common to catalogs throughout the world that the Library is frequently credited with the invention of card catalogs in general. In point of fact, thanks to Spofford's preoccupation with other matters, the Library of Congress was one of the last libraries to use them. Putnam grew up with such a tool—Boston Public put its catalog on cards in 1853, Harvard in 1856, and those two libraries had been printing their cards since 1879 and 1884, respectively. The Library of Congress's records were still being written by steel pen in book form as late as 1900, and when Putnam came aboard, he found that what few cards the Library did own were in manuscript and housed in a few drawers behind and below the issue desk.)

Putnam believed the libraries and scholars of the country had a right to know what was in the national library, and therefore, in the midst of his other accelerated programs, he began a series of published lists of "books about . . . " By the end of his second year as Librarian, eight such bibliographies, containing over 2,300 pages, had been printed, and the idea snowballed as the years passed.

Recognizing that as more and more libraries came to rely on the Library's cards, the Library's cataloging techniques would become the standard of the profession, Putnam joined with committees and representatives of the American Library Association to systematize the rules by which books would be described and identified. The numbers by which they would be classified and shelved, however, had to be done for the Library of Congress alone.

Young's catalogers had rejected Jefferson's forty-four categories as hopelessly restrictive and had turned to the Dewey Decimal System as the proposed basis for an enlarged Library of Congress classification scheme. After extensive study and long discussions with Dewey himself, they came to the disappointing discovery that the Dewey system was inappropriate for a collection the size of the Library of Congress's. Elaborate as the system was, the Library's holdings were already so vast that many single numbers in the Dewey tables would represent complete floors of books in the Library of Congress. The purpose of a classification scheme—to pull together volumes of similar contents and similar treatment on shelves, properly adjacent to correlative subjects but in themselves separate and distinct—broke down under such volume.

The catalogers therefore embraced a plan for an "expansive collection" invented by Charles A. Cutter of the Brooklyn Public Library and, using his principles, built their own classification scheme from the ground up. By Putnam's twenty-fifth anniversary in the Library, he could point with pride to the *Library of Congress Classification Schedules* containing over 5,000 printed pages of specific subjects, each with its matching call number. By the same time, eighty-some major libraries had abandoned the Dewey system and had begun to convert their collections to the Library of Congress classification scheme, and Putnam was selling over 7 million LC cards a year.

Putnam was obviously pulling the national library system toward the Library of Congress and doing so deliberately. There had never been any doubt in his mind as to the answer to the traditional question, Is it Congress's library or the nation's? In October 1900, he said:

> It is the National Library of the United States. It is thus a bureau of information for the entire country; and as to Americana for the entire world, for of all American libraries it will sustain the most active and intimate relations with libraries abroad; and through the Smithsonian with all learned societies abroad. It will maintain a corps of highly trained experts who will make known its resources and will aid in research. It will undoubtedly become the most active center of research, for the largest area, of any library in America. It will not merely draw students to Washington; it will by correspondence stimulate research all over the United States.

With such an attitude on the part of the Librarian, it is little wonder that Putnam began to hear murmurings from Congress about the Library's role in the legislative process. Except for a small room containing some reference books and a book delivery station, the Library's presence had disappeared from congressional halls, and its attention seemed to be distracted as well. A special room for senators and another for representatives had been built into the new building, but they were seldom used. By 1912, when a congressional committee queried Putnam about congressional use of the Library, he could point to an average of only "three or four" telephone calls a day from congressmen during the session. Only 93 members out of 490 had used the Library in any way the previous year, and that figure included all requests for novels and magazines as well as official business.

The increasing detachment from the parent organization might have gone unnoticed had it not been for an invention of the Wisconsin state government in 1901. The Progressives were in power in Madison, and in the process of challenging the establishment of the day, they found themselves blocked from access to the information and data needed to write the new legislation they wanted to press through the state legislature. They solved their problem by combining the resources of the Wisconsin State Library with the expertise of the University of Wisconsin faculty and came up with a device that became known as the Legislative Reference Bureau. The bureau searched for areas of potential government improvement; brought together the data, the solutions, and the experience of other states with similar problems; and then drafted potential legislation for correcting the matter. The device worked so well that within ten years, over two dozen other states had copied it, and it soon became an accepted fixture tied to state legislatures.

As time passed, members of those legislatures climbed the political ladder and arrived in Washington as senators and congressmen, expecting to find similar support available from Congress's library. The comparison between what they had known at home and what they found was distressing, and various members began introducing legislation to correct the situation.

By 1911, when seven such bills appeared, Putnam had resigned himself to the inevitability of the added service and reacted character- istically. He wasted no time on apologies but did a detailed analysis of the work and organization of all the known state bureaus and of what European counterparts there had been thus far. He described what would be required to set up a similar service in the Library and sent the completed report of over 20,000 words to Congress.

In 1912, Representative John M. Nelson of Madison pressed his bill, which would duplicate the Wisconsin idea on a considerably grander scale at the national level, and hearings were held. Representatives from various state legislative reference bureaus described their experi- ences, and Lord James Bryce, British ambassador to the United States, testified about equivalent services in the House of Commons. Repre- sentative Swagar Sherley of Kentucky, like other congressmen, felt that the bill-drafting should be left with the two houses of Congress, but

as to the reference bureau, there should be no great difficulty. You simply want here a corps of men sufficiently trained to give to Congress, or to a proper number of Members on request, data touching any particular question. In a sense the Library of Congress is supposed to supply that thing now. Practically it does not supply it at all. It may be somewhat the fault of Congress and the Members of Congress, but by having a small corps of men, whose duties pertain only to the demands of Congress, I think you could create a body that could gather together data—could be not the mind of Congress, but, so to speak, the hands and the eyes and the ears of Congress, because all of us, as our work increases with longer tenure, realize the impossibility of making the investigation that we would like to do before coming to a conclusion. No one desires to have Congress have some other body doing its thinking, but all of us would like to have the data collected that would enable us to arrive at better conclusions.

In 1913, six more bills were introduced, and at Senator Robert LaFollette's urging (he had been governor of Wisconsin when the prototype reference bureau was created), the Senate held hearings, again with the Wisconsin model in mind. In 1914, the idea of setting up a bureau by formal statute was finessed through a Senate floor amendment to the Library's budget for fiscal 1915. Quickly accepted by the House, the amendment read: "Legislative reference: To enable the Librarian of Congress to employ competent persons to prepare such indexes, digests, and compilations of law as may be required for Congress and other official use."

Thus the Legislative Reference Service (LRS) was founded. Today, under the name of the Congressional Research Service (CRS), it receives well over 1,500 congressional inquiries each day—rather than the "three or four" that had embarrassed Mr. Putnam.

The experience clearly impressed itself on Putnam's mind, and he never again slighted his legislative ties. From this point on, his congressional relations were flawless, so much so that by the 1920s, a conservative legislature was appropriating $1.5 million to buy the Vollbehr collection of 3,000 rare books, and by the 1930s, Putnam's appropriation requests were being passed exactly as he requested them, frequently with only the most cursory review.

By the end of World War I, Putnam had overcome his processing problems and had firmed up his congressional support. From then on, he concentrated on building and using the Library's collections. His library was to be "universal in scope; national in service," and, as he said when someone remonstrated that his expanding interlibrary loan program ran the risk of losing material from the permanent collections: "Some volumes might be lost to posterity. But after all we are ourselves a posterity. Some respect is due to the ancestors who have saved for our use."

He pursued every avenue to make the Library preeminent in Americana. Early in his tenure, Theodore Roosevelt had transferred all the so-called Revolutionary archives from the Department of State to the Library of Congress. These comprised the records and papers of the Continental Congress and the papers of Washington, Madison, Monroe, Hamilton, and Franklin. In 1921, the librarian of the Department of State suggested that the engrossed parchment copies of the Declaration of Independence and the Constitution also be transferred to the Library of Congress so the general public could see these fundamental documents. Putnam brought them to Capitol Hill and personally placed them in a special shrine in the Library's Great Hall.

A law was passed that authorized all federal departments to transfer to the Library all duplicate or superseded material, and this greatly strengthened the collections in documents of the executive departments and records of ongoing federal programs. There were limits, however, to what Putnam believed was appropriate to the Library's holdings, and he refused the records of the U.S. military occupation of Cuba on the grounds that they belonged more properly to a "national archives depository," which he recommended be established elsewhere.

Although Putnam emphasized Americana, he sought foreign material as well. He bought a complete library of Russian history and culture (80,000 volumes for a fourth of their true value), which was brought from Siberia across Europe in 500 specially built packing cases; he acquired 9,000 "carefully selected works" in Japanese and 5,041 volumes of the famous Chinese encyclopedia, *Tu shu chi cheng.* By World War II, he had assembled the largest collections of Russian, Chinese, Hebraic, Judaic, and Semitic materials existing outside their parent countries (a standing that still obtains today).

In 1925, he created a dramatic precedent by changing the Library's role from that of merely servicing the materials it has to one of producing new works for the nation. In that year, he accepted the offer of Mrs. Elizabeth Sprague Coolidge, the nationally known patroness of the Berkshire Music Festival, to build a 500-seat auditorium in the northwest court of the building. With it as a showcase, Mrs. Coolidge established a generous endowment to pay for free concerts by outstanding chamber music ensembles and to commission new compositions by famous composers. In 1935, the tradition was further strengthened by Gertude Clarke Whittall's gift of five Stradivari instruments and Tourte bows. She also paid for the construction of a separate pavilion to be built within the courtyard so the Strads could be properly housed and played. Whittall funds were also used to acquire such rare music manuscripts as Brahms's original score for his Third Symphony, Beethoven's final draft of the E Major Sonata, and the complete holograph of Mozart's Violin Concerto in A Major.

In like manner, Putnam brought in money with which to endow chairs of American history, fine arts, aeronautics, and poetry. As he explained, they were neither teaching chairs nor research chairs, but each was to be an "interpretive" chair, "whose incumbent will combine with administrative duties an active aid and counsel to those pursuing research in the Library and general promotion of research within his field."

Putnam was highly conscious of the Library's role in the intellectual life of the nation. He lectured widely before both the library and the scholarly professions, and he created an interesting device that frequently appears in the biographies of the period: the Librarian's Round Table. In those days, the Library's dining room was located on the top floor of the building overlooking the Capitol, and there was a private dining room off the public one. Here Putnam would preside over daily luncheons of writers, government officials, visiting intellectuals, diplomats, and his favorite library staff. The phrase "had a fascinating . . . stimulating . . . interesting luncheon at the Librarian's Round Table" appears in such diverse memoirs as those of H. G. Wells, Henry Adams, and the Supreme Court justices of the day.

Throughout his tenure, Putnam continued to divide and establish new divisions with a lavish hand—making each directly responsible to himself. In 1915, the Semitic Division appeared; in 1917, a Division of Classification was broken out of the original Catalogue Division; in 1922, a Binding Division was split off from the Printing Division, and a Building and Grounds Division appeared, as well as the Slavic Division; 1928 brought the appearance of the Division of Chinese Literature; 1929, a Division of Fine Arts and a new Disbursing Office (which also handled the funds for the Botanic Garden). In 1930, the Rare Book Room appeared, as well as the new Division of Aeronautics. The Division of Orientalia came in 1932; another fragmentation of cataloging came when the Division of Cooperative Cataloging and Classification was established in 1934; and in 1936, the Division of the Union Catalog was formed. As late as 1938, the Librarian created a Photoduplication Service (with Rockefeller Foundation Funds) and a Publication Section.

Like Spofford, Putnam first filled, then exceeded, the space he had inherited, and he ended his career by providing a new building for his successor. In 1928, he got land purchased behind the great gray building for an annex. In 1930, the new building was begun, and Putnam opened it in April 1939. It was solid, businesslike, and functional, holding twice as many books as the primary building and twice as large a working staff in a third less space, but with little style and less grace.

On June 7, 1939, after serving for forty years, Herbert Putnam retired to become Librarian Emeritus and was given an office "down the hall." There he held formal state for fifteen more years while his successors struggled first with World War II and then with the information explosion. At the age of ninety-two, according to a local reporter, he still "gets up at 6 A.M., prepares his own breakfast, takes a trolley to Capitol Hill, maintains regular office hours, handles his mail, receives

The north reading room on the fifth floor of the Adams building is shown here shortly after Ezra Winter completed his murals based on Chaucer's *Canterbury Tales.*

numerous visitors and is available for consultation." In 1955, at ninety-three, he passed away: vigorous, respected, and having viewed the activities of his successors with stern, detached disapproval.

Archibald Macleish

But Librarian Putnam had retired in 1939, and the Librarian's position had opened again for the first time in forty years. Who was to be next? It had been two generations since the argument over newspaperman Young, and the few professionals who gave it any thought assumed that of course the new appointee would be a professional librarian. They assumed the issue had been settled and that hereafter, the problem would simply be to decide who was currently the nation's leading librarian. Franklin D. Roosevelt, who had to make the choice, was unfortunately unaware of the tradition. Roosevelt's friend, Supreme Court Justice Felix Frankfurter, told him, "only a scholarly man of letters can make a great national library a general place of habitation for scholars," so, on June 7, 1939, Roosevelt nominated the poet Archibald MacLeish to be the ninth Librarian of Congress. The scholarly world seems to have been surprised but noncommittal. The library profession was completely taken aback—at first irritated, then vocationally furious. The president of the American Library Association, Milton J. Ferguson, sent the President a letter that began, "We think that the confirmation of Mr. Archibald MacLeish as librarian of Congress would be a calamity," and Ferguson pressed his point with such phrases as "Mr. MacLeish could not qualify for the librarianship of any college or public library in America which attempts to maintain professional standards," and "The appointment of a man as a figurehead would do no honor to the appointee." The letter concluded with the signatures of 1,400 librarians (who were attending the ALA Convention in San Francisco at the time).

Confirmed by the Senate, Mr. MacLeish took office on October 2, barely four weeks after the outbreak of World War II and the invasion of Poland. Within a remarkably short time, he had endeared himself to the Library's staff, earned their warm loyalty, and been so forgiven by the profession at large that he was accorded a standing ovation at a subsequent ALA Convention, where he was introduced as the best friend American libraries had. Anywhere.

Librarian MacLeish is remembered for two things. He reorganized the Library from top to bottom, and he faced up to the need for a rationalized order of not only what materials the Library should seek and keep, but—possibly more important from a working librarian's point of view—what it could throw away. As a corollary, he attempted to describe where the Library should invest its energies and what its priorities of effort should be. If you can't keep everything, what should you keep first? If you can't do everything, what should you do now? The reorganization followed the course of events rather than design. As MacLeish wrote:

> What actually happened in 1939 and 1940 and thereafter was merely this: that one problem or another would demand action; that to take action it would become necessary to consider the effect of the proposed action on related situations; that related situations had, in turn, their related situations; and that eventually it would prove simpler to change several things than to change one.
>
> At the beginning . . . there was no question in my mind of a "considered program for the institution as a whole." There was merely the question of survival.

As soon as he sensed the magnitude of the problems he faced, MacLeish set out to see what was causing them. He created, begged, and borrowed committees of every variety to study first one area and then another throughout the Library's system. Each committee was asked for an account of the status quo and for an enumeration of the changes that would be required to bring an area to top efficiency in its field. When the studies were completed, MacLeish had reports from eighteen examining groups, which included the leading names in librarianship of the day, federal agencies, professional associations, and the District of Columbia Fire Department. (An *obiter dictum* was also received from the CIO on the "underpaid and misclassified" status of the librarians.)

Astonishingly, the reports revealed a situation as bad as, if not worse than, when Putnam had taken over from Young. The Library now had an arrearage of 1,670,161 volumes (exclusive of maps, music, and manuscripts), and the arrearage was growing at the rate of 30,000 books a year. In one area alone, the Bindery Department, there were 373,721 volumes waiting to be processed, lying in bins and lost to use and circulation.

Considering the known skills and awesome reputation of MacLeish's predecessor, the obvious question was, How could this have happened? The answer appeared to be that at least three things had occurred so imperceptibly that Putnam had not noticed them. First, the Library had become big business, a major bureau of government. Second, Putnam's attention had been distracted; like Spofford, he had failed to keep the three responsibilities in balance. And third, the mass of material pouring into the Library—the result of all the copyright, gift, exchange, and bulk purchase agreements of nearly a century's accumulation—had built into an avalanche. There seems to be no doubt that the work of the Library had indeed been current in the early 1900s, but as Putnam's efforts turned to the reference and cultural activities of the institution, he simply lost track of—or did not care—what was happening on the processing side. According to a distinguished committee of librarians from Harvard, New York, and Chicago:

> The great complexity of the Library machine had prevented effective control of technical operations and had permitted great variations in the quantity, quality, and uniformity of work done in the various divisions and sections. It had been impossible to maintain qualitative standards of performance because of the enormous increase in accessions. The quality of administration had also declined to such a degree that administrators had been unable or unwilling to find solutions for the resulting difficulties.

Putnam had carried the principle of unity of command to its furthest limit. When he had inherited the Library from John Russell Young, it had 850,000 volumes and a staff of 134. When he passed it to MacLeish, it contained 6,375,000 volumes and there were 1,300 employees, all depending (in the words of the poet/administrator) "from the Librarian as the miraculous architecture of the paper wasp hangs from a single anchor." Every decision of any significance in any unit had had to be individually approved by Herbert Putnam. He had hired, fired, promoted, maintained public relations, secured funds, controlled expenditures, detailed programs, determined policy, and kept personal tabs on the most routine items. We are told by public administrators that the highest degree of coordination takes place within departments when they are broadly structured and that the greatest frictions occur between departments or at points where they overlap. If this is so, Putnam had built in thirty-five lines of friction, and MacLeish began by reducing them as quickly as possible.

In 1940, he sorted thirty-six units into five groups: a Processing Department with five divisions (Accessions, Descriptive Cataloging, Subject Cataloging, Catalog Preparation, and Cards); a Reference Department with twenty-one divisions (with staffs ranging in size from the hundreds of employees in the reading rooms to a handful in the Project F Indic Study); an Administrative Department with six divisions; the Law Library; and the Copyright Office.

Although the new arrangement reduced the Librarian's own span of control to five, it left the department heads with more than they could cope with, so in 1944, MacLeish did some readjusting, splitting the huge Reference Department into three large, internal units: the Legislative Reference Service, the Public Reference Service (with nine "type" divisions, such as Maps, Rare Books, Manuscripts), and a Circulation Service.

In the next thirty-five years only 3 substantive changes were made— Acquisitions was folded back into Processing, the LRS/CRS took on departmental status, and the "national programs" cluster became a department in its own right. The resulting structure exists today. (When we come to see how the Library actually works in our own time, we will examine its present organization in more detail.)

Of equal importance to his reorganization plans was MacLeish's rationalization of the Library's mission. The purpose was stated in his "Objectives of the Library of Congress." The character of the collections, he declared, was defined by the fact that they were

available for the use of three categories of users: first, the members of the Congress; second, officers of the Federal Government and the staffs of various government departments and agencies including the Supreme Court and its Bar; and, third, the general public—all comers from all places. Since it is impossible for the Library to "collect everything," selection of books must be made upon the basis of the anticipated needs of these three classes of users in the order given. To this end the Library adopts three Canons of Selection.

The Canons were as follows:

1. The Library of Congress should possess in some useful form all bibliothecal materials necessary to the Congress and to the officers of government of the United States in the performance of their duties.
2. The Library of Congress should possess all books and other materials (whether in original or copy), which express and record the life and achievements of the people of the United States.
3. [It] should possess, in some useful form, the material parts of the records of other societies, past and present, and should accumulate, in original or in copy, full and representative collections of the written records of those societies and peoples whose experience is of most immediate concern to the people of the United States.

These generalities were then applied to the thousands of specific subjects covered by the Library of Congress classification scheme, and specific categories were assigned. Some topics were to be collected comprehensively, others on a research level. Still others were limited to major works alone—and two areas, medicine and agriculture, were abandoned to the other national libraries. These priorities, further elaborated and continually revised, are still an integral part of the acquisition policies of the Library.

Such a rethinking of traditional procedures occurred in every department, division, and section. MacLeish brought a revitalization to the institution that generated its own momentum. Every element seemed to come alive. He achieved his hope that he had given "an increasing number of men and women the sense of participating creatively and responsibly in a work which all of them may well feel proud to share."

MacLeish served for barely five years. They were the World War II years, and not only was the Library of Congress itself swept into the war effort, but Franklin Roosevelt increasingly used MacLeish as a personal representative in affairs of state. While serving as Librarian of Congress, he was made the first director of the Office of Facts and Figures and then assistant director of the Office of War Information. He then served as representative to the founding meetings of what became UNESCO, and finally he was made Assistant Secretary of State, and to accept that post, he resigned as Librarian on December 19, 1944.

The employees he left behind compared the experience of having worked with him to having lived in the tail of a comet, but there was no question of their enthusiasm for MacLeish and for the adventure they had shared. In retrospect, there is no question that he pulled the institution into the twentieth century (albeit belatedly) and prepared it for the demands that would be laid upon it in our own time of accelerated information transfer.

Luther Evans

MacLeish was followed by Luther Harris Evans. Evans was a political scientist and an internationalist. MacLeish had brought Evans to the Library to run the Legislative Reference Service (LRS) on the strength of a remarkable reputation with the Works Progress Administration Historical Records Survey: Evans had conceived the idea of the survey, had sold it to the federal government, and then, as director, had got more results for less cost than had almost any of the other Depression amelioration programs. Evans had an M.A. from the University of Texas and a Ph.D. from Stanford, and he had taught political science at Dartmouth and Princeton—he had never been near a library school.

MacLeish had been so impressed with the way Evans had handled the LRS that he had promoted him to Chief Assistant Librarian and director of the Reference Department, and in 1943, he had made him full-time Assistant Librarian. When MacLeish moved to the State Department, he recommended that Evans be made Librarian, and President Truman concurred. The American Library Association accepted the appointment without demur, still so embarrassed over its treatment of MacLeish that it dared not mount its traditional "library professional only" assault.

Evans was a heavy-set, grizzly-bear kind of figure with a gruff, macho image, which he consciously projected to be certain no one confused him with the traditional librarian stereotype. He sometimes overcompensated for that threat, such as the time he told a roomful of Appropriations Committee members that he could drink any man in the room under the table (thereby losing the support of an unusually large number of Baptist and Methodist congressmen).

Evans became the tenth Librarian of Congress on June 30, 1945, halfway between V-E and V-J Days. He was deeply impressed with what he perceived as the lessons to be learned from the recent war. "No spot on the earth's surface is any longer alien to the interest of the American people," he said. "No particle of knowledge should remain unavailable to them." He set out "to revise and rebuild and reconstruct the Library to resolve for its own part and within the terms of its own duties, the problems which this new world [will] encounter."

Working closely with his middle managers (whom he knew personally from his days as Assistant Librarian), Evans designed a new, service-oriented expansion of the Library. He identified those aspects of the Library's programs that would help local libraries, and he sought out those tools and programs of the Library that would best cut down on duplication of research by state governments. His "Library of Congress for the postwar period" was carefully developed and costed out, and a special effort was made to show each member of Congress how money spent on the Library could save money for their own state universities, state legislatures, and constituents at home.

Once the plan was designed, it required an increase of the Library's annual appropriation from $5.1 million to $9.8 million. It was carefully presented to the House Appropriations Committee, which denied every increase requested except for some minor expansions of the Legislative Reference Service and the Copyright Office. The committee explained:

> The original purpose in establishing the Library was to serve Congress, however, it would seem that the Library has evolved not only into a Congressional library but a national and international library as well. . . . If it is the desire to build and maintain the largest library in the world which, according to testimony, the Library of Congress is at present, that is one matter, and if it should be the policy to maintain a library primarily for the service of Congress, it is quite another matter from the standpoint of fiscal needs.

In the absence of any such change in Congress's intent, expanded service to the nation was thereby and therewith disallowed.

This initial put-down characterized Evans's tenure. The Congress watched him intently, repeatedly asking, What's he up to now? Evans, in turn, tried to get support from outside groups—the American Library Association, the American Political Science Association, and the American Historical Association—to make the materials and services of the Library available to a larger audience. Evans believed that since the Library was the largest government library at the federal level, it should play a unifying role among federal libraries and provide single-point acquisition for all, shared cataloging, and union records for the individual agencies. Congress was distressed at his apparent inability to understand the principle of separation of powers—his eagerness "to give the Congressional library away to the Executive." As time went on, the mutual hostility went from distrust to resentment to the outright baiting of one another.

Evans was in office for eight years, and during this period, he found he could advance his plans in two areas: (1) Congress was sympathetic to anything that strengthened the Library's services to the Congress, so it supported steady expansion of the Legislative Reference Service, and (2) Evans found he could expand his bibliographic support to the library world simply by publishing the bibliographic tools the Library created for its own use. Frequently using private funds or foundation support as initial seed money, and then continuing publication on a revolving-fund basis, such series as the *Cumulative Catalog of Library of Congress Printed Cards, New Serial Titles, Rules for Descriptive Cataloging,* the *Southern Asia Accessions List,* and the *Monthly List of Russian Accessions* began.

Evans had victories and defeats with his cultural activities. He successfully opened a Poetry Office (with private, Whittall money), staged literary programs, began broadcasting the music series on nationwide FM radio, and began selling phonograph albums of leading poets reading their own works. On the loss side, the Fellows of the Library awarded the Bollingen Prize in Poetry to Ezra Pound, which in turn stirred up so much controversy in the literary world that the Joint Committee on the Library instructed the Library to cancel "all arrangements for the giving of prizes and the making of awards"—a prohibition that still holds today.

The treasures of the Library increased dramatically during Evans's time. He secured the papers of such significant Americans as the Wright brothers, George Gershwin, Woodrow Wilson, John Philip Sousa, and Gen. John J. Pershing; he acquired the early motion picture library of Mary Pickford, the Giant Bible of Mainz, Jean Hersholt's Hans Christian Andersen collection, Leonard Kebler's Cervantes collection; and the complete Rachmaninoff archives were secured from the composer's widow. Evans sent microfilming crews abroad, and they brought back copies of such disparate riches as the complete manuscript collection of St. Catherine's Monastery on Mt. Sinai, portions of the archives of the Japanese Foreign Office, and the majority of the official gazettes of the states of Mexico.

As Evans's tenure progressed, Congress became increasingly distressed with his "internationalism," which they saw in the Library's vastly increased overseas purchases, the expanding international exchange agreements, and Evans's frequent remarks about the legislature's conservatism and parochial attitude toward the world at large. Congress claimed that Evans spent too much time in Paris helping to create UNESCO and too little time running the Library. Thus, when Evans was offered the position of director general of UNESCO, the oversight committees wished him a prompt and hearty Godspeed. He resigned on July 1, 1953. Within fifteen years, almost all of the programs he had recommended but had been denied became a reality as a part of the national reaction to the Russian Sputnik.

L. Quincy Mumford

Lawrence Quincy Mumford was the eleventh Librarian of Congress, and he held the post for twenty years—1954 to 1974. Although we are still a bit too close to his administration to be sure we can see how history will remember him, it begins to appear that he and his two decades will prove to be the greatest paradoxes of the Library's first 200 years. His record is the kind that keeps public administrators humble and blunts the arrogance of their neatest maxims; his style and administrative techniques ran counter to most of the accepted rules.

Mumford was a quiet, very orderly man. He spoke with precision, communicating in single, subject-verb-object sentences, and once the purposed sentence was expressed, the thought was neither illustrated nor elaborated on. He dealt only with his personal staff and his immediate department heads, expecting them in turn to deal with the successive steps of the pecking order. Few members of the general staff ever saw him, and it was estimated that less than a tenth of the employees would have recognized him had they met him in an elevator. He did not believe in long-range plans; instead, he solved problems one at a time, worked out budget strategies a hearing at a time, and tended to rely on his managers for innovative suggestions.

What is remarkable is the fact that Mumford will certainly join Spofford and Putnam as one of the Library's "big three," and he will probably share the peak with Putnam as having done more for the Library in a single lifetime than any other leader in the institutional pantheon. When Mumford acquired the Library from Evans, it had a staff of 1,500 employees and a budget of $9.5 million. When he passed it on to his successor, Daniel J. Boorstin, it had 4,250 employees and an annual appropriation of $96 million.

L. Quincy Mumford was as much a librarian's librarian as Evans had tried not to be. Mumford was the first Librarian of Congress to have a library degree (from Columbia), had worked at the New York Public Library and Cleveland Public, and when President Eisenhower appointed him Librarian of Congress, was president-elect of the American Library Association. From the beginning, he had the fullest support of the library world.

The same could not be said of his relationship with the Congress. Without doubt, he inherited the worst legislative situation the Library had seen in a century. On the occasion of his first meeting with the House oversight committee, he was told: "The new Librarian should be mindful that the Library is the instrument and the creature of Congress. Its duties historically have been to meet the needs of the Members of Congress first and to limit its services to others to that which can be furnished with the funds and the staff available." The Senate counterpart told him it was less than enthusiastic about the way "the freedom of action allowed [Librarians of Congress] by law, their prerogatives of independent decisions, and the manner in which they discharge their daily duties leave more to their judgment what is owing to the job than what may be owing to Congress." They cited examples of this confusion. Concerning acquisitions:

> There appears some doubt . . . that the program of accessions should be as catholic and diversified as it is. . . . The scope of the collections . . . has been extended outward to cover many things which, on second glance, would appear to be completely extraneous to a Library of Congress. Furthermore, it does not appear that there has always been a proper selectivity of acquisitions, the tendency being to accept everything. A firm policy for the dumping of unsuitable or outmoded material also seems to be lacking.

Concerning services: "It is apparent that too often the Library seems to be submerged by its own good intentions. A stopping place—a final line—should be set beyond which its public services and those to the executive agencies cannot go. Indeed, a withdrawal of many of those services or their de-emphasis appears to be in order." And so on.

Mumford solved his problem with Congress by impeccable budgetary manners. He costed everything conservatively, was consistent in his avowed priorities, never padded, and never dramatized. He had an encyclopedic memory and could deliver figures, statutory citations, and "bottom lines" with precision, so year by year, he won the growing respect of his appropriation committees. Similarly, he was careful to keep his oversight chairmen closely aware of Library programs and innovations; he treated them with great respect and awe, and they, in turn, increasingly considered it "our" Library with a feeling of paternal protection. Congress soon came to trust him and ultimately became vigorously supportive.

Mumford benefited from the national inferiority complex that swept the nation when the Soviets launched a tiny satellite around the world. The federal government reacted by pulling every lever it could reach to "catch up" intellectually and technologically, and several aspects of the reaction impacted on the Library.

The first related to the fears, Does anybody know something we don't know? and What are other nations doing we haven't heard of? To protect the country against these unknowns, the Library of Congress was assigned the task of acquiring "all library materials of value to scholarship that are currently published throughout the world and providing catalog information for these materials promptly." "All materials" soon came to be interpreted quite literally as *all* materials, and soon the Library was receiving a copy of essentially "everything" published in Switzerland, Kenya, France, Brazil, Indonesia, et cetera. Library of Congress offices were opened in New Delhi, Tokyo, Oslo, Belgrade, and Cairo, and "all" the publishing of those countries was purchased. The material was cataloged on the spot by local librarians and then flown back to the Library of Congress via air freight. Once there, cataloging data was distributed to research libraries throughout the United States through monthly, published accession lists. Universities and public libraries could then order copies of the books or magazines directly from the issuing country or borrow the materials from the Library of Congress through interlibrary loan. This mass, foreign purchase program (usually paid for through blocked foreign aid currency) came to be known as the National Program for Acquisitions and Cataloging. It placed millions of volumes on the Library's shelves and expanded every aspect of the Library's operations: preservation (over half of the material had to be bound); publishing (the monthly union catalog volumes doubled and trebled in size); printed cards (these rose to more than 79 million a year, each one to be sorted, filed, or sold, one at a time).

A second shock wave rolled through the Library at the same time: automation arrived. The building of lists—pure, permanent data—was immediately recognized as a classic application of the computer, and in 1961, at the urging of Senator Leverett Saltonstall and the Senate Appropriations Committee, the Library began its long battle with what Mr. Saltonstall called "electronics." The first programs were designed to establish the basic format of the digitalized catalog card, and this was done in a form called MARC (for MAchine-Readable Cataloging), which was invented and expanded by the Library staff. In 1966, the Library began to distribute weekly reels of MARC data to libraries, business firms, and later, regional computer networks. This distribution had the effect of providing instantaneous bibliographic control of the world's publishing, and thus, with the MARC tapes, the Library had at last achieved the ultimate form of Herbert Putnam's 1898 dream of cataloging in a single place and letting all libraries copy the single prefabricated part.

Another innovation, the Cataloging in Publication (CIP) program, began under Mumford. This was the final fruition of yet another longtime dream of librarians, which had been discussed, debated, and explored for decades. For CIP, the nation's publishers would send galley

Books from Pakistan, purchased with PL 480 funds, leave the American Libraries Procurement Center in Karachi.

proofs of their forthcoming books to the Library; the Library would rush-catalog the contents and create the data for the author card, under which each book would be filed in libraries; the copy for the card would be returned to the publisher, who would then print it on the back of the title page in the book itself. Thus, when a library bought a book, it would not need to purchase printed or computerized cards or to spend time figuring out subject headings and an appropriate call number for itself. It could simply copy the data out of the book, data that was free and preprocessed by the Library of Congress. Within a year of the program's inception, over 200 major publishers were sending in galley proofs and publishing the card copy they received in return.

One of Mumford's greatest—and most exhausting—triumphs was the building of the huge James Madison memorial library. Spofford's original Library of Congress building had taken twenty-six years to plan, sell, and build; Putnam's annex had taken twelve years. When Mumford's turn arrived, he submitted his first specifications and drawings to the Architect of the Capitol in 1958. The building was then designed and defended and resurrected and modified and saved over and over again until it was finally occupied in the winter of 1980, twenty-two years later. But it is a tour de force of librarianship.

The Madison Building fills a complete city block six floors above and three below ground. Having no hollow core or courtyards, it is built of solid, weight-bearing concrete, and of all the federal government's real estate, only the Pentagon and the FBI buildings are larger. Within, the rare materials are housed at the most appropriate temperature in perfect humidity and dust-free air. Materials march through work-sequences in logical order. Computerized delivery systems crisscross the departments, and television and computer cables run through special ducts. In the performing arts rooms, motion picture and television viewing screens line special consoles, which are fed by closed cable from multiple remote sources, decks away. Music is placed on tape decks and turntables in cellar areas for listening on the proper floors of the library above. And so forth. The building now houses 4,000 staff members and plays host to half a million visitors and readers each year. With the opening of the third building, Congress passed a law formally terminating the traditional "Main" and "Annex" labels and declaring that henceforth these should be known as the Thomas Jefferson and John Adams buildings, respectively.

Quincy Mumford became enmeshed in one final issue, one that has pummeled every Librarian from the Civil War to the present: Just whose library is it? Congress's or the nation's? We will touch on this dilemma only briefly here, because it will come up again and again throughout the book, but Mumford was present at two of the major battles.

The first was an assault on the Library by Douglas W. Bryant, associate director of the Harvard University Library. In 1962, Senator Claiborne Pell of the Joint Committee on the Library asked Bryant for a memorandum on what the Library of Congress did and what it ought to do for the government and the nation in general. When Senator Pell introduced Mr. Bryant's resulting recommendations into the *Congressional Record*, he noted, "We have tended to take for granted our Library of Congress—our basic working tool which underlies all our useful schol-arship, the responsible work of our Congress, and the very culture of our nation."

Taking his assignment at face value, Mr. Bryant had recommended the unspeakable. He suggested that for the good of all concerned, the Legislative Reference Service should be broken off and given to Congress so it could provide the information Congress needed to govern. He urged that the Copyright Office be removed and be placed in the executive branch, presumably as a part of the Patent Office. The rest of the institution, "the national library," should either be handed over to the Smithsonian Institution or be set up as a cultural entity somewhere under the President—but in any event, removed from the legislative branch.

Having thus improved the environment in which the Library would work, Bryant then suggested that the national library should initiate new programs. He provided a list of examples: do basic "research and experimentation in the application of modern technology to library purposes," assist underdeveloped countries in strengthening their libraries and creating national bibliographies, build and operate laboratories to preserve research materials, supervise federal grants-in-aid to local libraries, and run scholarship and fellowship programs for library professionals.

The Joint Committee on the Library evinced some astonishment at this dramatic checklist but was reasonably sympathetic to its purpose; the staff of the Library, although ambivalent about leaving the legislative branch, was intrigued and excited about the vista of new horizons. Both sides were astonished when Mumford mounted a strong attack to discredit every suggestion that had been made from top to bottom of the memorandum. He prepared long, written rebuttals; he met with both congressional and library leaders to refute both the implied need and the suggested solutions; he gave out interviews to the library news media. By the end of many months of such activity, his efforts had achieved his aim. Congress began to feel that change would be more trouble than it was worth and lost interest in the whole discussion. The library profession wrote the argument off as another example of the Library's love for the status quo, and nothing further was heard of the Bryant Memorandum. But the debate left resentment on all sides.

This episode might have done serious damage had not ongoing congressional history taken the pressure off the argument. A swelling tide of congressional reform furnished a kind of solution to the problem. Throughout the fifties and sixties, Congress had grown increasingly resentful of a series of presidents who either ignored the Legislature or told it imperially how to act. Rather than being the primary branch, it had become the least and weakest of the Constitutional three. Congress began to correct the imbalance by streamlining its procedures and "breaking" the seniority system. It modernized its budgeting techniques and created a special budget office with two new budget committees, and then, to reduce its dependency on the executive branch for statistics, information, and policy choices, it decided to use the Library of Congress as a policy analysis center.

The reformers took the long-standing, nonpartisan Legislative Reference Service and added some 600 new subject specialists skilled in the full spectrum of public policy. These analysts, beholden to the congressional branch, not to the presidential cabinet agencies, were to calculate costs, explore legislative options, do future projections, and apply the latest techniques of computer modeling and matrix analysis to national social issues. The result of all the activity was that the renamed Congressional Research Service (CRS) not only trebled in size but also reassured the Congress that it was receiving massive support from "its library"; it no longer needed to worry about the Library being distracted from its legislative purpose. The Legislative Reorganization Act gave the CRS a separate budget and spelled out its "maximum administrative independence" from the rest of the Library. The oversight committees began to refer to "the CRS" and "the Library" as two equal and independent partners. The gain was to ease the resentment and the fear of a "national" library at the expense of the Congressional one; the cost was to drive a slowly widening fissure down the institution (a we/they, FBI versus Justice Department split) that has steadily worsened rather than being eased by time.

After twenty years of quiet, orderly service, L. Quincy Mumford retired at the close of 1974, and President Ford appointed Daniel J. Boorstin as his successor the following year. Boorstin had been a Rhodes scholar, was a Pulitzer Prize winning historian and an Oxford-trained lawyer, and was director of the Museum of History and Technology of the Smithsonian Institution when he was named as Librarian. Today's institution is Boorstin's working tool, and we will see the changes he has made in organization and purpose as we examine the present establishment.

*   *   *

We have now devoted as many words and as much space as we dare to the institution's history. We have skipped through 200 years like a spinning rock across a pond, but we hope we have given some suggestion of the way the Library arrived at its present form. Our chief interests in this book are how the Library works and what its future looks like, but for us to advance through this empire of large countries and small duchies with any kind of order, we need some kind of a road map. Let us therefore take a very brief glance at the organization chart to get the lay of the land.

3

THE ORGANIZATION OF THE LIBRARY

When a visitor tells a Washington cab driver, "Take me to the Library of Congress," the odds are that he or she will be deposited on a street corner across from the Capitol building with a casual, "There it is," and before said visitor can ask, *"Where?"* the cab will have sped away. Our visitor is faced with three enormous buildings, each occupying a full city block and each marked, "Library of Congress." This visual confusion is a splendid symbol of the organizational confusion inside. One building is wedding-cake Italian Renaissance, another is dazzling art deco, and the third is "General Services Administration Moderne." They seem to have no relationship to each other. The administrative units within seem equally independent.

The Library is divided into six great empires: the Congressional Research Service, which serves the Congress; the Copyright Office, which serves the nation's creative community; the Law Library, which serves the legal community; the Research Services cluster, which serves the academic community; the Processing Services divisions, which serve both the national library and the library community; and the National Programs cluster, which acts as a home office for programs that operate outside the walls and outside Washington.

Within these six nations, some eighty-five independent operations function, such as the American Folklife Center, the Near Eastern and African Law Division, the Network Development Office, the Licensing Division, and the National Referral Center. All of these operations employ between 5,000 and 6,000 staff members, depending on the time of year and the condition of the contracting programs.

From the point of view of the taxi passenger standing on the curb with his back to the Capitol, the first decision is simply, Which building should he enter? His decision is based on the following elements:

A view of the interior of the dome of the Main Reading Room.

1. If the visitor is a user of the Library in the same sense as a student approaching a campus library or a citizen going into the local public library, he should go into the great gray Jefferson Building—the Renaissance edifice with the green dome. Once inside, he should ask directions to the Main Reading Room, the circular center of the building, where he will be served by professional reference librarians. They will either care for him there or direct him to one of the specialized reading rooms distributed around the eighteen floors of the three buildings. (The buildings, incidentally, are connected by underground pedestrian tunnels, which in turn pass under the streets, over the subterranean railroad tracks of the Southern Railway, under the mechanical book systems linking the Library with the Capitol, alongside the vaulted crypt to the Supreme Court Building, and below the steam- and ice-

water tunnels running to a power plant nearly a mile away. These various passages crisscross beneath the dignified Library buildings and give a misplaced patron the sense of having walked onto a science fiction set.)

2. If the visitor is a senior researcher, or knows in advance that the information she seeks will be in nonbook material (like music, motion pictures, manuscripts, maps, art prints, or photographs), she should go to the newest building, the James Madison Memorial Library, and ask for directions at the information desk in the lobby.

3. If the visitor is seeking material in non-Roman languages, such as Arabic, Hebrew, Hindu, Chinese, Japanese, Thai, or Russian, he should go to the white, 1939 art deco, John Adams Building located behind the Jefferson. Similarly, scholars wishing to work in specialized and advanced science materials should go directly to the Adams Building. (Note: People familiar with the Library from 1939 to 1980 knew the Adams Building as "the Annex"; the name was changed by law when the Madison Building was opened.)

4. Visitors wishing to participate in the Library's concert series, attend its literary lectures, or see its exhibitions should go directly to the 1897 Jefferson Building.

5. Finally, those wishing to do business with the Copyright Office, the Congressional Research Service, or the Processing Department, will find those services in the Madison Building.

How could such a simple thing as a library have gotten so complicated? The answer can be found in those eighty-five self-sufficient little countries or cells, which the Library calls divisions. Organized around a special kind of work or a kind of collection or a specific program, they can be perceived either as the elements that make the whole Library possible—or the fractures that make its work very difficult. With the usual occasional exception, 90 percent of the divisions have a chief and an assistant, a secretarial support unit, and then the people who actually do the work or care for a particular kind of material or run a particular program. Most divisions have from 50 to 100 staff members, and most of these cells are astonishingly self-sufficient—the people who work in them have the same social sense as members of "the political science department" or "the library school" or "the music department" do on a campus. The division is the social as well as the administrative unit, and although neighboring divisions may be only a plaster wall's thickness away, one knows next to no names outside one's own division and has few opportunities for eye contact beyond the divisional limit.

The great majority of the 5,000 to 6,000 employees in these division-units are highly trained specialists. They are musicians, lawyers,

60

THE LIBRARY

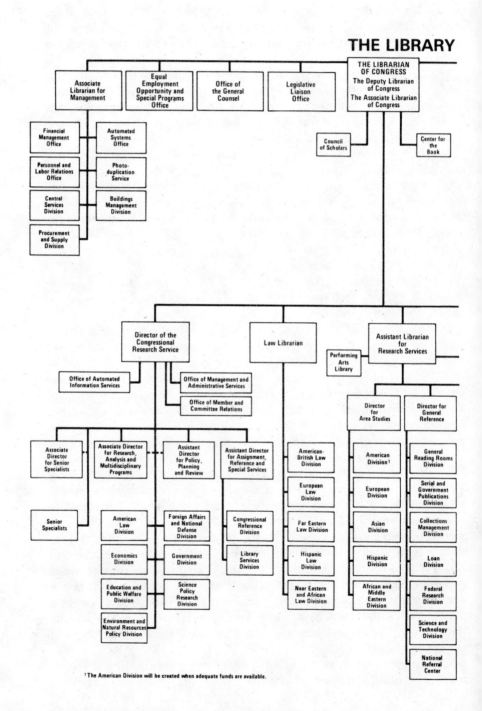

[1] The American Division will be created when adequate funds are available.

OF CONGRESS

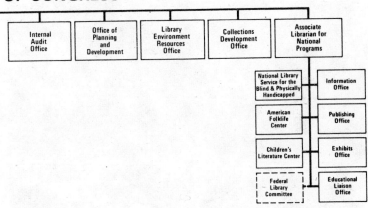

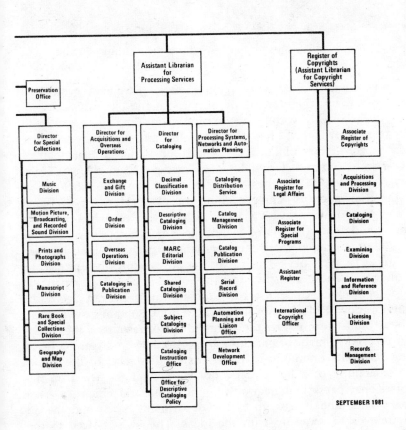

SEPTEMBER 1981

The John Adams Building, looking northeast from the Madison Building.

preservation chemists, computer programmers, petroleum geologists, Braille proofreaders. Therefore, unity of purpose and like skills (indeed, loyalties) focus mainly within the division. They link more gently to the department in which the division falls, and they relate rather distantly to the Library of Congress. The result is that a major part of the Librarian of Congress's energies must be devoted to giving a sense of unity of purpose—a "we-ness"—to the institution. The other aspect of the Librarian's role is simply running the place. How are decisions made and passed along in such a disparate environment?

One would think the answer would lie somewhere along the neat lines of the organization chart, but experience has shown that they are merely tracks or pipelines. Which way the power flows has proved to be an integer of the personality and the interests of the Librarians of Congress themselves. Under Herbert Putnam, the tracks ran rigorously from the top down. Most innovations came from Putnam's own office, and when conflicts arose over the commitment of resources, they were usually resolved in favor of enriching the collections and gaining favor with the research community. Under Archibald MacLeish, the tracks became something of a horizontal loop. He spread the word among his professional peers that he wanted innovation and efficiency from all departments, and it was up to the department heads and the ad hoc committees to come up with the ideas. The ideas flowed to the

The James Madison Memorial Building of the Library of Congress was formally dedicated in April 1980. The glass windows above the main entrance reflect the Italian Renaissance dome of the Jefferson Building across the street.

Librarian, and if they appeared to be appropriate, he supported them. Given conflicts and limited resources, MacLeish tended to embrace anything that improved the Library as an institution, and if he favored an elite, it was the cultural elite and the press.

Under Luther Evans, the tracks became vertical again. His interests were research oriented (politics and history in particular), and his innovations began in the area of service to the professional disciplines. The majority of the innovations were originated by Evans himself and were sent "down" to the departments and divisions as directives from on high. He relied as much on outside suggestions from the public as he did on his own staff. "Decision making" frequently amounted to getting Evans's attention and making a colorful or convincing case. Once he had embraced the idea, he galvanized the appropriate division into frightened energy. Formal decision patterns were limited, in spite of the fact that he organized the most complicated lattice of employee suggestion schemes and interunit communication of any Librarian before or since. Evans's ties were originally with the academic profession, so he first committed funds to support the services that pleased the scholarly associations, but as his tour of office developed, he moved toward internationalism and concentrated his energy (and the Library's) on reciprocal cultural relationships with like organizations around the world.

Under Quincy Mumford, the tracks or pipelines reversed direction again. He played the role of the arbiter and tried to stimulate innovation by his department heads. His style was to give his principal administrators maximum independence and to urge them to improve their own areas of responsibility; he then chose from among their competing demands those he wished to back with the weight of his office. Having selected the areas he wished to support, he begged the necessary funds from Congress and underwrote those innovations with the power of his position.

Boorstin is essentially project oriented, and he focuses on specific innovations in a deliberate progression, one at a time. He determines that something needs to be initiated or improved, gathers the managers involved, instructs them in what action he wants taken, and sends them out to get the job done. His attention then moves on to the next area he wants addressed, and he energizes all the elements connected with that source of concern. The power is again located in the Librarian's office and goes down to the program divisions. The result of all this ebbing and flowing is that the locus of power seems to change with every generation—and probably in a very healthy way.

But at this point, let's abandon any further thoughts about how or why the Library is put together and get directly to what it does for its clients and how it does it.

Part Two

THE LIBRARY WHEN
IT'S WORKING WELL

4

ACQUIRING THE COLLECTIONS

Where does it all come from? Ten million pieces a year; 27,000 pieces a day—the equivalent of a complete public library arriving to be processed every working morning. It pours into the Library in endless, undifferentiated streams. As it builds up in canvas tubs, on rolling trucks, in bins, in shopping carts, along decks of cluttered, ragged shelves, it gives the appearance of undisciplined, random confusion. At the arrested moment between receipt and processing, that is exactly what it is. Its presence in the Library, however, is intentional; the mass of material comes from four rather clear-cut sources.

The Copyright Office

The first source is the transfer of material to the Library from the Copyright Office of the United States—itself a part of the Library of Congress but a discrete, independent unit within the institution. In 1980, the Copyright Office received 532,678 articles deposited for copyright, and 368,813 of them were transferred to the Library for its own use.

Oddly enough, although this material is pushed and rolled into the Library on the same vehicles as the other 9.5 million items, copyright materials are easily identifiable; they actually look different from the rest. For our purposes, the copyright material can be divided into four parts. The first portion (130,000 pieces) is simply books. These are bright, colorful, mostly in English, and have the appealing look of the contents of a lively new bookstore. The second part (230,000 pieces) is periodicals, and they are less colorful, for although they include all the popular magazines from the newsstands, there are even more professional and trade journals, which somewhat dignify the mix. The third portion looks even less appealing, being tens of thousands of

Once a copyright claimant's certificate of copyright is embossed with the Copyright Office's official seal, his or her claim to the exclusive rights of the work is formally registered.

pieces of sheet music. Very little of this music will have been published, so the majority is handwritten sheets on all sizes and kinds of paper. In reality, those three categories add up to 96 percent of the copyright whole, but the final 4 percent is the most unusual: huge sheets of maps, motion picture canisters, mounds of telephone directories, 4,000 to 5,000 new phonograph records, computer tapes, ballet notations, and various odds and ends.

All of this material comes as a result of the U.S. method for protecting the ownership of creative works. Securing copyright involves two activities: registering the work and depositing two copies with the Library of Congress. Contrary to what one might expect, the primary purpose of the deposit element is to get free books for the Library. The deposits have no archival role in subsequent litigation, the Library can keep or discard what it pleases, and this somewhat cavalier method of creating a national library has existed for well over a century. (The British have exploited the idea even further. They require copies to be deposited with the British Museum, the Bodleian Library at Oxford, the University Library at Cambridge, Trinity College in Dublin, and the

National Libraries of Scotland and Wales.)

In order to receive a copyright, an author, composer, or artist must first write to the Copyright Office (Library of Congress, Washington, D.C. 20559) and obtain the proper forms. He or she should describe the kind of work that is to be registered—such as a poem or a piece of music or a poster—and the office will provide the correct forms without charge. Once the claimant has the right forms in hand, they should be filled out and placed in a single envelope or package with a money order for ten dollars and a copy of the work to be registered. If the work has already been published, the claimant is required to provide the office with two finished copies.

Once the library has received the forms, fee, and deposit copy (or copies), the Register's staff checks the forms to see that they meet the legal requirements, and if so, the ten dollars are transferred to the U.S. Treasury, and a certificate of registration goes back to the claimant. Record cards are made under author, title, and claimant, and the books themselves are made available to the Library's selection officers to determine which of the volumes are to be retained. The paperwork up to this point can take from six to eight weeks, depending on the backlog at the time of receipt.

Some unlikely things can be copyrighted. You can copyright maps prepared for sale, drawings, magazine advertisements, comic strips, billboards, and phonograph record jackets. "Useful designs" are patented (by the Commerce Department), but works of art are copyrightable and thus, each year, the Copyright Office receives literally thousands of plaster statues, carnival dolls, designs for lingerie lace, choreographic diagrams, place mats, and Charlie Brown or Snoopy in a bewildering variety of beach balls, night-lights, doorstops, and what have you. (You cannot, incidentally, copyright titles, slogans, calendars, or blank business forms.)

The Copyright Office offers all its receipts to the Library. As a rule, the Library selects two-thirds, and what it does acquire can be generalized simply. It takes the majority of the hardback books, but only a sampling of the paperbacks. It takes many college textbooks, but almost no texts for the elementary or high school levels. It takes all of the published music and most of the unpublished. It retains most of the maps it is offered and all of the prints and photographs.

Motion pictures are an exception to every rule. From the time of their invention, two copies of each reel have been deposited with the Library to secure copyright protection, and from the beginning, the Library has not quite known what to do with them. In the early Edison days, individual paper prints were made of each frame of the film and deposited for record. This procedure was soon recognized as cumbersome

The Copyright Office registers claims to the design of games as well as to the words of a literary work.

and expensive, but the film itself could not be easily stored. From the 1890s to World War II, film was made of a nitrate compound, which became violently flammable and ultimately explosive with age. Further, it had to be rewound regularly to keep the surfaces from fusing together. Even after the industry adopted safety film in 1950, the huge bulk of a year's film production exceeded the kind of storage the Library had available. Various solutions were tried, but in the mid-1950s, an agreement was worked out with the motion picture companies under which all films—feature, educational, and television—would be deposited for copyright, examined, and then returned to the producer with the understanding that if the Library later wished to acquire a copy, it could do so. Under this arrangement, the Library surveys motion picture activities in general and selects titles falling into a number of categories. It calls back the films that win the major prizes, the several dozen that appear on the "ten best" lists each year, the significant documentaries, films that represent the work of outstanding directors or involve innovative techniques, and a representative sampling of "run of the mill" productions. Under these criteria, the Library recalled some 1,800 films for inclusion in its permanent collections in 1979.

Any material rejected by the Library (other than motion pictures) is held in the Copyright Office forever. The retention is simply a courtesy to the claimants; it is not legally required. The records of the copyright receipt are kept on the three types of cards mentioned earlier, but the cataloging at this point is strictly for record purposes. The items selected by the Library of Congress are completely redescribed by the catalogers in Processing Services before being added to the Library's collections and catalogs.

The roughly 350,000 items copyright contributes to the Library each year represent barely 5 percent of the total receipts, but in terms of later *use*, the books secured by copyright are pulled from the shelves more frequently than those obtained from any other source. In addition, the deposit device is saving the taxpayer literally millions of dollars annually.

Government Exchange

The next source of receipt is government documents. They sound dull and may look dull, but from the point of view of original research, they are the lifeblood of a contemporary library. "Government documents" once implied a yellowing, thin paper report written by some obscure bureau and filled with production statistics of some unlikely—and probably unwanted—commodity. This image is no longer appropriate. With the government involved in practically every aspect of national life, these documents have become startlingly relevant.

Most of the nation's universities and art museums are supported by some form of taxation; thus, works of scholarship and culture appear as government documents. Great quantities of the nation's medical and scientific research are supported by the government; thus, the reports of such research are government documents. Every aspect of social issues and ills—drugs, urban blight, environmental pollution, housing, integration, the energy crisis—is analyzed, and the ameliorative successes and failures are duly described in government documents.

The copyright receipt brings in the commercial publishing of the nation; the government exchange programs bring in the records of all governmental affairs. And note especially: *all* governmental affairs. The Library must have not only the federal records but also the records of the states, the major cities of the nation, all governments abroad, and all supranational creations. This adds up to a vast operation, highly organized, which handles nearly 4 million publications a year.

Documents of the Federal Government

Obviously, the Library's first obligation is to have at least one copy of every significant publication of the U.S. government. In point of fact, it attempts to get and keep at least two. Traditionally, this has been done by assigning to the Library a quantity of all publications printed by the Government Printing Office (GPO) at the time of publication. Laws to this end have been in effect for 100 years, and in 1980, the GPO sent the Library 680,642 items. At one time, this enormous receipt would have meant that the Library had automatically received all the publications of all the federal agencies, but that is no longer the case.

With the invention of the office copiers and offset printing, more and more government studies and reports are being duplicated in-house or are being printed under contract by private printers at the instigation of an agency. The result is that in order to secure any degree of totality in its federal collections, a constant program of begging must go on by letter, telephone, and Office of Management and Budget directive to secure documents issued (from a librarian's point of view) "through the back door" of an agency.

The Library ultimately receives practically everything the federal government produces. It would like to get such material when it is new but will also accept it when it is old. The Library is aided in this quest for information by a law that says that no printed publication owned by a federal library can be discarded or destroyed. *Everything* must be sent to the Library of Congress for disposal. Thus, in 1980, 3,158,721 pieces flowed into LC from government agencies—the entire libraries of discontinued bureaus, consolidated field offices, closed military bases, mothballed aircraft carriers, and no-longer-funded welfare agencies. Thus, no matter how minor the publication of a government unit, if a copy was placed in its own library, someday it will come to the Library of Congress.

Documents of the State Governments

State government documents are considerably harder to acquire than are federal ones. In the past, their primary importance to the Library was for historical purposes—a means to the preservation of the American experience. Now, with the federal government deeply involved in block grants, shared funding, and interstate and intranational activities, state documents are required as daily working papers for the use of the Congress. State documents are received principally through agreements negotiated between the Library and whatever agency in a state is most likely to know about and have access to all of that state's publications. In some cases, this is the secretary of state, in some cases the state printer, but oddly enough, in most cases, it is the state librarian. The other officers come and go, parties and personnel change, agreements evaporate, but the state librarian tends to endure and seems to know whom to call. As an acquisitions librarian will point out, state librarians also recognize the absolute importance of unbroken serial sets and the need for prompt receipt of unemployment statistics, highway outlays, and welfare totals when an importunate legislator is pressing for materials.

Ironically, one of the chief motivations behind the acquisition of state documents is the very confusion and isolation of the publications and publishing sources in the field. State governments are eager to find out what other state governments are doing, and the primary source for this information is a publication prepared by the Library's Exchange and Gift Division entitled *Monthly Checklist of State Publications*. This catalog (itself a serial government document published by GPO) is now in its seventy-second year and goes out to over 4,400 subscribers. In order to be listed, a copy of a state publication must be received by the Library of Congress. Thus, in this case, an unusual form of exchange appears: trading a publication for a service.

In 1980, the above arrangements brought in 139,337 state documents, but this figure, *mirabile dictu*, has been shrinking steadily for the past two decades. Peaking with the Great Society programs of the mid-sixties, the number of state publications published has since declined each year at a fairly regular rate. Where the number will bottom out is interesting—conceivably at a very low level as more and more statistical reporting is kept in state computers and never printed at all. Indeed, we may already have seen something of the future in city and county document production. In 1970, the Library was receiving over 6,000 local publications a year. In 1980, only 835 appeared—whole series having disappeared into digital storage, microfiche, and in-house image processing—with their access either being held until needed on demand or limited to local, need-to-know users.

Documents of Foreign Governments

In most of the above instances, the Library's position is one of a supplicant, appealing to an organization for its materials for the use of the federal government or as a contribution to a central depository of U.S. history. The Library has little to offer in return except its own annual reports and some bibliographic publications, but when it turns to acquiring documents from foreign governments, it can deal from strength.

First, under terms going as far back as the Brussels Conventions of 1886, the major nations of the world have exchanged copies of their laws, their administrative directives, and their official journals. One hundred twenty-five copies of the *Congressional Record*, the *Federal Register*, and *Presidential Publications* are made available to the Library for this purpose. Library publications go out, other nations' publications flow back and are bound, classified, and added to the collections. To all intents, the Library thus has complete collections of the laws and legislative journals of all the nations of the world, received and continued with a minimum of effort.

Next, a series of statutes going back as far as 1840 have given the Library a steadily increasing number of copies of all GPO publications to be used as items of exchange in broad trading programs with foreign governments. This device has grown to the point where the Library is now conducting wide-ranging exchange programs with 45 nations and selective programs (limited to specific subjects or to the publications of specific agencies) with 38 more.

In the case of the 45 nations, a "full-set" agreement is common, under which the Library chooses the most significant publications of the U.S. government, draws copies of them from its allotments, and sends them off at convenient intervals to the exchange partner. A "full set" usually involves about 22,000 pieces a year.

The developing countries are particularly eager to keep abreast of U.S. solutions to modern governmental problems, but they simply cannot handle receipts of this magnitude (22,000 pieces would frequently fill the complete storage space of a young library, not to mention the manpower required to sort and identify the material so it could be of any use). To meet situations of this kind, GPO selects a "partial set" of approximately 5,000 pieces, containing the kinds of material that would appear to be the most useful to the particular exchange partner involved.

Recall, the purpose of any kind of exchange—full or partial—is to get the publications of the other country into the Library of Congress. Long experience has shown that it is almost impossible to do this a title at a time. The only hope is to set up channels—sluices!—for the material to flow through automatically.

The exchange programs are no respecters of ideologies. U.S. scholars seek "everything" (and so do their foreign counterparts). The State Public Library at Ulan-Bator in the Mongolian People's Republic submits its nation's documents in return for a selected group of U.S. publications. The National Library of Beijing receives a full set of U.S. documents and, in return, sends the Library of Congress thousands of Chinese materials each year. The Library of Congress receipts from Cuba are thought to be the most comprehensive of any North American library and thus provide a major window for Latin American scholars working in this field. But the Library's receipts do reflect difficult times. Longtime arrangements with Albania have recently evaporated, Haiti fluctuates from sending riches to trivia, and at the time of this writing, the centuries-old receipts from Persia/Iran have disappeared into the sand.

Scholarly and Cultural Exchange

The formal products of the foreign governments merge into the last form of government documents—those of private sector (but tax-supported) cultural and think-tank-type materials. In this category, there are over 14,000 individual agreements worked out with such dignified centers as Heidelberg University *(Sitzungsberichte der Heidelberger Akademie der Wissenschaften)* and the Louvre *(La Revue du Louvre)*. To such institutions as these, the Library offers limited lists of U.S. federal documents, from which the organizations can choose the U.S. publications in their own fields of interest in exchange for sending the Library their own publications.

These bibliographic "deals" cover the globe. In 1980, they brought in some 467,000 pieces of such glamorous or unlikely series as *The Warunda Review* (from the Warracknabeal and District Historical Society of Warracknabeal, Victoria, Australia), *The Adelphi Papers* (from the Institute for Strategic Studies, London), *Acta naturalia Islandica* (from Reykjavik), and *Poirieria* (from the Conchology Section of the Auckland Institute and Museum in New Zealand).

Gifts

With gifts, the third source of the Library's materials, we come to the glamour part. We need only scan the recent accession sheets to sense the importance of this port of entry. In the twelve months of 1980, the records show the receipt of the papers of Margaret Mead, Kurt Vonnegut, Senator Edward Brooke, Branch Rickey, and musical manuscripts by Charles Gounod, Andre Kostelanetz, Richard Rodgers, and Aaron Copland. During the same period, the Library received the papers of Joseph Wechsberg, author and writer for the *New Yorker;* Arthur Rothstein, noted photojournalist; Ursula and Reinhold Niebuhr; Harry Guggenheim; Lillian Gish; and Drs. Paul Elkish and Edith Jacobson from the Sigmund Freud Archives; correspondence, notes, and legal papers of O. John Rogge relating to David Greenglass and the Rosenberg case; the papers of Senator Abraham Ribicoff and Congressman Mendel Rivers; those of Judges Skelly Wright and Harold Leventhal; and additions to the Walt Whitman collection and to the Justice William O. Douglas and President William Howard Taft papers. The records of the National Woman's Party for 1920 through 1965 and those of the Legal and Educational Defense Fund of the National Association for the Advancement of Colored People came in during the year. And in the same twelve months, the noted book dealer Hans P. Kraus presented the Library with sixty breathtakingly rare pieces of Sir Francis Drake material, which included maps, manuscripts, printed books, medals, and portraits relating to the explorer's life and voyages.

It is obvious that the two great strengths of the Library of Congress are its size, which gives it the quality of comprehensiveness, and the glories of its unique collections—the only-one-of-its-kind manuscript, historical record, or creative work. The great majority of the latter are received through the Library's "gift source."

Most gifts are of a deeply personal nature. They are given to the Library for a variety of reasons: a recognition by the owner that he or she has something of value the nation's scholars will find useful, or the feeling that something will be left behind by which that person's contributions will be remembered. Many come as the result of long pleading by specialists on the Library staff, who finally convince some donors to part with their treasures for the nation's good; and others come because of the tax benefits that can be reaped in exchange.

Gifts to the Library are acquired or held through a variety of arrangements. Most personal papers, for example, are given outright for the benefit of scholars. Others are "deposited," which means that the donor continues to own them but is making them available for immediate use by the public. The deposit device is frequently used to insure the papers' preservation when a celebrity retires or breaks up housekeeping. It is also employed while litigation is being resolved between heirs and there are counterclaims to ownership—and in some cases, the donor simply cannot bring himself to give away his life's work and wishes to "try out" living without his personal files. Traditionally, deposited papers are placed in the Library for ten years or so and then are donated at the end of that period. In some cases, they are placed on deposit for the donor's lifetime and given outright at his death according to instructions in his will. In cases connected with the papers of national figures, restrictions can be placed on their use to avoid embarrassing private individuals who are discussed in the letters—or who actually wrote them in the first place. In these instances, the collection can be closed to public use until the death of the donor or for his lifetime plus a given number of years. Notwithstanding its attempts to be equitable, the Library tries to discourage any limitations on access, and such restrictions remain the exception with most gifts.

The tax-benefit aspect has recently passed through a change for the first time in a century. In the past, as in the donation of paintings to public galleries, the government permitted an individual to deduct from taxable income the fair cost of his or her papers—what they would have realized if they had been sold on the open market rather than given to the nation. In 1969, Congress changed the law so that although the old arrangement is still true for heirs or private purchasers, the individual whose papers they actually are cannot claim tax compensation if he or she produces words or music for a living—such as an author, composer, or statesman. Their donations are now limited to the cost of the materials involved: the ink and paper. The result is that some collections are now being sold on the open market in order to secure their cash value or, in the case of large or especially valuable units, are being broken up. Dealers are buying one letter at a time out of the whole, or research institutions are buying portions covering special time periods or subjects, so the papers, as a collection, are fragmented. This practice of splintering collections has not yet become common, but it is increasing at a rate that gives the Library concern for scholars yet unborn. Many donors cannot believe that the law will stand in its present form and so are "depositing" their collections for the moment, waiting to see how the situation will resolve itself before offering the papers for sale, in fragments, to individual bidders.

Gifts are an extraordinarily valuable source of the Library's materials and are in no way limited to individual donors. Some of the most useful, unique, and significant materials come from scientific societies, labor unions, church denominations, industrial corporations, and utility companies; groups like Rotary and Kiwanis clubs or the Red Cross, symphony and opera societies, and the national political parties. Altogether, their contributions make up the rarest portions of the Library's record of the national experience. In 1980, some 1,824,494 pieces were received as gifts.

Purchased Materials

What could possibly be left? With the copyright deposit bringing in the books other libraries have to buy, with exchange agreements bringing in the world's documents, and with gift arrangements gathering the rarities for preservation, what could be left over? The answer (in 1980): 3,082,924 items that could be secured in no other way but by paying for them!

The missing pieces fall into five rather clearly defined categories. The first is newspapers. Fewer than 50 newspapers in the world are copyrighted, and being in business for a profit, they are not likely to be donated as gifts. So the Library buys them. In the United States, it subscribes to some 330, which add up to all the major communities in the nation; abroad, it pays for more than 1,000 subscriptions to newspapers in all the national capitals and in the remaining largest cities around the globe.

The second category of purchase is foreign magazines in general. There is no shortcut to acquiring these, and the Library of Congress

More than 1,600 domestic and foreign newspapers and 130,000 serial titles are received by the Library every year.

subscribes to them in the same way any citizen would, the only difference being the quantity. It pays for approximately 30,000 continuing, foreign periodicals.

The third category is foreign books. In many respects, this is one of the most interesting sources of all the Library's receipts. As we have seen, Librarians of Congress have been trying to get the books of foreign countries for nearly 200 years. They first sought the publications of the nations from which U.S. citizens came, then China and Western Europe in general, and gradually, since World War I, the publications of all the nations of the world. To put it somewhat differently, for the past seventy years, the Library has deliberately sought all the significant nonfiction and representative literature of all the countries of the world.

If you consider the challenge of this effort, it poses an intriguing problem. Suppose you are a librarian in the United States who has never been anywhere except on a three-week bus tour in Western Europe, yet you are expected to secure everything of significance being published in, say, Indonesia, Peru, and Guinea-Bissau. How would you go about it? Press runs are short, and books go in and out of print in matters of weeks, but you are expected to have all of the works published by those countries this year, next year, and on into infinity. The answer is the same as it was for foreign document exchange: Don't look for individual titles, don't bother with individual publishers or individual arrangements. Try to set up sluiceways that will deliver rivers of books, and then throw away what you don't want.

In the many countries that have no book trade, the usual approach is to go to the largest library—the national university library or the national library of the government—and ask it to buy a second copy of anything it gets and send it to the Library of Congress. LC then pays the library for the publications it sends, plus a little for the cost of handling.

In countries that have booksellers (France, Switzerland, Brazil, et cetera), the Library of Congress selects a single, reputable dealer and sends him a "scope list" which explains what LC wants and what it does not want. The Library essentially gives him a blank check (officially called a "blanket order"), which says in effect "Send us one copy each of everything of substance published in your country, and we will pay you for it."

This technique sounds terrifyingly open to fraud and waste, but experience has shown it instead to be remarkably safe and efficient. By now, the Library has norms by which to check if shipments are too low or charges too high. Further, once respectable dealers are located, national pride (and the possibility of a continuing source of dollars) has resulted in long-term, highly professional relationships. The Library monitors the incoming material closely and reports back which items were not added to the collections, so the dealers become highly skilled in identifying what LC does want. In the few countries that have national bibliographies, the shipments received are checked against the known national production, and the dealers are required to explain why missed items were not included. This mass channeling of the world's commercial publishing brought in 615,257 pieces in 1980.

There remain two more blocks of purchased materials. The fourth category is the miniature research library continually being assembled for the Congressional Research Service. In 1980, this came to over 4,500 volumes. These were "rush processed" and hastened to the appropriate CRS subject specialist so Congress would have the very latest information available as quickly as possible.

Why would you need a library for Congress in Congress's library? Because of the competition. In the 1950s, the competition for the usual copyright copies was becoming so intense that it was impossible to find the books the congressional committees needed to prepare new legislation and confirm appointees. Competition with whom?—the executive agencies in Washington who had been told to limit the growth of their departmental libraries and rely on LC. In any one year, a quarter of a million volumes will be borrowed from LC for outside use. Scholars throughout the country borrow 50,000 volumes through interlibrary loan, and the hundreds of thousands of scholars in the various reading rooms will have vast quantities of books off the shelves, at any one time. This race for the volumes became intolerable, so the CRS began to build a Congress-only library within the Library to support the Congress. Competition was dramatically reduced, and (if nothing more) the bitterness among all parties was minimized.

The fifth and final block of purchased materials is probably the most surprising of all: those purchased for the blind and the physically handicapped. In 1980, for example, the Library bought 1,919,462 volumes in braille or on tape cassettes for loan to those groups of people. These volumes are sent out of Washington and circulated throughout the states, so the pieces do not become a part of the permanent collections of the Library. They are purchased with book acquisition funds, however, and the statistical strokes appear in the incoming tables of annual reports—but fail to reappear in the "added to the collections" tables, thus causing considerable confusion in library school papers and at appropriations hearing time.

Including this last category of materials, we find that in 1980, the Library spent $40.1 million for the purchase of 3,082,924 pieces of material. Not including the materials for the blind and physically handicapped, it spent $5.6 million for 1,163,462 items purchased for the general collections of the Library.

So you've got it. What are you going to do with it? We have thus seen how rivers of material stream into the Library, swelling to a mass of 10,020,460 pieces in 1980. The material was vigorously sought, laboriously checked in, and now lies in a great undifferentiated mass. Let us now consider how the Library gets it under control for use by its ultimate customers.

5

CONTROLLING THE COLLECTIONS

Let us first consider the problem of bulk. When a research library decides to add a volume to its permanent collections, it in effect contracts to house that book, to keep it appropriately warmed and cooled, to provide it with light and with dry, dust-free air, and in general to care for it—forever. This sounds self-evident, but in fact it poses a savage administrative problem. If you were to give up a bedroom in your home just to house books, you would have in effect built a room costing roughly $10,000, which would hold (even if stored on floor-to-ceiling shelves set so close together you could barely pass through) scarcely 7,000 books. The Library of Congress adds that many volumes to its collections every working day. Ten thousand dollars to store 7,000 books—and once on those shelves, there they would stand for generations to come until their paper turned to dust. Needless to say, the same amount of space is even more expensive in a fireproof library building.

The point is that not only is the myth that "the Library of Congress has one copy of every book ever printed" demonstrably untrue, but it signifies a luxury the Library dare not even approach. In point of fact, a great deal of the Library's energy is spent in throwing away as much material as it can, while still struggling to achieve the mission articulated by Archibald MacLeish forty years ago. You will recall he set the Library the task of securing the materials that Congress and the federal government need to govern, of preserving the materials that express the life and achievements of the people of the United States, and of acquiring the records of those peoples whose experience is of the most immediate concern to the nation.

So let us examine how the 10 million pieces acquired each year

Senior shelflisters search for serial entries under the subject of child care.

are reduced to the 1.5 million that actually become a permanent part of the Library's collections.

The Selection Process

The first aspect to keep in mind is that the streams of material are endless. The staff doesn't face up to a static group of books quietly sitting on the shelves waiting to be considered in a structured, logical way. They try, instead, to control cascades of books that never stop. Ten million pieces a year is an enormous amount of bulk; you dare not let it accumulate. (Harvard University has only 10 million books and bound periodicals, and it has been collecting for nearly 350 years.) So the Library of Congress's selection process starts with controlling, dividing, and directing the flow into discrete channels.

The first divisions are based on format or script. The broadest channel is given to all printed matter in English or one of the Western languages—French, German, Swedish, Dutch, et cetera. This stream is shunted off to a three-person team called "the selection officers," and this cut reduces the total by one-half right at the outset. Next, the unusual formats are directed into separate streams: maps go to the geographers; phonograph records, tape cassettes, and open reels are sent to the sound specialists; motion pictures, television tapes, and videodiscs are channeled to the performing arts people; manuscripts, to the historians; and music, to the musicologists. This leaves hundreds of thousands of items in languages that are absolutely unintelligible to the average receiving clerk (the Library receives 516 magazines in Hindi, 43 in Kannada, 34 in Telgu, 120 in Gujarati, 34 in Oriya, 70 in Marathi, 300 in Urdu). These materials are grouped by language family: Oriental languages go to the Asian Division; Arabic and Hebraic publications, to the African and Middle Eastern Division; et cetera. The result of these activities (and recall, this sorting is going on constantly, eight hours a day) creates rivers of materials pouring toward dozens of selectors, all of whom are choosing and discarding simultaneously all over the Library.

So how does the Library get any uniformity in what is kept? How does it avoid having each specialist collect what interests him or her and junk the rest? The answer lies in the sacred Acquisition Policy Statements. For nearly a hundred years now, the Library's staff has been asking, "What should we keep of books about _____?" (fill in the blank—asphalt highways? aldehydes and esters? gypsies? religious tracts from small cults?). Astonishingly, the selectors have made decisions in each case and written them down. These decisions now fill two massive binders—over 800 typewritten pages—which are placed in the hands of selecting officers throughout the Library, and all selection officers are required to conform to the basic dicta.

Unless a specific exception is made, a decision on a subject cuts across all formats and languages, so if the Library decides it will keep books for the layman on the effects of fluoride applied by toothbrush, it will keep such books in Tagalog, Norwegian, and Swahili; it will keep documentary films on fluoridated toothbrushing from China, Canada, and Rumania; it will keep cable television specials on dental care in—wherever.

The Acquisition Policy Statements go far beyond the simple level of yes or no. They first tell the selecting librarian at what level to take a subject. There are four levels of retention: comprehensive, research, reference, and minimal. "Comprehensive" obviously means that the Library will attempt to secure, catalog, and retain any material in all editions and languages that contributes to the understanding and history of that topic. Examples of fields in which the Library collects comprehensively are law, American music, and aeronautics. "Research" means that the Library will limit its acquisitions to the major works, the major primary resource material, and the significant documentation of the assigned field. In practice, this tends to mean mostly books and documents but comparatively few pamphlets and next to no "near-print" materials such as mimeographed and multilithed reports. (Great quantities of the last will be used as working data in such units as the Federal Research Division òr the Congressional Research Service, but there they will be employed for possibly three to five years and thèn pulped. They will not be added to the permanent collections of the Library.) Examples of subjects that are retained at the research level are politics and government, economics, and U.S. history.

The "reference" category retains only the most important single volumes—often simply a representative sample of commercial publishing—in subjects in which the Library feels no obligation to provide research depth. Subjects collected at this level include religious sermons, military manuals, and histories of fraternities and sororities. The "minimal" collection is obvious and embraces such categories as insurance company annual statements and books on real estate and fortune-telling.

Having set the broad level of a subject, the Acquisition Policy Statements then get down to specific decisions within a subject. Examples: Municipal documents issued by foreign cities—the decisions say yes for such-and-such cities in this country; no for all others. They will say, "Keep all documents issued by the Pan American Union regardless of subject but only in English and Spanish; do not retain those in French or Portuguese." They will say, as in the case of the fluoride hygiene, "Keep medical publications directed to the layman; transfer medical treatises directed to the medical profession to the National Library of Medicine."

The medical instruction is an example of another series of instructions in the policy statements: decisions by bloc category. As we saw in relation to the copyright receipt, the Library keeps very few textbooks, no matter what their subject is (next to none below the college level); it keeps only a few mass-market paperbacks and even fewer reprints. It keeps almost nothing in the medical or agricultural fields, sending materials in those areas to the National Library of Medicine or to the National Agricultural Library at the Department of Agriculture. It keeps U.S. doctoral dissertations only on microfilm, fewer master's papers, and foreign dissertations only in the field of law. It rarely keeps translations from English into a foreign language (although if it cannot secure a piece in English, it will take translations from a "difficult" language into an "easier" one—Hindu into French, or Russian into German), and except for family genealogies, it rarely keeps publications from vanity presses or privately published works.

Finally, having made all the above yea or nay decisions, the selecting officer holds in his or her hands a piece that has been chosen for eternal retention by the Library and, at this point assigns it a cataloging category. The officer tells the catalogers how important this volume is to the collections and in what order—priority—it is to be processed. First priority goes to books needed by Congress. Only when all of them have been cataloged do the catalogers go on to second-priority items, English-language material of high research value. Third priority is assigned to English-language material of medium research value plus foreign-language material of high research value. And so on through five levels.

A footnote should be inserted here. When it comes to the million magazines received each year, the selecting officer sees only the first few issues. The yes or no decision is made on the basis of these, and once that decision is made, every issue thereafter is either ignored or is dutifully bought, paid for, checked in, and bound as long as that title shall last. The initial decision is chancy in the extreme. With only a pair of issues in hand of a new teenage periodical or *Occasional Study Number One of the Citizens' Land Use Committee of Montana*, the selection officer must decide yea or nay forever. Once a library commits itself to a periodical, it rarely abandons it in midstream, and conversely, it is almost impossible to buy a periodical in reverse—that is to work backward from present holdings. A publication that looks fairly ephemeral in its early issues, like the *Village Voice* or *Playboy*, can take on unusual social significance as it ages, and failing to save the title from the beginning can leave a library with an impossibly broken set. The problem is equally irritating with the publications of small-town junior colleges. Departmental series that looked questionable when the school was one year old with a class of thirty freshmen may later mature into major scholarly series when the school becomes a campus of the state university with an enrollment of 30,000. The assessment of serial futures requires the prescience of a successful stockbroker.

As can be seen, the acquisition process is both complicated and enormously important to the Library. It creates what the Library is: It determines what cards will go into the book catalogs and what entries will be loaded onto the computer tapes going out to five continents. Something missed or discarded is rarely recovered in this business. The perpetual question of a dedicated selection officer is, What will the user a hundred years from now wish we had kept today? But the end result of all this effort is to reduce the 10 million volumes to the 1.5 million to be retained in the permanent collections of the Library of Congress.

Searching

The winnowing process has yet one more step to go. In spite of the selection officers' having approved a volume for retention, there is always the possibility that another copy of the same work may already have been received and processed by the Library and may now be sitting on a shelf. To test this, each selected volume is handed to a "searcher" who checks the piece in the Library's records. Searching through every possible way in which the item might have been identified, he or she will discover, astonishingly, that *one-third* of the works approved for retention will already have been received and processed!

This does not mean that all of this third will then be discarded. On instructions from the selection officers, many of the duplicates will become second copies for the main collections or additional copies assigned to various specialized reference collections. This matter of duplicates does dramatize, however, the variety of ways in which materials are received. Duplicates can be generated by the combination of copyright deposit, publishers' sending volumes for early cataloging and early preparation of printed cards, by the receipt of discards from other federal agencies, by the acquisition of complete collections donated to the Library, and so forth. In 1980, the first round of elimination (by the selection officers) and the second round (preliminary searching) reduced the 10 million items received to 1,457,676 items that were actually processed and placed on the shelves for perpetual preservation. (We can only hope they were the very best, for processing is expensive and space is dear.)

Processing

Processing is simply getting control of the material—by describing what it is about so the user may know what is available and by preserving it in some order so it can be found when it is needed. Processing is about one part for the benefit of the library and two for the reader who comes through the front door. The library must know what it owns, and the user must be able to find what the library has— either by an author or a title already known or through a subject he seeks but whose authors or titles he has not yet learned. This adds up to bibliographic control, and it starts at the point where the selection officers have finally said, "This shall be preserved: describe it, identify it, and store it in a place where it will be of the greatest use."

In a small library, the material would be processed by a single librarian who would do all these things himself. In a larger library, there would probably be a division of labor—English-language material would be handled by certain catalogers, foreign-language material by others. In a yet larger library, subject specialists would appear: A lawyer would be hired to do the law books, and a scientist to handle physics and chemistry. In the fullness of time, the lawyer becomes increasingly expensive, so someone else is assigned the "routine" parts of his work and he is saved for professional content analysis. The scientist grows increasingly restless, so he is removed from all descriptive activities. The end result is productive use of both brainpower and money—up to a point. The cost is that each person who deals with the book must start afresh. Even though each worker has only a small task to do, it always overlaps the task before and the one behind, and each person does something over again; if the whole job had been given to a single person there would have been considerably less slippage and duplication.

The Library of Congress, whose holdings represent the ultimate in variety of material, has been driven to the ultimate in specialization. All of its material is processed in a formal progression, each piece being passed from hand to hand along the way. A routine volume will normally be worked on by thirty different specialists. In fact (staggering statistic), if you include the people who sort the books by language or subject, the messengers who place them on trucks and move them between processing stops, and the technicians involved in the inputting of the digital data, three-fourths of all books processed will be touched by over sixty different people—each making a contribution toward getting the record into the catalog and that one volume on the shelf! The first step in the processing is that each piece of material—be it a book, magazine, phonodisc, or government document—is first described.

Descriptive Cataloging

The Descriptive Cataloging Division describes a book as an entity; these catalogers do not care what the book is about. They describe it precisely, so the resulting record matches one book and one book alone. They carefully establish who the author is, what the title is, what edition is represented, who the publisher was, where the book was published, when this particular volume was published, and how many pages it has. Its height is given in centimeters, and any special parts are pointed up that might be useful to scholars, such as maps, bibliographies, or illustrations by noted artists. The result of this quite formal description is a single, complete catalog card, which is known as the main entry. This card or record then becomes a module, and it can be used in an endless number of ways. By simply writing additional information across its top, it may become a title card, a subject card, or an insurance record (to be stored in a fireproof vault), but all these manipulations are done with a single main entry. And the main entry is basically an author entry.

That fact hardly seems worth noting. How else would you catalog a book except by setting up an author card? Oddly enough, many experts consider the author device to be a U.S. invention. European libraries came to it very reluctantly, and the Orient still does not fully accept it. Foreign librarians would say that a book has only one clear-cut title but its author(s) can be infinitely confusing. Rachel Carson was a civil servant in the Department of the Interior when she wrote the department's *Food from the Sea* document. Who is the author? When you go to look for the document, would you expect to find it under Rachel Carson? the Fish and Wildlife Service? or the U.S. Department of the Interior? The famous *Report of the President's Commission on the Assassination of President Kennedy* was actually written by a lawyer, J. Lee Rankin. Would you expect to find the report under the commission's name or the man's? And so forth, through nameless government reports and numberless symposia. (When the Japanese began to move toward using author entries after World War II, they described the practice as "progressive" and "democratic," since it "recognizes the worth of an individual," but, they added, regretably it is "not as logical as the single title" by which books are commonly known.)

The greatest value of the author entry is that it instantly brings together the works of a single author in a single place for a single look in a catalog tray. The difficulty is that there are already almost 3 million names in the Library of Congress catalog, and without the catalogers' help, it is almost impossible to tell which is the precise author the reader is seeking. If you look for a tract by the abolitionist John Brown, you will find there are no fewer than 249 John Browns, 69 of them without a middle name or initial. There are nearly 1,500 books by or about the 249 John Browns. Unless the cataloger can sort out and distinguish which John Brown is which, the idea of bringing books together by the man's name is lost. (The problem is not limited to common U.S. names either; a chess enthusiast discovered 109 different Hans Müllers in the same catalog drawer.) The difficulty is resolved by "establishing" an author, which means ferreting out the birth date and the years of the author's creative work ("flourished 12th century" is a typical description when the trail vanishes in the mists of time), and when an author dies, the death date is added and the entry is "closed."

Such is the flowering of the literary spirit that one out of every two books newly received in the Library of Congress is by an author as yet unlisted in the catalog. And of those, nearly one-half require some creative research to differentiate a particular author from others of the same name in the drawers. Each new author receives the same treatment. The book itself is scanned for internal evidence, and bio-graphical directories are searched. In extreme cases, the catalogers may send letters of inquiry to the authors themselves. This procedure is followed regardless of the fame or anonymity of the author and regardless of the language of the work or of the author's country of origin.

Interestingly enough, the major element used to organize the mechanics of descriptive cataloging is not the country in which the book was published or the subject the book is about, but what language it is written in. At the present time, two-thirds of all the material received by the Library is in a foreign tongue, and the Library actually employs specialists to deal with some 50 languages routinely plus another 200 on an occasional basis. The descriptive cataloging divisions employ some 307 professional librarians and 114 subprofessionals to produce a single product with a single purpose.

It is the task of all these catalogers to create the main entry, the "catalog card," we used to say. Now in the computerized world, we have to say "the record," since the information is stored in machine-readable form and the catalog card is only one of a number of by-products, but these basic records, no matter what the thing described may be, all come out looking very much alike. Films and filmstrips are established under their titles, even if the scenarist is known, but all the other odd forms end up looking like the usual card of any book in any public library. Phonograph records, for example, are entered under the composer of the music, and the card comes out just like a book card except the "imprint and collation" read "New York: Columbia Records, c1982. 1 sound disc (50 min.)," instead of "Boulder, Colo.: Westview Press, 1982. 350 pp.," or whatever.

The task of establishing an author is time-consuming and expensive, but the cataloger will pursue it until he or she has either satisfied all the questions or exhausted all the research sources. An average book will absorb anywhere from two to five hours of professional staff time as it moves through the complete cataloging sequence. When the cost of acquiring the book is added in, the total cost of processing a book from receipt to shelf can easily exceed $100 a volume. Descriptive cataloging accounts for a substantial share of this cost.

Once the author is established and the work described, the draft catalog record is inserted in the book. It is reviewed by a senior cataloger/librarian for accuracy and consistency with the Anglo-American rules for cataloging, after which it leaves the Descriptive Cataloging Division for the Subject Cataloging Division. There they establish not *which* book it is, but what it is *about.*

Subject Cataloging

If a reader seeks a book by its author or its title, the work done by the Descriptive Cataloging Division will successfully lead him to the

Principal access to the Library's current bibliographic data base is through a computer terminal with a CRT screen. No new printed cards have been added to the Library's card catalog since December 31, 1980.

volume. But if he is seeking a book by its subject, he must rely on the skills of the Subject Cataloging Division, which will try to get the reader and the volume together by two different devices: first, by arranging the books on the shelves so that books on a single subject will stand together (with related subjects on either side) and then by loading the catalog with copies of the descriptive cataloger's original main entry, now filed under the most appropriate subjects for the book's contents. Subject cataloging requires different techniques from descriptive cataloging.

Each work day the descriptive catalogers pass some 850 books on to the Subject Cataloging Division where the books are distributed according to skills, interest, and language. The professional life of a subject cataloger is beset by frustration. He is cribbed and confined by the limits of mass, money, and time. As a subject specialist, he would love to read each book he handles and to explore its smallest detail. He cannot. Hundreds of books a day are remorselessly flowing into his unit, readers are waiting for the volumes to reach the shelves, libraries all over the world are waiting for the cataloging data. So he is instructed *not* to read the book! He must limit his analysis to the table of contents, the introduction, the preface, and the publisher's blurb on the dust jacket. He would love to put the book in a dozen places in the library so it will be a part of a dozen involved subjects. He cannot. He must select *one* subject, convert it to a numerical code, and give the book the resulting *single* call number that will place it most appropriately on the shelves. He would love to spray subject cards all through the catalog, to lay a road map of headings so the reader would be led to the volume from dozens of points of access. He cannot. To prevent both the catalogs and the users from being paralyzed by a mountain of splintered indexing terms, he is limited to two or three, at most a half a dozen, subject entries.

In addition to those troubles, the subject cataloger is engaged in a philosophical tug of war with the user. For the past seventy years (ever since the principles for subject cataloging were made firm), readers have gone to card catalogs and looked up what they wanted by the broadest, most generalized term. And subject catalogers have entered it under the most *precise* term. The reader wants a book on canaries, so he looks up Birds. The cataloger puts the card in the catalog under Canaries. No place else. The reader wants something on income tax, so he looks in the Ts for Taxation. The cataloger puts all books on income tax in the Is under Income tax. The reader wants something on jukeboxes, so he looks under Phonographs, Musical instruments, Coin machines, Record players. The cataloger puts jukeboxes in the Js under Jukeboxes.

This long-standing feud, now entering its eighth decade, merits a little elaboration. From the cataloger's point of view, almost any conceivable subject is part of a much larger frame of reference. Consider a book on the return of the Panama Canal in 1977, for example. The event is an aspect of U.S. history, U.S. foreign relations, Latin American affairs, President Carter's administration, President Torrijos' administration, and the history of the Canal Zone. But the book is not entered under any of these categories. It also concerns maritime law, naval defenses, shipping routes, and national sovereignty, but you won't find it entered there, either. The cataloger would say it is hopeless to try to draw a level of subject description so that each of the above subject headings in the catalog would include every book that dealt with all the ramifications of the topic. All the subject cataloger can hope to do is to describe a particular volume precisely and rely on the reader to come to the topic in the course of his or her search. In the case of the return of the Panama Canal, books on that topic are placed under Panama Canal treaties. Period. They do not even go under Panama Canal, which is located 300 cards away and in another drawer.

The result of this cataloging decision is that subject headings in a catalog are always focused on the lowest point of a scale of correlations.

For example, if you have a book on Erasmus, it is given a subject card under Erasmus. The book is at least half about his great friend, Sir Thomas More. It clearly involves British history, the Reformation, the history of the Catholic Church, and *In Praise of Folly*, but the book will not be listed under any of those subjects. Conversely, if the reader is researching Sir Thomas More, even though the volume on Erasmus may have half a dozen chapters on More, it will not appear under More. The catalogers say it is up to the reader to know enough about More to know that if you really want to know all about More, you had better also look in books about Erasmus (and about Catholic Church history, the Reformation, et cetera). The librarian cannot and does not supply see-also references for every subject dealt with. The reader is expected to do that for himself.

Attempts were once made to do that sort of thing by inverting the subject headings. (Backward ran descriptors till reeled the mind.) Thus, although the librarian insisted on having a specific heading for automobile insurance, life insurance, and property insurance, an attempt was made to keep these very clear-cut subjects from being swallowed up in a morass of cards, and the librarian tried to link them together in the catalog trays, alphabetically, by inverting the heading. You would find Insurance, Automobile; Insurance, Life; Insurance, Property—to remind you that there are all sorts of *insurance* to be considered. The idea was tried for several decades (just long enough to get library users accustomed to thinking backward when they confronted a card catalog) before it was abandoned. Why put property insurance in the Is under Insurance, Property, instead of in the Ps with Property taxation, Property assessments, Property management? Why put Automobile insurance in the Is, when it clearly belongs in the As along with Automobile accidents, Automobile repairs, Automobile design? Nowadays, subjects are entered under the most precise form possible and are described by the phrase most commonly used. (Incidentally, if that reader who wanted a book on canaries had looked under Canaries, he would have found canaries. However, if he had wanted a book on canaries, lovebirds, and parakeets, he would not have found that one under Birds either. It goes under Cage-birds—the most specific subject possible!)

Library of Congress Subject Headings and Classification Schedules

If the subject catalogers cannot assign headings in every direction, they are still sufficiently challenged simply by keeping up with their single, precise terms. Each day, new books appear on their desks discussing new subjects—the discovery of a new insect, the development of a new tax, a new uprising in Africa—for which no subject heading yet exists. It is the cataloger's duty to research the topic to determine the importance of the new subject, its scope, its validity, and its relationship to other subjects already established. Once the cataloger is convinced the subject is a genuine expansion of man's experience, he or she determines the most appropriate words to be used in describing it and defends the recommended heading through various formal review procedures. If it is accepted, the heading eventually becomes a part of the 2,591-page *Library of Congress Subject Headings.* Approximately 9,000 new subject headings are established each year.

The subject heading list is a basic tool of librarianship and is used throughout the Western world. It includes terms that can be used as subject headings in the Library's catalogs and, equally important, contains the terms that must not be used. (Is it to be Pornography or Obscenity? Is it Robbery or Larceny or Theft?) Subject headings can be established in all varieties of forms, but once determined, they must be used uniformly throughout the topic. Subject headings can be single nouns (for example, Radar, Contracts, Trade-unions), adjective plus noun (Agricultural credit, Irish literature), or complete phrases (Extrasensory perception in animals, Radio in navigation). They can be compound headings to express a relationship (Church and education, Law and ethics) or paired terms (Strikes and lockouts).

The *Library of Congress Subject Headings* has its twin in a second cataloging tool of almost equal importance: the *Library of Congress Classification Schedules.* These contain the subject numbers that go on the spines of the books to bring volumes on like topics together on the shelves. Most users of libraries are familiar with the Dewey Decimal System, which divides all the world's knowledge into ten major headings and uses numbers to divide and subdivide those headings into tens of thousands of increasingly detailed topics, going from the broadest to the most specific. It was devised by Melvil Dewey, one of the founders of librarianship, and was developed, almost literally, while he sat in an armchair with his fingertips together, trying to figure out some way in which knowledge could be rationally organized. The Library of Congress classification scheme (which relies on numbers *and* letters) was created in a different manner. It was designed to organize the collection of almost a million volumes that Librarians Young and Putnam found already sitting on the Library's shelves. It thus differs from Dewey's system in that Dewey's forms a logical progression from level to level of specificity. The Library of Congress's scheme is arbitrary and essentially one of convenience: If there were a lot of books on a lot of topics, those topics were given a lot of numbers. If there were very few books on a lot of topics, those topics were lumped together so as not to use up numbers too fast.

After over eighty years of use, the Library of Congress Classification Schedules have grown pragmatically until they, too, are now a very complete statement of man's knowledge. They divide all experience into thirty-two volumes of descriptions and tables. The letter A covers general works, the letters B through P serve the humanities and social sciences, Q through V cover science and technology, and Z is bibliography and library science. By doubling letters and adding numbers, the system has become vastly detailed, and where Dewey provides a number for a common subject and all works about it are so labeled, the Library often provides a separate number for every minor aspect or element. Thus, the Social Sciences are given the single letter H; Economics is HB, Economic history is HC, Commerce is HF. Within Commerce, you find Tariff policy (HF 1701 through all kinds of ramifications to HF 2701) and Advertising (HF 5801 through 381 steps to HF 6182).

Under the Dewey Decimal System, Economics and Commerce would be further and further subdivided under the same general numbers. In the Library of Congress system, when another substantial part of knowledge appears, numbering simply starts all over again. Finance, instead of being a small part of Commerce in the HFs, is HG. One might expect that Public finance would be a subdivision of Finance in the HGs, but not so. Public finance starts over again as HJ and has fractional topics; for example, Income and expenditure (Budgets) is HJ 2005 through 2347, and Taxation is HJ 2240 through 5957. This all adds up to thousands of specific numbers for thousands of specific topics. The result is that the Library's books are organized with great precision—but without any particularly logical progression. Under Dewey's system, once you know the general idea of his scheme, it is possible to guess fairly closely what the proper number will be. Under the Library of Congress classification scheme, there are no rational shortcuts; the cataloger and the user must "look it up" each time—once again, the price that must be paid for size. And like the subject headings, new classification numbers must be continually created to reflect a changing world. Each year, some 3,000 new numbers are put together, described, and added to the classification schedules.

The Shelflist

Finally, the Subject Cataloging Division is responsible for what is called the shelflist. This is a huge catalog of 9 million catalog cards, each one of which is filed according to the classification number on a book's spine. The shelflist thus exactly represents all the books on all the shelves throughout the Library and becomes a complete inventory of the Library's holdings. Books on the shelves are checked against it to be certain that all the volumes are in place or can be accounted for. The shelflist serves one additional purpose beyond simple organization and inventory.

The subject call numbers bring all books on the same topic together, but no matter how precisely the number can be focused—MT 68 is Improvisation, a fragment of the larger Musical composition, which in turn is an element of the still larger Music instruction and study, which is but a subelement of Music in general—in a collection as large as the Library's there will still be dozens of volumes carrying the exact same classification number (there are 188 different titles under MT 68). To sort books within a subject, they are made separate and discrete from each other by the use of a Cutter number, which is determined and assigned by the Shelflisting Section of the Subject Cataloging Division. Cuttering is a complicated system by which letters and numbers—plus dates—are used to sort out all the volumes, arranging them by author or place or industry or edition (whatever order seems most appropriate to the topic) and assigning each book a number like (in the case of a book on music improvisation as an aspect of instruction and study) MT 68. D2125 1954a—about par for the length of an LC call number.

The Final Steps

We have thus taken a book from the mail bag, decided if we wanted it, checked to be sure we don't already have it, created a record of it for the computer, given it a call number, and left clues in the catalog as to where it can be found. We have entered it in the inventory, and from this point there is little left to be done before the book is placed on a shelf. If it is unbound and paperbacked (half of everything received will be), it will go to the Binding Office for shipment to an out-of-city contractor, who will bind it in thick cardboards covered with heavy buckram cloth and return it to the Library. Records will be cleared, "secret" Library of Congress identification marks will be punched into an inside page, the classification letters and numbers will be labeled on the spine, and the book will be trucked into the stacks for shelving. A new best-seller takes an average of three to four weeks to move from receipt to shelf. An unbound book or document requires many months. "Rush" material for congressional requests or Research Services requirements can go through in as few as three or four days.

The Serial Record

All the things we have processed so far were single entities, which are complete in themselves—books, phonograph records, government documents—each a single "it," which (in the case of printed material) a cataloger calls a monograph. We must also note the control exercised over an even more elusive form of material, the "serial," which is any publication issued in sequence in a series. The interval between issues does not matter. It can be the daily *Treasury Statistics*, the weekly *New Yorker*, the monthly *Bluebook of Used Car Values*, the quarterly *FBI Crime Statistics*, the annual *Report of the National Education Association*, or the biennial *Who's Who in America*. A serial can be federal bulletins that appear without any regularity at all, so long as they are numbered as a series and have a single point of issue.

The Library sorts this mass of sequential fragments in a unit called the serial record. This is housed in a block-long room of the Madison Building and presents one of the most chilling sights in the Library of Congress. Row upon row of flat-drawered, steel cabinets are tended by a staff of 107 people who sort and record over 6,000 pieces of printed material every working day.

The trays are filled with check-in sheets showing the title, the source, the way each item is received (gift, purchase, exchange), and from where. The sheets tell which section of the Library has custody over the loose fragments while they are accumulating toward a complete volume and what call number the volume should be given when enough fragments have arrived to be bound.

The serial record itself is so vast that every two or three accessioners are assigned to a *single* letter of the alphabet, and they check in publications whose titles begin with that one letter and only that letter every working day of the year. Some accessioners have spent a decade specializing in the letter G! Traditionally, the Us have the greatest status, being exceptionally complicated and encompassing both the United States and the United Nations.

Remember, the selection officer decides whether a serial will be kept or discarded. Since publications pour in from so many sources, it is essential to keep track of the decisions that have been made. To this end, the serial record carries entries for approximately 348,000 serials that are currently kept, checked in, and prepared for binding; but it also has cards for 142,000 serials that are to be discarded if received. An interesting footnote relates to the ever-present problem of foreign languages. Although 70 percent of monographs are in foreign languages and 30 percent in English, serials break down into 55 percent in English,

9 percent in Spanish, 8 percent in German, 3 percent in Russian, and 3 percent in Italian.

The Computerized Catalog

One last device must close our look at how the Library's materials are controlled: the catalog of the Library of Congress. For nearly a hundred years, that sentence would have read, "the card catalog of the Library of Congress," and the LC card catalog is almost certainly the largest the world has ever seen. As it sits frozen in perpetuity now, it contains over 20 million cards in 25,548 drawers, and surely nothing so defines a "library" as the card catalog to its collections.

But on December 31, 1980, the last card was added to this monument, and on January 2, 1981, the Library became totally dependent on its computer for the foreseeable future. Since this computerized tool is both new and having a great impact on other libraries around the world, it bears some elaboration here. How it came to be and the trouble it has caused will be explored in Chapter 14, but *what* the computerized catalog is, is as follows.

As we have learned, all the records of LC materials were based on single catalog cards: the main entries—which, in turn, were usually the author cards. With the computer, the main entry is still the basic record. It stands alone in the computer's memory, and it is displayed on the television screen (cathode ray tube, CRT) of the 2,000-plus terminals distributed around the Library of Congress and on Capitol Hill.

The basic record is almost exactly the same as the traditional catalog card. The only difference is that it can be found in many more and different ways. The old paper card could be found in only three ways: under the author's name, under the book's subject, and sometimes under the title. Using the computer, you can still find the record under these three points, but you can do a great many other things as well. You can say, "Give me only English-language books about so and so." You can say, "Give me all the books about the Iraq-Iran war printed in English that have maps in them." You can say, "Give me a list of all the books containing prefaces by Daniel J. Boorstin, regardless of who wrote the books, for the past ten or fifteen years." The Library has been putting its Western-language books and documents into the computer since 1968, so searches such as those just described can be run with confidence to find materials placed in it for a decade.

What can't you do with the computerized catalog? Obviously, you can't find much in it that was printed before 1968. Thus, to make a list of books by James Michener, the reader must both look him up in the frozen card catalog and then go to a CRT terminal and call him up on the flickering screen. But equally obviously, each successive year, there will be less need for the printed cards than there was the year before. Well over half of all books sought in a card catalog are books published in the last five years.

One of the most ironic frustrations about the computerized catalog is that since it looks so magical, users expect unusual things. They are therefore distressed to find that the only copy of a periodical is on microfilm or that the only copy of a thesis is on microfiche; they expect it to be in the computer. It isn't, but it wasn't in the card catalog either. The great card catalog was an index to the book and magazine collections of the Library. Loose manuscripts, music, microfilms and microfiche, much law material, and all visual materials—motion pictures, prints, photographs—were always controlled solely by handmade cards in the specialized divisions. When the basic tool was the card catalog filling four huge rooms, the user said, "Well, you can't expect the Library to make a card for everything." Now, when the same user is using the cathode ray tube, he says, "I thought this was the catalog to everything in the Library." Regardless of tradition, one's sympathy is with the user.

In fact, using the magic tool, one's sympathy is frequently with the user. The computer is vastly skilled at making lists. When the user wants "all the books about _____," it can pick and choose, alphabetize, date, and organize with great accuracy and intelligence. It does not do so with unusual speed—it gathers and rejects rather deliberately—but it does the work well.

The computer is clumsy and time-consuming, however, for simply finding a single call number. The traditional question, "Do you have a copy of _____?" is far too trivial for the "power" of the machine, and it demands so many decisions to get the single answer that in most instances, the traditional find-the-drawer, look-up-the-card process is considerably faster. But the computer is the way of the future. Undoubtedly, it will become faster and more flexible as both the users and the programmers understand each other better. And no matter what anyone thinks, there is no going back.

In Conclusion

In this chapter, we have taken a superficial glance at how the Library's material is sought and acquired. We have noted how it is arranged for maximum use and recorded for later retrieval. These steps employ the technical processing skills of librarianship and involve what most people think a librarian does for a living. It is essential to recall that the acquiring and cataloging of a library is not done simply because it is the traditional thing for a librarian to do. It is pursued with the single justification of *use*. A librarian gets the material his particular library's clientele will need to use and arranges it and controls it so it can be found when its time for use arrives. Use. The cataloger is tied as tightly to use as is the reference librarian who will put the book in the requester's hands. The obligations of use are shared equally by all members of the staff of the Library of Congress. Keeping this in mind, we will now turn to the "reference" departments of the Library, where the specialists who deal directly with the Library's users can be found.

6

USING THE COLLECTIONS: THE RESEARCH SERVICES

Back in the days when Jefferson's library was up for sale, one of his friends learned it had been offered to the Congress, and the friend was distressed. He knew it to be a splendid collection—he was particularly awed by its strength in the sciences—and the idea that it should be buried in a government library "where it cannot produce any benefit to them or to the World" gave him deep concern, for there in Washington, it must "become motheaten upon the shelves" and lost to the world of knowledge. The library, of course, did go to the government, as did all its succeeding particles, and it is the responsibility of the three Library of Congress *research* departments to see that these riches do not sit upon the shelves and turn to dust. The three departments serve three audiences: Research Services serves the general public and the scholarly world, the Law Library serves the legal world, and the Congressional Research Service serves the Congress.

Each element of the three departments has in turn three responsibilities. First and foremost, each must act as a bridge between the users and the collections—to be the "experts" who know what is where and put it into the hands of the requesters who need it. Second, the research units must act as the custodians of the particular parts of the overall collection that they serve. Although Processing Services accumulates the material and organizes it for use, once the material is passed on, it is the reference librarians' responsibility to care for it, preserve it, and keep it available for immediate delivery. Finally, the specialists in each subject area are required to act as recommending officers to see that the collections do in fact have what is needed by the users. It is their responsibility to request through the processors the further acquisitions needed to keep each collection balanced and

Some 640,000 readers used the Library's general reading rooms in 1980.

complete. Use, preservation, and enrichment. The Manuscript Division demonstrates these elements especially well, so let's start with it.

The Manuscript Division

Here we must admit our own bias. Each person who knows the Library of Congress cherishes a portion of it that ceases to be simply a federal warehouse and becomes an area of pure emotion. Some find it when the Library's Stradivari violins are lifted from their cases and the Julliard String ensemble begins a Beethoven quartet—playing from a Library score in Beethoven's own hand. We've seen the same sort of quiet tension in a visiting mapmaker when he carries a portolano that belonged to Vasco da Gama to the light, knowing that this particular piece of parchment may have gone around the Horn with the great man. For the authors, the most moving portion of the Library is the Manuscript Division.

One can walk through rows of stacks and be surrounded by names that read like an opening stanza of Benét. An alphabetical sample: Nicholas Biddle, the Breckinridges of Kentucky, Salmon P. Chase, Andrew Jackson, George B. McClellan, Robert Morris, James K. Polk, Edwin M. Stanton, Martin Van Buren. Women's Lib? Here are the most personal and private papers of Clara Barton, Susan B. Anthony, Carrie Chapman Catt, Margaret Sanger, Clare Boothe Luce. Located nearby are the papers of Frederick Douglass, Booker T. Washington, and Cordell Hull. Another aisle: Sigmund Freud, Lillian Gish, Samuel F. B. Morse, Alexander Graham Bell, Louis Untermeyer, and Daniel Chester French. The shiny silver boxes containing the papers of the LaFollette family seemingly stretch on forever: thirty bookcases, seven shelves high, seven boxes to a shelf. And of course the papers of the Founding Fathers: Washington, Franklin, Jefferson, Madison, Monroe (indeed, twenty-three of the presidents from Washington to Coolidge), plus long rows of papers that belonged to the signers of the Declaration of Independence and the Constitution. As one of the division's leaflets explains, these shelves bear "the papers of those men and women who, throughout the centuries, have most profoundly influenced the lives and destinies of their coun-trymen." Notwithstanding our own awe of these particular decks, they are just another part of the operation to the Library as a whole, so let us examine them as such.

What are "personal papers"? David Mearns, one of the past chiefs of the division, has described them as:

> an individual's or an organization's correspondence (both letters received and retained copies of letters sent), memoranda, notebooks, journals and diaries, logs, orderly books, commonplace books, drafts of speeches, articles and monographs, trial lines, scrapbooks, reports, press releases, ephemera; in short, writings (inherently unique) of whatsoever sort or kind that possess evidential value, illuminate a personality, or provide a basis for scholarly judgment on actions and events.

All such bits and pieces from, to, and about an individual are kept together and referred to as the Lincoln Papers, the Oppenheimer Papers, and so on. There are over 10,000 such individual collections housed in the division.

What do they look like? They stand on the shelves either in bound volumes or in vertical cardboard boxes. The George Washington Papers, for example, are preserved in huge red-leather, tooled, and gold-stamped folios, each in its own slip case and each weighing ten or fifteen pounds. The volumes' pages are heavy rag paper on which the Washington material is mounted, one item to a page; each item is hinged on the left side so (in the case of a three- or four-page letter) each leaf can be turned and read in sequence. The George Washington Papers occupy 163 linear feet.

There are, on the other hand, 443 feet of the Booker T. Washington Papers. These, like all modern manuscripts, are packed in manuscript boxes, which are metal edged and deacidified so nothing touches the papers that would threaten their preservation. The manuscript stacks are themselves a huge vault which is fireproof and humidity controlled.

How are the manuscripts used? How would you yourself have access to them? First, you would have to have some serious purpose behind your request, such as the preparation of a book or some specific research quest. The materials are far too valuable to make them available for general browsing. A piece of paper with nothing but George Washington's signature on it is worth at least $400 in today's market; the Library's holograph draft of his first inaugural address is worth well over $100,000.

Assuming that you have a serious need to examine some material, you would present yourself at the register desk where you would be asked to sign in and identify yourself. After explaining what you sought, you would be introduced to a reference librarian, who would discuss your project in terms of the Library's actual holdings so you can know what papers are available for your purpose and how to ask for what you want.

Manuscripts are kept in one of two ways: either chronologically by date of creation or alphabetically by the persons who wrote them or to whom the originals were sent. The materials are rarely accessible by subject (although individual collections of papers may have subject files), so if you are working on the driving of the golden spike in Utah, you must know beforehand who was there, who might have been involved, and when the event actually happened. If you are trying to trace the letters Hamilton wrote the afternoon before his duel with Burr, you must not only know when it happened in order to search the files under his name, but must also guess to whom he might have written in order to search those peoples' collections for the same date. (In this case, for example, you would come on Hamilton's tragic, final letter to his wife in the Hamilton collection, but his other communications would be among the papers of his contemporaries.)

All of the Library's papers are preserved in some logical order and indexed in an author catalog, but in addition, the staff of the Manuscript Division has prepared some 1,200 detailed, individual "registers." Each of these is a small book analyzing a single collection. A typical one will first have a statement of "provenance," which tells how the Library came to get the collection. Some of these are straightforward records of legal deposition by the owner, but others are dramatic stories of lost trunks found, of shattered collections laboriously reassembled over the years, and of similar treasure hunts.

A register will next describe the status of the literary rights—or "copyright interest"—in the materials. The 1976 copyright revision changed the law so that an individual's rights to manuscript materials are now protected by statutory rather than solely by common law. The person who wrote the manuscript (or that person's heirs) owns the copyright interest in the writing, even though the Library owns the manuscript itself. If the copyright interests have been dedicated to the public, you can quote verbatim. If not, you will be able to use only small portions directly—following the rules of "fair use"—paraphrase the material, or use the information for background understanding. The register then tells how many pieces the collection contains, what kinds of materials are in it, and their overall arrangement—down to the contents of each individual box, book, or filing folder.

With one of these registers in hand, the reference librarian can steer you very precisely to the parts or particles you need. If it turns out, however, that the object you are pursuing is a difficult one—some obscure premise you are trying to prove or possibly a hunch you are trying to substantiate—the reference librarian may well pass you on to one of the division's resident historians. There are six of them, and each is responsible for a particular specialty: early American history to 1825, the national period to 1861, Civil War and Reconstruction, twentieth-century political history, cultural and scientific history, and Afro-American history and culture. (Cultural history covers the papers of such figures as Walt Whitman, Archibald MacLeish, and Edna St. Vincent Millay; scientific history encompasses the works of individuals such as the Wright brothers, Sigmund Freud, and Alexander Graham Bell.)

Each of the resident historians is knowledgeable about his assigned period and the contents of the Library's papers that concern it. Thus, if you are trying to reconstruct an event or are challenging some piece of conventional wisdom, the resident historian can tell you quickly whose papers might discuss what you are seeking and how to search the specific recommended areas.

Although the division's own collection of original manuscripts is comprehensive, its collection of copies of manuscripts from other institutions is equally broad. Since as far back as 1905, the Library has sent copiers (and now microfilm technicians) around the world to duplicate materials in foreign archives that bear on the development of U.S. history. Great quantities of material have been reproduced and brought to the Library of Congress from such depositories as the Archives of the Indies in Seville, which record the Spanish colonization of America; early British colonial reports preserved in the Public Record Office in London; and the records of the Society for the Propagation of the Gospel, which contain minutely detailed reports sent to England from individual parishes on the American frontier in the seventeenth and eighteenth centuries. Other copied collections contain correspondence from foreign diplomats to their home governments during the Civil War, German records of the Hessian mercenaries in the Revolution, and the like. Remarkably enough, because of the widespread destruction of two world wars, some of the duplicated European documents are now the only extant copies, and European scholars are coming to the Library of Congress to use duplicates of their country's own papers.

Any of the above materials would be available to you as a researcher. You can bring your typewriter or tape recorder or camera into the reading room and, within the limits of the specific collection you are working with, copy away. The Library also maintains a Photoduplication Service, which will reproduce whatever you wish as Xerographic hard copy, photostatic enlargements, glossy photographic prints, or microfilm and microfiche miniatures. Indeed, many of the most frequently used collections have already been microfilmed and are for sale to libraries and individuals by specific time periods or as complete collections.

No matter when you might visit it, you would find the Manuscript Reading Room humming with activity. In 1980, 8,966 researchers used it, some for a single afternoon, others spending many months pursuing some specific research project. Direct reference services (in person, by telephone, by letter) totaled 35,887 in the same year. The division has fifty regular staff members, nearly half of whom organize and describe incoming materials. And to answer the most asked question: Yes, the scene is under continual surveillance to be certain nothing is stolen, nothing defaced—and that no one uses a wet-ink fountain pen (ball-point pens are tolerated).

The division's activities in "use" and "preservation" are obvious. Its obligations in "enrichment" might bear stating, because very little of the material simply comes to the door, begging to be admitted. It is the obligation of the curators to determine who in their areas of assigned responsibility have indeed met the criterion of having "profoundly influenced the lives and destinies of their countrymen." The curators recommend; the administrators weigh, reject, endorse; and then the division sends a representative to the author or statesman or family of the national figure. In this day of spirited competition for research papers, some institutions can offer more cash for specific items than the Library of Congress can, but few can offer the associational ties of having one's papers preserved alongside the most noteworthy representatives of the national experience.

Beyond preservation, the Library's greatest contribution to scholarly collecting is the spread, the spectrum, of the individuals whose papers it seeks to include in the collections. Political and literary types are expected and traditional, but if the Library is truly the holder of the nation's memory and experience, it must have the record of its commercial leaders, technologists, medical pioneers, scientists, philosophers—its dissenters and its innovators; indeed, all who have most profoundly influenced the lives of our countrymen. Enrichment of the collections alone is not the point. It is the enrichment of the scholarly source data that matters. Why? So that the Library's users can mine those materials to enhance everyone's understanding of national traditions, achievements, and, on occasion, failures.

The Geography and Map Division

In many respects, the Geography and Map Division is similar to the Manuscript Division. Although many of its materials are duplicated somewhere else and thus are not as unique as manuscripts, they are not found in many other places, and indeed, some are available nowhere but at the Library of Congress.

The first catalog of the Library in 1802 listed 9 maps and charts and 6 atlases. By 1980, the numbers had grown to 3.6 million maps and 45,000 atlases. The Map Division is omnivorous. There is none of the "just take the best representative samples" here. The division will take anything it does not already have and thus, without doubt, has the largest collection of cartographic material of any institution in the world.

When a map (land) or chart (water) is received, each one is examined and, depending on age and condition, either encapsulated in Mylar or placed in an acid-free folder to protect it from wear and tear. The maps are then stored flat in huge steel cabinets with the maps laid out in drawers four feet wide and three feet deep. The cabinets themselves are housed in a room two floors below the street that stretches the length of two football fields—more than two acres of map cases!

The maps cover the history of the art. The division has vellum charts drawn by Italian, Spanish, and Portuguese cartographers in the fifteenth and sixteenth centuries. It has Champlain's original map of Canada on parchment (1607) and an early map of Manhattan Island (1639). Forty percent of all its holdings relate to the Americas. There are literally thousands of individual maps of the colonial and Revolutionary periods, both in manuscript and in print, and many of them came to the Library with intriguingly complicated pedigrees.

The so-called Faden collection (which, among other things, contains 101 maps of the Braddock Expedition and the French and Indian War) was first put together by William Faden, map publisher of the 1700s and geographer to the king of England. A Reverend Converse bought the collection from Faden's estate, Nathan Hale—the hero's nephew and father of Edward Everett Hale—bought it from Converse, and the

Joint Committee on the Library of the U.S. Congress bought it from Hale for $1,000 in 1864.

Similarly, the Hummel collection was purchased by Andrew Mellon in 1930 from Arthur W. Hummel, who had collected maps for many years in China. Mellon in turn gave them to the Library. They include two atlases of "all China," one containing twenty maps drawn in the Ming period (1368–1644) and another from 1662; a huge wall map of China drawn around 1673; and a vast and complicated road map of the "great and ancient highway from Sian in Shensi to Ch'engtu in Szechuan Province."

In 1975, some 8,000 maps and charts, the largest remaining portion of the Hauslab-Liechtenstein map collection, came to the Library by transfer from the U.S. Air Force Cambridge Research Laboratories Library in Massachusetts. The collection was originally assembled during the nineteenth century by Franz Ritter von Hauslab, one of the Austro-Hungarian Empire's most distinguished students of military science, cartography, history, and art. Although some of the rarer items were sold off over the years, the collection is still very strong in large- and medium-scale eighteenth- and nineteenth-century European topographic maps. It also includes groups of printed maps and plans of fortifications, maps of selected European cities, early lithographic maps, and a selection of historical maps, facsimiles, and tracings that illustrate the history of cartography. Since the Library of Congress did not have a separate map department until 1897, the Hauslab-Liechtenstein collection adds considerable depth and strength to the Library's map collection.

How do you find a map to use it? Oddly enough, until 1969 there was no single catalog of the maps in the Library's collections. Instead, there were endless published lists of special kinds of maps ("Fire Insurance Maps of North America," "Descriptive List of Maps of the Spanish Possessions Within the Present Limits of the United States, 1502–1820," "A Descriptive List of Treasure Maps and Charts"); there were indexes of special publishers (the Army Map Service, the National Ocean Survey, the British Ordnance Survey), and "finding lists" like those generated from the annual record of all maps deposited for copyright ("Catalog of Copyright Entries, Fourth Series, Maps"). Those lists, of course, are still invaluable as guides to the older materials in the division, but with the birth of the computerized MARC data base in 1968, it became possible to catalog current receipts of maps and enter them directly into the computer. Some 70,000 entries, controlling approximately 250,000 individual sheets, have now been entered in the cartographic data base and are available on-line in the division's reading room. (All of the atlases, incidentally, are under bibliographic control, and an eight-volume *List of Geographical Atlases* in the Library of

Congress directs the user to the appropriate atlas for the information needed.)

The modus operandi, therefore, in this division is for the reader to describe to the librarian what he wants and how it is to be used. Then with astonishing speed, he finds himself facing large sheets of paper depicting the area he is seeking. The "area," it should be noted, can be maps of the bottom of the sea, census tracts, logging trails, the incidence of cancer, mine fields, glacial moraines, annual income, ethnic antecedents, or the back of the moon. The division has thirty-six staff members and helped researchers 21,467 times in 1980. Half of those reference assists were provided to in-person users who took the trouble to find the Geography and Map Reading Room.

The Rare Book and Special Collections Division

Manuscripts, maps, and bibliophilia. The final member of the "treasure house triad" in Research Services is the Rare Book and Special Collections Division. At the beginning of this book, we noted some of the early collections the Library acquired, which later became the base on which the rare book holdings were built. Prime examples are Jefferson's library (of which, in spite of two fires, some 2,400 volumes still remain), the Peter Force collection of early Americana, and the Joseph Meredith Toner collection of biography and medical history. Since then, rare books have been added by the tens of thousands, and they fall into two fairly clear-cut categories: They are either distinctive, unified collections of books and pamphlets about a single topic and accumulated by a single bibliophile ("special collections") or individual books that were come by in the normal course of library business but that are of such value or form that they need special preservation techniques and protection. Many of the individual items in the special collections category may indeed be unique—and thus rare as well. More often, though, the individual elements are relatively common but were assembled because of a unifying theme. Once gathered together, a special collection such as the Stern collection of Lincolniana assumes a rare status of its own, simply because no other collection can match its comprehensiveness.

The term *rare books* immediately suggests either pristine first editions in hand-tooled slipcases or huge volumes of vast age. There has been a years-old argument in the library profession over whether it is appropriate for a public institution to hoard volumes merely because of their publication date. (In point of fact, 95 percent of *any* library is composed of first editions simply because libraries buy books when

Lincoln's first draft of the Gettysburg Address is one of the Library's unique treasures.

they appear and few books ever go beyond the first edition!) But there is seldom an argument over the appropriateness of an institution's accumulating the earliest examples of printing and bookmanship because libraries are almost by definition museums of the printed word. Such early examples are costly and rare. The most intriguing of all are those books printed between the invention of movable metal type around 1440 and the end of the fifteenth century. These are called incunabula, and the Library owns 5,600 of them. Of all the incunabula, none is quite so dramatic as the Gutenberg Bible.

The Vollbehr Collection

The Vollbehr collection was assembled by Dr. Otto H. F. Vollbehr in the 1920s and was purchased by the Congress in 1930 for $1.5 million. It contained some 3,000 incunabula, making it one of the richest collections of fine and early printing in the world. Among its treasures was a copy of the Gutenberg Bible—one of the three perfect vellum copies in existence. This splendid work is, of course, the earliest known Western book to be produced by movable type. Its fame rests, however, not only on its age but equally on the fact that it would have been a masterpiece of bookmanship no matter when it was printed. That it was cast so near perfection at the very birth of the art boggles the mind.

Not much is known about Johann Gutenberg, the man. He came from a family of goldsmiths in Mainz and seems to have gotten his idea for a process that would duplicate the written word in 1435. He borrowed money to develop his invention, and it presumably occupied a good deal of his time for the next twenty years. But nothing came of it until Johann Fust, a local lawyer who was one of Gutenberg's creditors, got fed up with the endless delays and foreclosed on Gutenberg in 1455. Fortunately, the project was essentially completed, so the Bible was actually printed by Fust, with the help of Gutenberg's type designer, Peter Schoeffer. They deserve considerable credit themselves, because the printing took them three hard years and often involved running six presses twelve to fourteen hours a day. We know of at least 30 vellum copies they printed during this time, plus 180 copies on paper.

The Library's vellum copy was one that Johann Fust took with him to Paris to sell in 1458. It was purchased there by a group of Benedictine monks, who took it home with them to their abbey at St. Blasius in the Black Forest of Germany. During the Napoleonic Wars, their copy was moved from one house to another in Switzerland and central Europe and finally to the Abbey of St. Paul in eastern Carinthia, Austria. There it remained until the monks sold it to Dr. Vollbehr for $370,000, the most money ever paid for a single volume up to that time. Although one of the other perfect vellum copies (in the Bibliothèque nationale in Paris) carries two scribbled dates, August 15 and August 24, 1456, the Library's copy is undated in any way. The third perfect vellum copy is in the British Museum in London.

The Bible is bound in three volumes totaling 641 leaves, each leaf being about the size of a tabloid newspaper sheet. Most of the leaves carry 42 lines of type in double columns (hence the appellation "the 42-line Bible"), and the text is in Latin from Saint Jerome's translation of the fourth century. Today, over 500 years after the Bible's production, the vellum is still dazzling white, the ink rich black, the initial letters deep velvet blue and red. Each page is almost sublimely proportioned— margins, spacing, type size simply could not be improved by even the finest adjustments. The type itself, instead of being the primitive, chipped elements we are accustomed to seeing in colonial printing, is full bodied and graceful with delicate serifs and uniform color. Nothing symbolizes "rare books" quite so must as this single work, which seldom fails to awe both the sophisticated scholar and the visiting tourist.

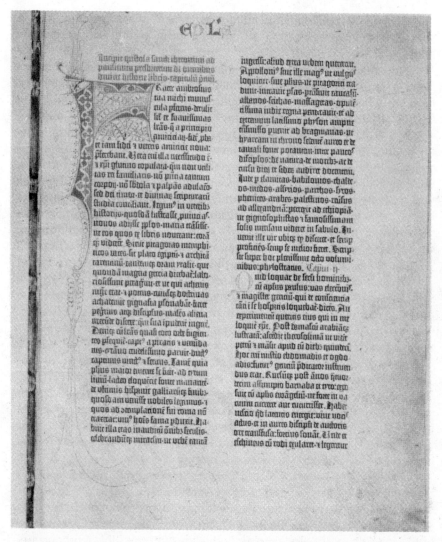

The Library also owns one of the perfect vellum copies of the Gutenberg Bible. It is continuously on display in the Great Hall in a special case that monitors heat and humidity.

The Lessing J. Rosenwald Collection

In our own generation, the Library has received one of the greatest collections of bibliophilic treasures ever assembled through the gifts of the late Lessing J. Rosenwald of Jenkintown, Pennsylvania. The collection was initially given to the Library in 1943, with the proviso that much of it would remain at Rosenwald's Alverthorpe Gallery in Jenkintown during his lifetime. He continued to add to the collection, and by 1978, the rare book portion consisted of more than 2,600 separate editions, with a considerably higher number of individual volumes. Slightly fewer than 600 of the volumes are incunabula.

The strength of the Rosenwald collection lies in showing the historical development of the illustrated book. Lessing Rosenwald started his collecting life in the 1920s as a print collector, and it was a natural progression to expand the scope of his collection from fine examples of woodcut prints to the masterpieces of the woodcut art in the form of book illustration. The collection's holdings are strongest in the illustrated books of the fifteenth, sixteenth, and twentieth centuries, but it has representative examples of illustrated Western printed books from the fifteenth century forward, supported by block books and a small but choice group of illuminated manuscripts of the twelfth to sixteenth centuries. Among the collection's treasures is the two-volume manuscript "Giant Bible of Mainz," which has important links to the Gutenberg Bible (and is displayed across from the Gutenberg in the Library's Great Hall); the *Catholicon* of Johannes Balbus, printed at Mainz in 1460; the 1462 Fust and Schoeffer Bible (the first dated edition of the Scriptures); and sixteen extremely rare works by William Caxton, the first English printer. It also includes what is generally regarded as the finest collection of William Blake's illuminated books in the United States.

Lessing Rosenwald himself was a great advocate of collecting rare books for a purpose; they were not to be stored away in a locked vault but were meant to be examined, touched, and used. In his own gallery, he brought out the Caxtons and the block books to show students and other groups so that they could look at and learn from them firsthand. He once commented, after one of his prints was damaged by insects while being exhibited in South America, "Better to be seen and eaten than not seen at all."

The Drake Collection

Treasures and rarities continue to come into the Rare Book and Special Collections Division. In 1980, a unique and remarkable collection relating to the life and explorations of Sir Francis Drake was given to the Library by the rare-book dealer and bibliophile Hans P. Kraus and his wife, Hanni. Intrigued by the enormous profit Sir Francis Drake and Queen Elizabeth made from his famous three-year voyage around the world, Kraus began to look into Drake's life and set out to collect all the contemporary materials he could find relating to Drake's lifetime. The result is a collection of maps, manuscripts, printed books, medals, and portraits of the period that, for its size, is unequaled. The fact that Kraus didn't begin his quest until the late 1950s undoubtedly only added to the challenge of bringing it off. Among the items in the collection is a letter written in 1580 by Gerard Mercator to Abraham Ortelius (two of the greatest mapmakers of all time) speculating on the route Drake might have taken around the world; a 1581 engraved map of the circumnavigation; and a 1589 silver medal engraved with Drake's route (one side shows Europe and Asia, and the other North and South America), which carries the name of the cartographer and engraver, Michael Mercator (grandson of Gerard). This collection was actually the second major gift the Krauses made to the Library; in 1970, they donated a group of 162 manuscripts relating to the history and culture of Spanish America in the colonial period (1492–1819).

Special Collections

In addition to the "treasure" rarities, the Rare Book and Special Collections Divison services and preserves many other individual collections assembled on a single topic or about a famous figure. It has a block of almost 14,000 children's books; it has 16,907 different early American volumes printed before 1801; it has 1,500 books, pamphlets, and broadsides published in the Confederate States between 1861 and 1865; and it has a number of collections relating to individual authors.

The William Montelle Carpenter collection of Rudyard Kipling contains manuscript copies of many Kipling stories and poems including "Mowgli's Brothers" (the first story in The Jungle Book), a long series of letters and photographs, and an unusually complete set of first editions of Kipling's works. The Jean Hersholt collection is a remarkable assemblage of Hans Christian Anderseniana, including the manuscripts of ten of the original fairy tales, an annotated transcript of Andersen's autobiography, and long runs of his first editions. The Bitting collection contains 4,300 volumes on the "sources, preparation, and consumption of foods, and on their chemistry, bacteriology, and preservation from the earliest times to the present day"—a gastronomic library. Finally, we should note the library of Harry Houdini, which contains 4,350 books and pamphlets on conjuring, magic, and spiritualism.

All of these literal treasures are housed in a huge, fireproof, multilevel vault, which is kept at 68 degrees Fahrenheit and 50 percent humidity. The special Rare Book Reading Room is modeled after a room in Independence Hall in Philadelphia and is served by a staff of twelve. Its collections currently contain some 500,000 pieces, and they were drawn upon 16,633 times by scholars in 1980.

First-time users of the Library of Congress stop at the Research Guidance Office on their way into the Main Reading Room to find out about the resources available and to get assistance in plotting the course of their research.

General Reference Services

The three divisions of rarities—Manuscripts, Maps, and Rare Books— are inherently dramatic and serve highly specialized audiences, but the Library also has a group of "plain, ordinary" library divisions similar to those in any large research library. They provide the basic operations that in fact serve most of the users of the institution. One specialized unit, the Federal Research Division, performs contract research for other federal agencies, relying in large part on the scientific and technical collections of the Library of Congress. The division is staffed with linguists and technical specialists who digest these materials for particular agencies with an interest in foreign economics and technology.

General Reading Rooms Division

Who can use the Library's reading rooms? And how do they go about it? The answer to the first question is quite straightforward: any person above high school age. The answer to the second is a bit more complicated, largely because of the fact that the Library's collections are so vast. But the general user should begin his or her visit in the Main Reading Room in the Jefferson Building. Indeed, many readers will be able to do all their research in this room, using the 40,000-volume reference collection around the walls and calling for other books from the Library's general collections. Other users, whose research projects will keep them at the Library for a longer period of time, will take advantage of such special study facilities as reserved bookshelves and study carrels.

First-time users of the Library of Congress will want to consult with the reference librarians in the Research Guidance Office (just inside the main doors to the Reading Room), who will orient them to the facilities and resources of the Library and help chart the course of their research. Other reference librarians are on hand to assist readers in deciphering the subtleties of the more than 20 million printed cards in the catalog and to educate novices in the technicalities of the computer terminals.

There is a second general reading room on the fifth floor of the John Adams Building, the Thomas Jefferson Reading Room. (The reasons why the Thomas Jefferson Reading Room is not in the Jefferson Building, and why the Thomas Jefferson Reading Room is decorated with Chaucer murals instead of the murals depicting the life of Jefferson that can be found in the room next door, are the kind of historic anomalies that so delight our British cousins.) The point to remember is that it is to the reader's advantage to work in the building closest to the collections he or she wishes to use, because the books can be obtained more quickly.

A digression is perhaps in order here. The opening of the new James Madison Memorial Building and the subsequent move of staff and collections mean that almost every book in the Library's collections has been or is about to be moved. This, clearly, is both a challenge and an opportunity. The Library has decided to make the most of the opportunity side of this equation and, over the next few years, will seek funds to restore the Jefferson Building to its original 1890s glory and at the same time make the Library of Congress an easier place to do research.

All of the reading rooms will have more and better space for readers, and as the collections are moved, they will be inventoried (for the first time ever) and relocated on the decks nearest the reading rooms they are most closely associated with. The Main Reading Room, of course, will remain where it is and continue to be the central hub of a wheel whose spokes extend out to other disciplines in the three-building complex. Also in the Jefferson Building will be a Local History and

Genealogy Reading Room (the nucleus of a new American Division) and expanded Rare Book, Hispanic, and European reading rooms.

In the John Adams Building, plans call for the current Science Reading Room to move into "real" reading room space (it now occupies a kind of anteroom between the two reading rooms on the fifth floor where the second card catalog used to be); the other reading room on that floor will be a Social Sciences Reading Room. The African and Middle Eastern Division and the Asian Division will also have greatly expanded reader facilities in the Adams Building. The Law Library will be in the Madison Building, along with the Geography and Map Division (both already in place at this writing), the Newspaper and Current Periodical Reading Room, and a Performing Arts Reading Room (a new entity combining music, motion pictures, theatre arts, and recorded sound).

The crucial link tying the buildings, the collections, and the formats together is the reference librarian. In the general reading rooms, the twenty-four person staff provides three services: It helps the visiting scholar use the catalog and reference tools so he can find answers for himself; it serves as a referral point to get the visitor into the appropriate specialty division (such as Manuscripts, Asian, or Law Library) where the proper specialist can serve him; or it directs the reader to information sources outside the Library of Congress if his research could be more usefully pursued somewhere else. All reference librarians are skilled at knowing shortcuts to answers. They carry with them a vast memory of what is where, which books have what in them, and in the absence of previous knowledge, how to find out what they didn't know before the question came up. (And once a fugitive fact is found, the model reference librarian never forgets where he or she located it!)

At the Library of Congress, the majority of the patrons are themselves skilled researchers, so much of a reading room librarian's time is spent helping the scholar plot an efficient course through the literature he is searching. The librarian brings him in contact with the bibliographic tools he will need and tries to make his research time as short and as profitable as possible. How well this is done is determined by the librarian's knowledge of the collections and the ways in which they are organized. Since the visitor can be anyone from Aunt Sarah working on her genealogy to a prize-winning novelist, each "May I help you, please?" starts a new story with a new challenge.

Not everyone can visit the Library of Congress in person. The Telephone Reference, Correspondence, and Bibliography Section responds to the reference inquiries that come into the Library by phone and by mail, roughly 250 questions a day. The Library expends skilled reference time on something better than half of these inquiries; the rest are referred elsewhere or returned to the sender with a recommendation that a local librarian be consulted for the answer.

This section's apparently arrogant approach is the only realistic way the Library can operate, and many believe it is actually more beneficial to the user. Since the Library of Congress comes close to having the world's greatest collection of information, it follows that it could theoretically come close to providing answers to most of the world's questions. But it has to draw the line somewhere, and it does this under the banner, "The Library of Congress should be the point of last resort." This policy means that if a citizen or scholar is seeking a fact, he should first try his local library or his nearest university or his state or regional reference facility, since that is what they are there for. The Library of Congress has made specific agreements with a number of state libraries so that if a general inquiry comes into LC that does not require the unique resources of the Library, it will be immediately referred to the cooperating state or regional library for attention. The result is that the letter (or phone call) gets a quicker response, the local library earns Brownie points, and the Library of Congress staff members are left a bit freer to deal with the questions that only they can answer. There are plenty of questions that meet that requirement; in 1980, the section wrote 12,336 replies to inquiries and handled 68,570 telephone calls.

The "bibliography" part of the section's title refers to the printed guides to Library materials the unit prepares for visitors and the general public. Examples include *Guide to Genealogical Research*, a seven-page handout that is vastly popular with family history buffs; *Pickaxe and Pencil*, a guide to the published writings on the WPA projects of the thirties; and *Revolutionary America*, a massive compilation of everything written on the whole Revolutionary period published by the Government Printing Office. In addition, this section has coordinated the preparation of booklists for distribution in connection with the LC/CBS "Read More About It" series. The idea behind this cooperative venture is to let television viewers know what books they might want to borrow from their neighborhood libraries or buy at their local bookstores if they want to learn more about the topic of a TV special; for example, if they want to learn more about the Warsaw Ghetto after watching "The Wall."

The General Reading Rooms Division is also keeper of the microform collections of the Library, and many people believe that they represent the future of the great research collections of our time. At present, the Library uses 1,020,615 reels of microfilm, 205,016 microcards, 457,318 microprint sheets, and 4,031,225 pieces of microfiche. Essentially all the Library's newspapers are kept solely on microfilm and so are the doctoral dissertations. Many books and serial collections now come into LC only as microforms; and in 1980, the Library's Preservation Office made 3,460,294 exposures of pages of brittle books and magazines in order to perserve their contents before they completely crumble to dust.

These kinds of materials can be used in the Microform Reading Room, which is located near the Main Reading Room. Special catalogs and guides help researchers find what they need, and microfilm and fiche readers are available. Many of the reels and cards are stored right in the room, and others are on the decks nearby. As the technology of image processing becomes more and more sophisticated—videodisc, laser disc, floppy disc—more of the Library's collections will be stored in this mode, and retrieving from a microformat (of whatever type) will be an integral part of much of the research done in the library.

Collections Management Division

The Collections Management Division shelves and inventories the books in the general collections (that is, all of those that are not in the custody of a specialized division such as Rare Book and Special Collections or Geography and Map), brings them to the readers in the two large reading rooms, and moves and adjusts *all* of the Library's collections whenever necessary. (Moving the Library's collections is a bit like painting the Golden Gate Bridge; it's a job that is never finished.) The general collections now contain over 10 million individual volumes, of which roughly 1 million will be called for each year by the 640,000 readers coming into the reading rooms.

The mechanics of requesting a book are relatively simple: Look up the book in the catalog, fill out a call slip, submit it at the central desk. It is then up to the 108-person book service staff to locate the book on the shelf and get it to the reader. Considering that there are some 332 miles of shelves in two buildings (soon to be expanded to more than 500 miles in three buildings), this is not always an easy task. And it takes time—too often a lot of time—which distresses the readers and Library management alike.

The call slips are transmitted to the central control decks in the two buildings through pneumatic tubes, the kind you used to see in department stores, and they arrive at their destination in less than a minute. In the past, the books were sent from building to building in the same kind of tubes (but larger) at the same speed. As the old tube system aged, though, it began to break down more and more frequently, parts were hard to get, and the Library finally decided to replace it with a book conveyor system that could accommodate many more outlets (or stations) and tie all three buildings together. That system is now in place, but it takes longer—speed had to be sacrificed for flexibility and unity. Fortunately, that is not the end of the story, because service in the reading rooms has actually improved, not deteriorated, in the past couple of years. And there are a number of reasons why.

Item: In the late 1970s, everyone in the Library was frustrated by the "NOS," or Not-on-Shelf, problem. Why was it so difficult to get a requested book from the Library's shelves? What would it take to do something about the problem? A small committee met for about a year under the auspices of the Library's Planning Office and discussed every conceivable aspect of the problem. They agreed it was complicated, but not insolvable. The happy coincidence of a general administrative reorganization in the Library and the willingness of a few key managers to take some risks made it possible to begin to chip away at the NOS nightmare. Before long, the Collections Management Division was able to implement almost every one of the NOS Committee's ideas.

Item: No inventory of the general collections of the Library had ever been taken. The NOS Committee made a strong pitch that it was high time someone did—it was fundamental to providing better service. With the forthcoming move into a third building and the need to move all of the collections anyway, Library management decided the time had come to face up to a real inventory of the collections. A new section was created in the Collections Management Division to begin the task. Now in operation for about two years, that section is relentlessly working its way through the collections, class by class. It checks to make sure that the book is on the shelf where it is supposed to be (comparing the shelved volumes with the cards in the shelflist) and that the label on the spine matches the number on the verso of the title page. The section devised shelf markers (self-sticking labels that go on book-sized pieces of heavy cardboard) to replace volumes that are missing from the shelves. The markers are even color coded: blue if the book is missing and can't easily be found (with five boxes to check each time someone asks for it so that it can be reordered if there is sufficient demand); green if the book is assigned to a reference or folio shelving area; red if the book is available on microform. In the best of all possible worlds, some of this kind of information should be recorded on the basic catalog record, but in a collection the size of the Library of Congress's, that procedure is impracticable if not impossible. Library staff involved in the inventory are also checking the books for preservation purposes (coding with colored dots those that should be rebound or repaired), and they send all volumes printed before 1801 to the Rare Book and Special Collections Division for safekeeping.

Item: What about the reader from out of town who has only one day to spend at the Library of Congress and can't find the book he or she needs? The Collections Management Division expanded its special search staff and stations someone right in the Main Reading Room to respond immediately to this kind of reader frustration. Trained over the years to know where to look for elusive books, the searchers turn up about 60 percent of them on the first try. If they don't find the item, they keep looking and ultimately send the request to the Collections Development Office (to decide whether to buy another copy) if the book isn't eventually found.

Item: Automation is coming and will one day allow the reader to type a request for a book into a terminal and get a report back in minutes as to whether it's on its way. The computer will automatically search the central charge file to determine if the item has been loaned outside the building.

A reader who uses the Library of Congress general reading rooms with a little forethought—early in the morning, during the quieter months of summer or midwinter, in the building closest to the books needed—can expect to have books delivered within twenty to thirty minutes. But demands at peak times will always result in a wait of an hour or more between request and delivery.

The Collections Management Division no longer speaks in the negative acronym of NOS; it now looks to the request success rate (RSR) and the shelf accountability rate (SAR) for its indexes of productivity. As the inventory progresses through the collections, both rates are expected to rise—along with reader satisfaction.

The Loan Division

All books requested from the shelves must be used within the reading rooms; the institution is not a lending library—with certain exceptions. The Library, being Congress's library, loans practically anything in its stacks to Congress at the request of members and their staffs. Notwithstanding the occasional reader who complains, "But I thought Congress had its own library!" the Congress borrows some 55,000 volumes a year through the Loan Division.

Further, the *libraries* of the various federal agencies throughout the government have the right to borrow books (but not magazines or newspapers), and libraries throughout the world have the privilege of borrowing from the Library of Congress's collections materials that are not available in their home communities. These so-called interlibrary loans amounted to 51,000 volumes in 1980 and may merit some elaboration.

Except for Library and congressional staffs, the Library does not lend directly to individuals. It does make its collections available for two-week periods to libraries both in the United States and abroad, which are then responsible for the materials while they are being used by researchers in their own institutions. Although in the minority, there are a few kinds of materials the Library will *not* lend. It resists requests for materials that ought to be in a hometown library (it will not send out copies of the King James version of the Bible or the *World Almanac*); it limits loans of materials that a small library should be able to borrow from nearby state or college libraries; and it refuses requests for some unique items, pre-1801 imprints, and common federal documents that should be available in the 1,400 document depositories distributed throughout the country. Except for these limitations, LC will loan almost anything in English that cannot be bought from a local bookstore and will loan pretty much anything in a foreign language, across the board. At the rate of 106,000 loans a year, the loan service is one of the Library's greatest strengths—and one of its biggest problems.

By congressional instruction, many federal agencies have been urged to borrow from the Library of Congress rather than build duplicate collections under their own roofs—yet the books so borrowed are frequently the very volumes Congress itself needs to study the legislative aspects of the problem being explored by the executive agency that borrowed the books. Similarly, many scholars come to the Library expecting its collections to be comprehensive, only to learn that the books they were expecting to find are on loan to a college library 3,000 miles away. The converse, of course, is that one of the major justifications for building a comprehensive national collection is to make it conveniently available to the nation's research community when and where it needs it. The situation makes for a dilemma.

One step that the Library has taken in recent years to help alleviate the problem is to send photocopies of the needed pages, instead of the whole volume, whenever possible. Another positive development is the more accurate pinpointing of the location of materials made possible by the proliferation of regional computer-linked networks. If a librarian in Seattle knows, after a quick check of her desk-side CRT, that the book a reader wants is located in a library in Portland, Oregon, she will ask for it from there rather than shooting the request directly to the Library of Congress. And the Congressional Research Service in the Library, finding itself so often frustrated as it tried to locate books on the shelves to analyze a particular issue for a member or committee of Congress, has built up its own substantial library collection of some 1 million volumes over the years—thus taking a bit of the pressure off the Library's general collections.

Serial and Government Publications Division

So far we have discussed only the book collections of the Library of Congress. Newspapers and periodicals, along with serially issued

U.S. government publications, are in the custody of the Serial and Government Publications Division. It is the largest collection of its kind in the United States (more than 1,600 domestic and foreign newspapers and 130,000 serial titles are currently received, with extensive holdings from the eighteenth through the twentieth centuries), and the division's Newspaper and Current Periodical Reading Room is the busiest specialized reading room in the Library of Congress. In 1980, 111,111 users came through its doors, and the staff responded to almost 100,000 reference queries.

The reading room is heavily used because many of the materials are truly unique and they are relatively easy to get to. You can help yourself to the microfilm reels of the *New York Times*, the *Washington Star*, or the *Los Angeles Times* from the drawers along the walls, roll them onto an available microfilm reader, and set to work. Catalogs and finding aids direct you to other parts of the collection. Materials that do have to be retrieved from the decks for you generally appear in less than half an hour.

Government documents are a special case. As anyone who has tried to use them knows, they are hard to describe, hard to locate in a classed catalog, and hard to find on the shelf (just determining the "author" or main entry of some government documents is an exercise of paralyzing frustration!). In the interests of efficiency and common sense, the division has abandoned efforts to keep current U.S. government publications in order by LC classification number. Instead, a complete depository set comes directly into the division and is maintained in SuDocs (Superintendent of Documents) number order sequence. This collection now includes about 75,000 pieces. The staff prepares awareness lists of recent federal documents in the collection to help users find what they need. Some recent examples include "Alternatives to Traditional Transportation," "Nuclear Energy and Power Plants," and "Sources of American Election Statistics."

Area Studies

Four divisions of Research Services are identified by the language of the material they serve: the Asian Division, the European Division, the African and Middle Eastern Division, and the Hispanic Division. They have staffs of twenty-eight, twenty, twenty-one, and fourteen, respectively, and together they served a total of 44,681 readers in 1980. Each of these divisions is staffed by specialists who have made a life's work out of the language and the literature of their subject area.

Although the language/geographic groupings make some sense as they stand, each division is subdivided internally to serve the differing

The reading room of the Hispanic Division is a dramatic tribute to Hispanic and Latin American culture. Given by the Hispanic Foundation, it includes Spanish decor and furniture, a hammered silver chandelier from the Escorial, a huge coat of arms of Ferdinand and Isabella, and four floor-to-ceiling murals by Cândido Portinari.

cultures covered. The Asian Division includes Chinese and Korean, Japanese, and Southern Asia sections. The European Division spans the continent, covering the Western European nations as well as Russia and the Baltic, central, and Eastern European countries. The African Division is tied together more through geography than through cultural identity and includes an African Section, a Hebraic Section, and a Near East Section. The most homogeneous of the group, the Hispanic Division, involves the Spanish, Portuguese, and Latin American worlds of books and culture.

Each of the four divisions maintains its own reading room, each has its own catalogs and reference tools, and all of their staffs are, by definition, multilingual.

There are other parallels. Major portions of the collections of each of the four divisions are unique in the scholarly world. Each division prepares printed bibliographies (sold by the Government Printing Office), which have become basic tools of the research trade, and each is headed by internationally famous scholars. And finally, the overall responsibilities of the divisions are basically the same: to develop and improve the collections in their area; to facilitate their use by scholars; and to explain and interpret the collections through published guides, bibliographies, and studies.

A sampling of some of the publications of these divisions gives an idea of the scope of their activities: *Las Casas as a Bishop: A New Interpretation Based on His Holograph Petition in the Hans P. Kraus Collection of Hispanic American Manuscripts; The United States and Africa: Guide to U.S. Official Documents and Government-Sponsored Publications on Africa, 1785–1975; Arab-World Newspapers in the Library of Congress; Diplomatic Hebrew: A Glossary of Current Terminology; Japanese National Government Publications in the Library of Congress: A Bibliography; The USSR and East Central and Southeastern Europe: Periodicals in Western Languages.*

Although the materials in the several area-studies divisions appear strange and dramatic to the untrained eye—with flowing calligraphy and unintelligible scripts—they are as much the stuff of research as the *New York Times* and Galbraith on economic policy. They are an essential part of a major research library.

Science and Technology Division

Let us conclude our hurried glance at Research Services with a look at the chromium and glass world of the Science and Technology Division—brave but not new. The Library of Congress projects a baroque image of history, culture, and literature, but not only are its scientific holdings now extraordinarily strong, they have been so almost from the beginning. Only the Philadelphia community could challenge Thomas Jefferson's collection of eighteenth-century experimental records, and with the addition of the Smithsonian collection, from 1866 onward, there has been no institution in the United States that could approach the Library of Congress when it comes to scientific holdings. The collection started rich because of the interests of the founders; it has gotten richer because of the way research has been funded in the United States. Somewhere along the line, it became routine to write into federally financed projects, "Copies of the results from this experimentation shall be deposited with the Library of Congress," and thus there is almost no area of applied science in which the Library is not as current as yesterday's mail.

Science Is Different

A scientific library both looks and operates differently from one in the humanities. The Science and Technology Division relates to some 3 million books in the Library's collections, but it lives out of its 3 million technical reports and nearly 48,000 current scientific journals.

In the *soft* sciences, research goes forward, and once a research project is concluded, the scholar puts it all together and interprets its meanings. He then attempts to prove that what he has learned is sufficiently important to justify its publication for the profession—he hopes as a book, if not, as a journal article. Either way, the scholar engages in a long drawn-out task of "selling" his product.

The *hard* sciences operate differently. As work progresses, a researcher is expected to share the results of his successes and failures with his fellow researchers at frequent intervals along the way; further, there is much less pressure to prove that what he has done is of towering significance, since any new data may be useful to someone, so his own profession supports him with its publication and dissemination. The product, however, appears in tiny transactions—offset and mimeographed documentation, microformed reports—all pouring out in great quantity and requiring immediate, uniform indexing so they can be made quickly available to ongoing researchers in parallel fields. Thus, life in the Science and Technology Division is unique.

Services to the Scientific Public

The division operates with approximately thirty-three staff members, the majority of whom are professionals, and since Russian, German, and Chinese experimentation is just as important to its customers as Anglo-American (if not considerably more so!), the staff is broadly multilingual.

The division operates a Science Reading Room for in-house assistance, and business has skyrocketed in the past ten years. Its in-person use has increased from 12,361 to 38,151 readers, and reference librarians provided a total of 37,727 answers to reference queries in 1980. The division also operates a highly refined bibliographic search service for out-of-house help. Scientific projects, in both the government and the private sectors, start with the question, What do we know so far? Thus a search of the literature "as of today" is essential. The Science and Technology Division provides such service through the publication of reference guides (called *Tracer Bullets*) that are targeted to the literature of a particular topic. They are designed to get the researcher started and to lead him to the basic texts, bibliographies, state-of-the-art reports, conference proceedings, and government publications he will need—and they are free for the asking. A recent listing of more than 125 titles ranged from "Acid Rain" to "Women in the Sciences" (and even included an unlikely one called "Hyperlipoproteinemia"!).

The division pursues its own publishing program so the various professions can know what is available in the Library of Congress as well as what is going on in appropriate fields. Recent examples are a 1,000-entry *Directory of Information Resources in the United States: Geosciences and Oceanography* and *Wilbur and Orville Wright: A Chronology Commemorating the Hundredth Anniversary of the Birth of Orville Wright*. Still in process is a definitive bibliographical work on Halley's comet, which will cover everything published about that mysteriously reappearing comet since it was first mentioned by Chinese astronomers in 240 B.C.

The division frequently works jointly with federal scientific agencies on a contract basis to support some major area of government research. The products of these arrangements have taken such forms as a *Bibliography on Cold Regions Science and Technology* and the *Antarctic Bibliography*. (The latter runs to ten volumes, almost 5,000 pages, and like most of the division's studies, is available from the Government Printing Office.)

The Collection

Books are an obvious part of the science collection, but technical reports may not be. Nowadays about 80 percent of the 120,000 technical reports added to the collections each year are received and kept solely on microfilm or microfiche; thus, the literature search is mechanically different from the usual "look it up in the catalog," and the use of the material itself involves row upon row of great, hulking microreaders in a dimly lit room. The kinds of subjects the reports cover are revealed by their sources (scientific bibliography is strong on acronyms): 471,926 AEC/ERDA/DOE; 412,926 AD; 235,800 NASA; 178,404 ERIC; and 140,368 PB reports.*

A specific example of the usefulness of technical reports may intrigue you: During World War II, the Germans were seriously, and secretly, investigating the potential of synthetic fuels—in their case, producing oil from coal. As the Allies moved into captured areas at the end of the war, a U.S.-British Technical Oil Mission was organized to visit

*A[tomic] E[nergy] C[ommission] E[nergy] R[esearch and] D[evelopment] A[dministration]/ D[epartment] o[f] E[nergy]; A[rmed Services Technical Information Agency] D[ocuments]; N[ational] A[eronautics and] S[pace] A[dministration]; E[ducational] R[esearch and] I[nformation] C[enter]; [the federal] P[ublication] B[oard].

plant sites where the research had been carried out, talk to the personnel involved, and evaluate the results of their work. The mission's reports (TOM reports) are contained on 307 reels of microfilm, plus a register and an index, and make up part of the division's technical reports collection. Recognizing the revived interest in synthetic fuels research as a result of concern about the world's energy supply, the Science and Technology Division sent out notices reminding interested researchers of the availability of the TOM reports. It is possible that this old data, examined in the light of recent findings, might kindle a spark in someone's mind that will lead off into new directions.

The National Referral Center

The reading room and bibliographic staff try to bring the reader in contact with the proper printed material. The National Referral Center, until recently a part of the Science and Technology Division, tries to bring people seeking information in contact with people having that information—throughout the country.

The center has queried over 12,000 institutions, departments, and individuals working in the major fields of the physical, biological, social, and engineering sciences to find out who knows what. The results of these surveys are loaded into the Library's computer, and the nation's research community is invited to use the service as a crossover directory. When a researcher is pursuing a topic, he writes or phones the center and states his query as precisely as possible, and the Library then spins its tapes through various search programs. The reply comes out with names, addresses, telephone numbers, and brief descriptions of the sources shown. It tells the researcher about people and places, not about books and articles in the usual library manner. A referral specialist will take up where the computer search leaves off, making calls and checking other sources if the response is not right on target. Some examples of search requests: Who is working on He^3 neutron detectors and cross sections of He^3? Who keeps track of tide measurements in Boston Harbor? Who has test data on the vibration-damping properties of thermoplastic materials with induced vibrations between 500 and 5,000 cycles per second? Who knows what attracts termites? Who has information on the effects of disarmament on innovation and invention?

The service is free to all comers, and the center currently handles more than 6,300 questions a year.

7

USING THE COLLECTIONS: THE CONGRESSIONAL RESEARCH SERVICE

The Antecedents

The Library of Congress started as simply and solely Congress's library. Then, mostly because of an acquisition policy that seemed to accumulate anything covered with dried ink, it became a national library, and to be certain that Congress was not forgotten, the Legislative Reference Service was formed in 1914 to concentrate on Congress's library needs.

The LRS gave the legislature what library support was expected until 1946, when Congress faced the demands of a postwar world and felt it needed not only the books and documents that carried the information it required, but also specialists skilled in understanding, interpreting, and applying the knowledge to legislative solutions. Thus, under the Legislative Reorganization Act of 1946, subject specialists were added to the librarians and the lawyers who had previously made up the LRS staff. What these new people did differed philosophically from what the Research Services people do, because instead of helping the inquirer do the research himself, the LRS handled the query completely and presented the inquirer with the finished product—searched, compared, projected, and packaged.

This approach worked with steadily growing success until the 1960s when Congress became frustrated over a constitutional problem. The Founding Fathers had decreed that there should be three equal and in-dependent branches of the federal government: the legislative, the exec-utive, and the judiciary. But rather than this combination producing an ever more efficient and smooth-running machine, the imperial presi-dencies of Kennedy, Johnson, and Nixon left the congressional branch feeling ignored, bypassed, and denigrated. The Supreme Court's tendency

The Madison Congressional Reading Room, with space for 65 readers and a 5,000-volume reference collection, is available to members and their staffs whenever Congress is in session.

to make more law under the Warren Court than Congress was making across the street was the last straw. By the end of the decade, the legislature had had enough, and it lashed back with a series of dramatic reforms designed to do a number of things at the same time.

The legislators wanted to speed up their own procedures so they could react quickly to executive initiatives: They therefore modernized their rules, shattered the seniority system, and streamlined their committee process. They wanted to recover their control of the budget process, so they established an overall Congressional Budget Office plus two supporting budget committees, placed on either side of Capitol Hill. They wanted to free themselves from the one-sided information provided by the executive agencies, which always seemed to add up to the single solution advanced by the White House, so they trebled the size of the Legislative Reference Service in the Library of Congress and expanded all the obligations it had been acquiring since 1914.

The result is that the renamed Congressional Research Service is now doing what its founders in Putnam's time envisioned—in spades. In 1980, the CRS responded to 340,000 congressional inquiries, which ran the gamut from simple legislative histories extracted from the

computer to complicated impact projections of possible legislative solutions. What the CRS does and how it does it is as follows.

The Idea

The concept behind the whole process is the conviction that there
is no single solution to any social problem. Congress is in place to
further peace, prosperity, and the general welfare of the nation, and
when any trouble threatens, Congress should take such action as is
required to correct it. The major flaw in this scenario is that all the
simple problems have already been solved. There are no easy answers
left. Thus, the difficulties brought to the Congress today are of shuddering
complexity.

The Congressional Research Service has three responsibilities as its
share of the challenge. First, it is required to draw together as many
possible solutions to any national problem as it can identify. Strangely
enough, it is specifically instructed *not* to identify the best one. Rather,
it is supposed to enumerate every possible solution, cost each one in
terms of social and dollar expense, anticipate the problems each solution
might create, evaluate their effectiveness, and identify the motivations
and possible self-interests of their advocates. So doesn't that process
automatically identify the best option? Very rarely. Variables that only
the legislators can know also influence the decision. Congress genuinely
believes that politics is the art of the possible and that the trade-offs,
the possibilities of support, the probables, and the worst-case recognitions
are the skills of the members. The Congressional Research Service is
instructed to identify as many solutions as it can find—and hand them
quickly and coherently to the Congress. The legislature will make the
decisions.

Second, the Congressional Research Service is expected to stand
immediately behind the members and their staffs with information. This
is a logical and obvious extension of the original idea of a library for
Congress: Simply have the facts already assembled and waiting so these
facts can be available to Congress when it needs them. In the old days,
the facts were in books and documents. Now they are in computer
data banks, on the floppy discs of the word-processing machines, on
microfiche and in video/laser readers, but they are there in vastly
greater numbers and have to be assembled, indexed, and stored in
anticipation of the congressional requests. The congressional session is
so short and the breadth of national issues so wide that each issue
receives a blinding scrutiny for a very short space of time. A potential
20,000 members of the legislature and their staffs fix their attention on
an issue, and then, frequently in a matter of days, hearings are held,

the bill is marked up, the debate rushes to a vote, and the issue is finished. It may be joyously passed or roundly defeated, but in either event, the issue will not be addressed for at least another session—and frequently not before another Congress two years away. The CRS must have anticipated the questions before they are asked; it will not have time to pursue much added data while the issue is at full pitch.

Finally, the CRS is expected to make Congress more efficient very quickly. The least-appreciated characteristic of the legislature is its shortness of tenure and its truly vast turnover. In any one year, the number of old staff leaving and new staff coming in now runs to more than 10,000 highly trained specialists. Committees bring in teams to help prepare a particular piece of legislation, and once the bill is resolved, these specialists return to their home governments, their campuses, or their corporations, and new teams take their place. Staff from district offices come to Washington to work with the member or senator for six months to a year until they "get the feel of the office," and then they return to the district or state. Young specialists with the new master's or doctorate degrees come to work for a year or two before they take up their next, extended careers. And then there are the waves of "interns" who come for a few weeks to a semester to work on Capitol Hill—in 1980, nearly 4,000 of them made their pilgrimage to the Library.

The Congressional Research Service is expected to fulfill a substantial role in training all of these various newcomers. It gives them crash courses in congressional procedures. It runs continual seminars on public issues so the appropriate people know what legislation is already on the books, what solutions have been tried and found wanting, and where an issue stands *now*. And the service conducts training in how to use the CRS most efficiently along with the other legislative support offices. Congress has major skills available to it from its General Accounting Office, its Office of Technology Assessment, and its budget offices, and a major part of the training programs is to explain the division of labor among these support units—which are all designed to make Congress work faster, more efficiently, and more productively.

How the Purpose Is Achieved

If options, information, and training are what the CRS is expected to provide, many of the techniques used to answer the annual 340,000 inquiries are unique, innovative, and now highly refined.

In-depth Policy Analysis

The techniques are accretive like a snowball or an onion. They start small and quick and build to larger and longer. When a new problem bursts on the scene—a sudden international crisis, a national strike, a fruit fly outbreak, or a dramatic breakthrough in genetic engineering— the CRS can expect several hundred requests for background briefings within the first forty-eight hours. (These, of course, are solely from the legislative branch; the CRS responds only to the Congress.) Once the problem arises, the CRS will quickly search its clipping files, its computerized data banks, and the resources of the Library's collections. It will place calls to the known experts around the country and then quickly pull this initial data into an Issue Brief. An Issue Brief is a document with a specific format that is kept in the computer and broken into specific parts. It starts with a definition of the issue, then it analyzes the options apparent at the outset for solving the problem, describes what legislation is already on the books, lists the printed hearings and reports that are appropriate, and presents a chronology of the events that led up to the problem. There are over 2,000 CRT terminals spread around Capitol Hill that are linked to the Library's computer, and any of these can display the Issue Brief in the callers' own offices or print it out on paper at their command. Keeping the document in the computer means that it is instantly available to the 20,000 legislative employees, but more important, it can be updated as quickly as changes occur. During the Iranian hostage crisis, for example, the basic Issue Brief was updated three or four times a day to keep track not only of developments in Iran, but of State Department announcements, congressional hearings and briefings, et cetera.

Once the basic Issue Brief goes on-line, the CRS subject specialists move to the full-dress CRS Report or white paper. This report will usually run to 50 or 100 typewritten pages and give a more analytical, balanced, and historical treatment of the problem than the Issue Brief can. In a report, the solutions can be costed out, the rationale for each described and analyzed, and the full spectrum of options developed. Broad areas of concern like health care, disarmament, energy, and taxation can be elaborated upon and explored. It will take a matter of weeks to develop and print these extended reports, and then they will be stockpiled to await congressional inquiries. At any given time, the computer will hold between 700 and 800 updated and current Issue Briefs, and the storage shelves will hold 800 stockpiled CRS Reports and white papers. Twice a month congressional offices are provided with a list of what materials are available (although most studies are

The Congressional Research Service prepares a variety of printed products to alert members and committees to the kinds of specific services CRS has to offer and to provide background information on current legislative issues.

used to answer inquiries for background material on such and such a topic, not as a response to a request for a specific publication).

No Propaganda

From the beginning, Congress set specific rules for CRS studies and products. The service was never to distribute its materials on its own initiative. No study could be sent out of the Library except in response to a specific, individual request. Every study was to be nonpartisan, objective, detached, and confidential.

Those near-cliché labels have a number of interesting aspects when applied to the CRS. The "confidentiality" element, for example, is linked to the fact that many requests for briefing on an issue are from a member who wishes to know "the other side" of a position he himself supports. Senator X knows his and his own party's position; he is frequently more interested in knowing "the enemy's" posture. Does the opposition have a better solution that should be absorbed? What challenges might be raised in a television interview to embarrass him? What will his answer be to all the other positions in the spectrum? If he is to be interviewed, the senator will want to have thought out these questions before the red light appears on a camera, but it would be time-consuming to have to explain to the press why he asked the CRS for information on the "wrong" side. On the other hand, once a member has chosen the option he thinks is best for his constituency, he frequently wishes his potential vote or position kept confidential to prevent preemptive strikes from his opposition. If he had to defend even a query for information from the Library, it would soon be easier simply to drop that source of information—thereby denying himself a better understanding of the problem.

Congress has frequently declared that the Congressional Research Service's greatest strength lies in the fact that "we've got to have *some* source of information we can trust." The CRS therefore strictly follows a policy of "We don't care which way the issue is decided; we simply want to be certain you have all the options before you; you make up your own mind." Astonishingly, during its many decades of work, the CRS has managed to sustain its detachment in the emotion-charged congressional scene and is used equally by both parties and by proponents of both sides of the issues. When the 340,000 requests for information are analyzed each year, they invariably reflect the vote count of the members of Congress, neither more nor less of liberal or conservative, "ins" or "outs." (The White House party versus the "outs" is also a source of some surprise; one might expect that the "outs" would use the Library and the "ins" would use the executive agencies for briefings or data. Experience has proved that no matter which party is in power, the "ins" are as suspicious of the case put forward by their own departments as they are of the opposition's!)

While speaking of objectivity and detachment, a word might be said about Washington lobbyists. The CRS has discovered that the professional lobbying organizations are excellent sources of accurate information. The secret, of course, is to be certain to identify the source (and its possible biases)—clearly and explicitly. However, lobbyists expect to be around a long time, and the only way they can maintain credibility with the members of Congress is to be certain that their statistics hold up in public and do not embarrass the members who use them. When the CRS provides its usual spectrum of options, it finds it usually ends up drawing about equally on government sources, university sources, and lobby organizations.

Multidisciplines

One of the most important contributions the Congressional Research Service makes to the understanding of a public issue is its ability to apply multidisciplinary knowledge to each problem. Organizationally grouped by subject specialization, the CRS has an American Law Division, an Economics Division, and divisions for Education and Public Welfare, Environment and Natural Resources Policy, Foreign Affairs and National Defense, as well as one for Government and for Science Policy Research.

Each of those divisions, obviously, is filled with trained specialists covering the full spectrum of each area. The 650 CRS researchers all have graduate degrees, and the senior analysts have written and published extensively and are recognized national figures in their fields. There are, in addition, a group of 35 analysts who carry the statutory title of senior specialists and are paid the highest federal salary possible for nonsupervisory personnel. In point of fact, their salary category places them at the level of a college dean or president, and as a result, the CRS has been able to make available to Congress some of the nation's leading specialists in the following fields:

agriculture
American government
American public law
congressional organization
conservation and energy
constitutional law
education
election law
energy resources
engineering and public
   works
environmental policy
futures research
housing
income maintenance
information policy and
   technology

international affairs
international economics
labor
mineral and regulatory
   economics
national defense
price economics
public administration
science and technology
social welfare
Soviet economics
space and transportation
   technology
taxation and fiscal policy
transportation

All of the researchers become "Congress's people" and approach their subject fields from the legislative point of view. They help members and committees set up hearings; they suggest who should be brought to Washington to explain an issue, who around the country have some innovative solutions, and who are trying new approaches. The specialists help the members determine what questions to use in hearings to bring out the particular expertise of a witness. Equally, the specialists point up the weak points in supplicants' arguments so a facile presentation does not mask a questionable solution.

All of these CRS subject specialties are brought to bear *across* disciplinary lines. Experience has proved that the majority of the legislative mistakes made in the fifties and sixties came about because of a failure to take into account the side effects of a cure. The social security solutions of the social scientists got into trouble because of unfunded indexing procedures, which should have been caught by the economists. Innovative interstate beltways denuded the centers of cities of tax revenue. Upriver dams permitted salt water to rise in the valleys. And so on.

The CRS, therefore, requires that every paper and every briefing be reviewed by specialists outside the subject specialty of the authoring division. Any major study has a multidisciplinary team at the very outset, not at the end, and there is a division of labor among the specialties before the first words are written. Every congressional question coming in becomes two questions within the CRS: What options are available right now to solve this public issue? and What will we wish, ten years from now, we had recognized today? As a rule the peripheral specialists can monitor the latter question better than the primary specialists doing the study can.

Protecting the Producers

The analysts and the subject specialists are very expensive. Before the Legislative Reorganization Act of 1970, the CRS was staffed by type specialists—water people, welfare people, tax people, atomic energy people. Since that act, however, the CRS still has "water people," but they specialize in one particular area so there are specialists in dams and hydroelectric power, specialists in river development, specialists in water quality, specialists in estuaries, and specialists in oceanography. The CRS still has "welfare people" but some are now experts in social security, in income maintenance, in medical care for the aged, in unemployment insurance, and some in the care of the family. The atomic energy section now has specialists in atomic energy generation, waste disposal, international export and monitoring, et cetera. Each of these experts is costly, and all of them are overworked. Even with a trebled staff, a single committee could keep the subject-related CRS people so busy that the rest of the Congress would be denied access to them. To prevent such bottlenecks, techniques have been developed to extend the reach of each specialist to the utmost.

Once a specialist has prepared the basic papers—an Issue Brief for the computer, a CRS Report, and backup reading materials—the materials are passed to the Congressional Reference Division of the CRS, which prepares a list of materials called InfoPacks. InfoPacks are essentially sets of five to ten pieces of reading material that add up to written briefings on some 100 public issues.

An InfoPack will have whatever reports the CRS specialists have prepared, but it will also include appropriate congressional committee prints and hearings, position papers from the executive branch, a representative sample of lobby group materials, and a fully developed bibliography of materials available from the Library of Congress collections. The idea is to give the requester a layered choice of information from which the requester can select and use as needed. The user can stop at any point, or if he becomes interested in some particular aspect of the problem, he has leads to further material he can explore himself. Samples of InfoPacks topics are gun control, social security financing, governmental grants and foundation support, and federal options in crime control. From the managerial point of view, the InfoPack protects the specialists from being swamped by what are essentially duplicate queries. When requests for briefings come in, the InfoPack provides a first response on a general level without the specialist being interrupted. Once the reader has gotten an overall understanding of the problem, he or she can then call back with a precise, targeted query that is passed through to the—expensive but limited—specialists.

Information

Facts. Statistics. Who? What is? When was? The congressional establishment generates literally tens of thousands of these queries each year, and the Library has been answering them since 1800. The majority of these queries are now answered by a group of librarians in a CRS unit called the Congressional Reference Division. (Note: Less than 10 percent of the CRS staff is composed of librarians; most of the researchers are lawyers, economists, biologists, engineers, et cetera.) These librarians work from a 5,000-book reference library and the largest newspaper morgue in the country, they have access to some 200 computer data bases rented from all over the nation, and they are connected to the congressional offices by telephone and by hourly messenger deliveries. "Outposts" of the unit are set up in five of the seven congressional office buildings, where further computer terminals, reader-printers, and facsimile machines are available along with smaller reference collections and trained librarians. These outpost units help member and committee staffs do their own research plus getting the answers for them when requested.

The end result of this network is that congressional staff members have CRS information material available within a series of circles:

In Their Own Office. In their own office (usually on their own desk), a computer terminal has five CRS data bases available for instant display. The CRS *Digest of Public General Bills* contains each piece of legislation introduced into either house of Congress, and it provides an abstract of what each bill is about and a record of its progress through the Congress. Each bill can be called up by number, sponsor, or subject.

The computer contains the CRS Issue Briefs, which can be called up by subject, and the index to the Daily *Congressional Record*. The computer also contains the CRS "SDI"—an index to some 4,000 magazines that identifies all significant articles and government documents relating to public issues. They are retrievable by author, title, and subject, and if the user wishes to see the full article, a "hard copy" can be secured by a telephone call. Finally, the computer plugs directly into the main catalog of the Library of Congress and gives the user access to its 1 million entries from 1968 to the present.

In Their Office Building Reference Center. The second ring of information support is the CRS Reference Center, which has offices on the ground floor of the Capitol and in all but one of the House and Senate office buildings. (The missing one is the Cannon Building, which is located next to the Library of Congress itself and is connected to it by an underground tunnel.) The Reference Centers stockpile CRS publications as well as providing rented computer research programs.

In the Congressional Reference Division. The third ring lies with the Congressional Reference Division librarians in the Madison Building.

In the Main Collections of the Library of Congress. The final circle is represented by the full staff and collections of the Library of Congress—on which the Congress always has first call.

Training

The various congressional training programs of the Library are of interest because they point up the complexity of working in the congressional establishment in the present political age. The day in which the most distinguished citizen of a town went to Washington to represent the community for three or four months—or a state's ex-governor went to the U.S. Senate for the same short session—and then returned home for the rest of the year is long gone. Being a member of Congress is now a full-time task based on the finest corporate model.

We have noted the startling rate of turnover in congressional staffs, which means that the CRS has only a short time to help in bringing that personnel "up to speed." The first layer of training is via television tapes written and produced by the CRS and shown on the closed-circuit television channel displayed in each congressional office. These CRS training videotapes cover such topics as "Congressional Operations and Procedure," "Preparation and Use of Legislative Histories," "Statutory Research," and "Senate Parliamentary Procedure." These pro-

CRS conducts seminars and workshops for congressional staff members to help them do their jobs better. Topics covered range from an explanation of day-to-day legislative procedures to a discussion by expert panelists of AWACS or social security financing.

grams run from one to two hours each and are shown at repeated intervals.

The next level of training involves audio cassettes that discuss the pros and cons of current public issues. These cassettes are designed for listening in automobiles and at work stations via portable cassette players. The cassettes are issued continually and are available free to members in the same way a CRS Report would be.

The more formal training programs come next. Once a week, training classes are held for permanent congressional staff members on how to use the CRS and the Library's Law Library and on how to handle constituent mail, legislative publications, et cetera, in the offices.

At repeated times throughout the year, the CRS stages a one-day Legislative Institute designed to help staff members handle legislative and procedural questions and to point up the various support services available to all staff members on Capitol Hill. On four different occasions each year, the CRS runs a two-and-a-half day seminar for senior staff that goes into the budget process, advanced congressional procedure, and the intricacies of congressional and executive branch relationships.

Periodically, the CRS also stages District/State Institutes. Several hundred "home" staff workers are brought to Washington, and for two and a half days, the CRS gives them a crash course in running a congressional office back in the home state.

Finally, the CRS stages more than a hundred seminars each year for which it brings in reputable advocates from outside Washington to present their particular solutions for the public dilemmas under consideration. These issue seminars are both popular and noted for their verbal free-for-alls between the advocates and congressional staff members once the formal presentations are over. In 1980, 5,100 congressional employees attended one or more of the issue seminars.

What the CRS Won't Do

What won't the CRS do? Several things that it once did. In the past, it would write speeches for members; now it will only provide briefing materials. It used to provide charts and graphs and help with the graphics for congressional publications, but no longer; it does those things now only when related to a CRS study.

The CRS does not—indeed it never did—draft the text of bills; that is a function of the offices of legislative counsels. It also does not do casework (search for a social security check, trace a veteran's claim, recover money for the fence a tank tore down during maneuvers).

And then there is the matter of constituents. A legend once got started that Congress could ask the CRS to write term papers for constituents. That was never true, but apparently the myth came from a rather frequent practice of members asking the CRS for information in order to reply to constituent letters ("Our college is debating U.S. withdrawal from the United Nations; please send material on _____"; "Our League of Women Voters study group is working on water programs for the Arkansas Valley; please _____"). If the CRS has already prepared a study on whatever topic is required, it will make a duplicate copy available. Congressional staff members frequently take their morning's mail to the nearest Reference Center and pick out CRS materials that will answer the queries in hand. Studies have suggested that as much as 15 percent of CRS replies are used by congressional offices to respond to constituent letters (and there are those who think the true figure may run as high as half that number again). The CRS answers no constituent queries directly (they must be both received and sent out through the members' offices), and the CRS has never knowingly prepared a study in response to a constituent inquiry. Its work must be tied to current, ongoing legislative activity.

Summary

The work of the Congressional Research Service continues the tradition of the first Librarians of Congress. In the 1800s, the Library was on the same floor of the Capitol as the two chambers of the legislature. During committee meetings and during debates in the two houses, members would rush off the floor to get data to support their cause or to frustrate their opponents. For nearly a hundred years their library and the facts that it contained were only steps—scarcely minutes—away from where the members worked. With the coming of the twentieth century and the new building, Congress and its information were both psychologically and geographically apart for eighty years. Now, in our own time, computers, image-processing techniques, and skilled Library staff scattered throughout the congressional office buildings mean that the Library of Congress is again only steps—barely seconds—away from its users. Every Senate office and almost every House office has a tabletop terminal tied to the main computer of the Library of Congress. By phone, or in person, the members and their staffs turned to the CRS 340,000 times in 1980. The nineteenth-century idea of providing unlimited information to the legislature from a *legislative source* would appear to be one of the few government ideas that got faster and better through the years.

8

USING THE COLLECTIONS:
THE LAW LIBRARY

The Law Library is the smallest of the seven departments of the Library of Congress, but it is by far the oldest, antedating any of the others by a good half century. It has the largest collection of legal materials of any institution in the world, and it not only covers the full story of U.S. jurisprudence (captured as it all happened), but its strength in foreign law is so great that its reputation is enhanced by its nondomestic holdings and staff.

In any logical explanation of how the Library of Congress is put together, the Law Library acts as a bridge between Research Services and the Congressional Research Service. The CRS cares for the Congress, and Research Services helps the public, but the Law Library works for both. It handles all the questions Congress asks concerning foreign law. (In 1980, it prepared 868 major congressional studies—18,521 typewritten pages—exploring how foreign governments used the law to solve their particular social or political problems.) Its collections are heavily used by scholars, the federal executive agencies, and the courts, and hundreds of students from Washington's five law schools seem to consider it part of their school campus. In 1980, almost 100,000 readers used the Law Library Reading Room.

You will recall that the Law Library was the first unit of the Library to be split off and set up as a separate department. In 1831, the Senate told its Judiciary Committee to look into the feasibility of putting all the law books from the general library collection into a separate law library. The committee found the idea good, and in 1832 a law was passed moving the appropriate books into "an apartment near to, and connected by an easy communication with that in which the Library of Congress is now kept. . . ." According to the act, the justices of the

The Law Library Reading Room in the James Madison Memorial Building.

Supreme Court were to make such rules and regulations for the new library as they saw fit, so long as they did not restrict its use by the President, the Vice-President, or the members of Congress. In those days, the Supreme Court was itself housed in the Capitol, one floor below the Library of Congress. The justices were given $5,000 to expand the collection, plus $1,000 a year thereafter to buy whatever books they wished for their law library. No doubt the separation was helpful to the Court, but by accident it was a greater boon to the nation, since most of the original Library of Congress burned to ashes in the fire of 1851, whereas the satellite law library was spared. The present collection of 1.6 million volumes is thus the oldest continuously developed collection in the Library. "In the Library" is appropriate, because when the whole Library of Congress moved out of the Capitol, the Law Library went with it and was reabsorbed under Library of Congress control. No books have been selected for the Law Library by the justices since the end of the nineteenth century, although the two institutions continue to maintain a close working relationship.

But the historic ties with the Capitol have not been severed altogether. The Law Library still maintains a small working collection of U.S. law reference materials in space adjacent to the Senate Library in the Capitol. By law, that collection is open whenever the House or the Senate is in session, and thus it is accessible should legal questions come up during debate on the floor.

The legal collection has always been heavily used. Understandably, the Supreme Court has used it during the Court's annual sessions, but the Congress has used it just as much—not for interpreting the laws but for making them. From the beginning, the amelioration of many of the nation's ills began with the question, How are the British doing it? Nowadays, the question is more likely to be, What are the Japanese doing about it? But the tradition persists.

Not surprisingly, the early collection of legal materials in the Law Library was heavily weighted in favor of Anglo-American and common-law traditions. Beginning in the 1900s, the law librarians began consciously to correct this imbalance, first by adding materials on the law of European nations, then of Latin American countries. Finally, in the years following the Second World War, they aggressively went after legal works concerning developing nations in all areas of the world. The basic philosophy of the Law Library is to collect primary legal materials—such as official gazettes, constitutions, codes and compilations of laws, court decisions, session laws, and administrative rules, regulations, and decisions—on an intensive rather than a representative basis from all around the globe.

The Law Library today contains works on all ages and all systems of law. In addition to their reference and research duties, the Law Library specialists help to develop the collections they require for their work, which involves seeking out specific items, organizing nonclassed materials, and surveying existing holdings. A staggering 1.2 million pieces are received by the Law Library each year, and an average of about 30,000 volumes are added annually to the Law Library's permanent collections.

The Law Library's 1.6-million-volume collection is one-third U.S. and two-thirds foreign law. The library's shelves contain rows of volumes in the traditional fields of jurisprudence, legal history, and legal philosophy, but they are filling even faster with the law of the Common Market, nuclear defense agreements, and multinational programs for developing countries. Similarly, the law classification schemes embrace thousands of volumes of Roman, medieval, feudal, canon, Islamic, and Jewish law as well as materials on the common, civil, and socialist law systems. Easily overlooked is the fact that some of the rare volumes in the Law Library's collections are beautifully illustrated—from the hand-painted miniatures found in a manuscript version of the customary laws of Normandy (produced in the 1400s and bound in green velvet)

Some of the rare volumes in the collections of the Law Library contain brilliantly hand-painted miniatures, like this manuscript version of the customary laws of Normandy, which dates from the 1400s.

to the lavish watercolor and gold decorations of a nineteenth-century folio edition of the Magna Carta.

Organization

For the better part of the twentieth century, the successive Law Librarians have found it convenient to organize their staffs and collections around language/area legal systems. This method has produced five divisions: The American-British Law Division of twenty-two staff members copes with U.S., British Commonwealth, and Irish Republic materials; the Hispanic Law Division, with a staff of seven, covers Latin America, Puerto Rico, the Philippines, Spain, and Portugal; the twenty-person European Law Division handles the remainder of Europe, including the USSR; and there are nine on the Far Eastern Division staff and seven staff members in the Near Eastern and African Law Division.

Even more than most other disciplines, the question of timeliness assumes vast importance in the legal field. Yesterday's court decision in Malawi may have invalidated a whole series of recent government actions, and a law approved by the Bundestag a month ago might have climaxed a year-long effort to modify West Germany's basic law on abortion. Legal specialists must have immediate access to the official reports of these kinds of actions if their research—for Congress or for other public officials—is to have any validity. The processing of these kinds of unbound, ephemeral materials, however, has a relatively low priority outside the Law Library, since the Library of Congress's Processing Services must give its first attention to hardbound trade and scholarly volumes likely to be in high demand both at LC and around the United States.

How to resolve this conflict without too much duplication of effort? Compromise: A small processing staff in the Law Library takes on the task of refining the partially classed works as they are received from Processing Services, applies labels to the spines, and puts the books on the shelves. Additionally, many of the official gazettes, digests, and loose-leaf materials come directly to the Law Library in the first place. Result: The legal specialists can get their hands on these essential materials as soon as they arrive at the Library of Congress—and the users of the Law Library can be assured that the information they receive is as up to date as possible.

The extraordinary complexity of evolving law is bad enough, but when you add the fact that foreign law—of the developing nations particularly—lacks the detailed indexing and control systems we are familiar with for U.S. law, it means that the selection of individual staff specialists is especially important in this department. The Law Library tries to get professionals who have actually been trained as lawyers in at least one of the countries they are paid to oversee. Each specialist must have passed a bar examination in his home country, and, to the extent that this is possible, each specialist is expected to have had experience as a lawyer, a judge, or an administrator abroad. Thanks to the distressing turbulence in twentieth-century world politics, the Law Library has been able to secure some of the world's leading jurists from an astonishingly large number of foreign nations. At the present time, its staff specialists work in more than fifty different languages.

Along the more traditional lines of service, the Law Library has a staff of legal reference specialists, primarily trained in law and/or library science, who handle the bulk of inquiries on a day-to-day, face-to-face basis. They not only man the reference desk and the telephones, but they also respond to most of the queries received from the judiciary, lawyers, law libraries, the press, and John Q. Citizen. Their responses range from preparing legislative histories and bibliographies, identifying cases or providing legislation information, to answering questions like, Can you send me a list of all your law books?

What Do You Use a Law Library For?

Obviously, it depends on who you are. A congressional subcommittee holding hearings on environmental health hazards may need a detailed study of criminal negligence violations of health and environment-hazard rules in Commonwealth countries. A member of Congress planning a fact-finding trip may need to be briefed on the legal systems of the various countries he or she plans to visit. The foreign specialist from a federal agency is more likely to be interested in commercial law relating to foreign taxes and trade incentives, the labor laws of the country the agency is dealing with, the regulation of private business within that country, the different treatment afforded foreigners (like Americans)—and the laws on motion picture censorship of exported U.S. films.

The visitor from the Supreme Court or the Justice Department is likely to be seeking some loose-leaf service relating to state and local statutes. The endless insertion into binders of literally tens of thousands of advance sheets, pocket parts, slip laws, decisions, and loose-leaf pages keeps several Law Library assistants busy on a daily basis. Attorneys need journal articles and textbooks. Legal historians struggle with the great vellum codices.

The 104,000 day-to-day queries placed at the public reference desk in 1980 covered the full spectrum of legal research. In a recent year-end summary, the foreign legal specialists noted questions relating to:

> the sale and export of ancient Egyptian artifacts, Liberian shipping laws, the North Borneo law of 1962 on the recognition of Chinese customary marriages, inheritance rights of illegitimate children in Trinidad and Tobago, marriage contracts under the Muslim personal law of Pakistan, presumption of survivorship under the laws of Guyana, marriage and legitimation in certain Mexican states, common-law marriage in Panama and the Cape Verde Islands, murder and homicide under the Cuban criminal code, statutes on bribery in Latin America, tort liability in a tram accident in Spain, community-property law in Bolivia, legal education in Latin America, liability and compensation for wrongful acts under Thai law, registration of births in Tibet, immigration laws in Singapore, contracts between Japanese and Peruvian firms to build an oil pipeline through Peru, recognition of divorce under Tanzanian law, marital obedience and child custody in Abu Dhabi, and smuggling laws of the People's Republic of China.

The Law Library, like any research-oriented group, strives for a wider dissemination of the results of its work through publication.

Reports on topics of more than passing interest become offset-printed studies that can be distributed to others looking into the same issue. Government financing of national elections, political parties, and campaign spending in various countries, for example, clearly fit this mold. A relatively new departure for the Law Library is the production of bibliographic guides to U.S. law materials in other languages to help answer the oft-asked question: "I can't read English; are there any books on U.S. law in my language?" The first of these guides, in German, was published in 1981. More substantial volumes, basically foreign legal texts or guides to foreign laws, are published as hardbound books and sold by the U.S. Government Printing Office.

The K Classification

Since 1960, the Law Library has been the scene of an unusual exercise, the like of which has not been seen in librarianship since the nineteenth century. The Gay Nineties and the ensuing turn of the century were the days of the great efforts to "organize knowledge" into vastly detailed classification schemes, of which the Dewey Decimal System is the most famous and the most pervasive. Dewey's system was only one of many at the time, but when the smoke finally cleared after several decades of experimentation, only it and the 5,000-page Library of Congress classification scheme had survived. The Dewey system has been embraced by most school and public libraries and is fully developed from 001 through 999, covering all the ramifications of the human mind. The Library of Congress system is used most heavily by the nation's research and special libraries and by 1948 was complete from AC 1 to Z 7999—except for the letter K! This category had been reserved from the outset for the development of numbers to organize the subject of law, but for fifty years no one got around to doing anything about it.

The "K exercise" sounds trivial, but in the world of books and libraries it represents a fairly high order of irony. Most of the earliest American libraries *began* as collections of law books, yet from the early eighteenth century to 1967, few major law or research libraries in the country had developed a fully expanded subject classification for legal materials.

How did they handle the volumes they had? The traditional private law office library was always organized by the kinds of books on the lawyer's shelves. The Library of Congress followed that procedure at the start, then as the legal volumes grew from hundreds to thousands and then tens of thousands, LC placed "temporary labels" on the spines and simply elaborated its basic form-sorts. From 1800 to World War

II, the books were divided first into countries, and then within countries into ten kinds of books (constitutions, session laws, compilations and codes, judicial decisions, simple legal treatises, and rules, regulations, decisions, and orders). Within each kind of book, the volumes were arranged either chronologically, numerically, or alphabetically, depending on which system seemed appropriate. Considering that the collection had grown to over a million volumes (many floors of stacks of books) before anything was done about it, this arrangement would appear to have been confusi..g and clumsy. It was. Someone looking for books on divorce, for example, was forced to pick them out of thousands of legal treatises arranged simply by author from A to Z.

The legal profession was slow to complain about the situation, which was duplicated throughout most of the nation's law libraries, but when it finally faced up to the problem, it concentrated its resources and expertise on developing the solution. Although the American Association of Law Libraries and the Library of Congress worked in concert—combining skills through committees, volunteer teams, and full-time personnel from the Library—it nevertheless took over twenty years to develop the detailed classification tables to the satisfaction of the many groups of users.

The sixties and early seventies saw a flurry of activity at the Library of Congress in the development of Class K. The classification scheme was first applied to current acquisitions in 1967 for subclass KF (law of the United States) and continued for subclass KD (United Kingdom and Ireland) in 1973, subclass KE (Canada) in 1976, and K (General) in 1977. The Library expects to have the law of Germany (subclasses KK, KKA, KKB, KKC) completed by mid-1982. Classification tables for Latin America and France are in the development stage.

It has become increasingly clear that Class K is a mixed blessing and will probably never be carried through to total completion. It is an expensive process (over a million dollars has been spent by the Library of Congress alone), and the high interest in the project that was expressed in the late sixties has long since disappeared (although the 1979–1980 A. D. Little study of the Law Library, mentioned later in this chapter, did indicate it would be nice if all the law collections carried a K-class number). The budgetary—and human—resources to pursue the project are hard to come by, and the development of individual schedules for every country in the world would take longer than the books being cataloged will last. Many people in the Library now feel that it makes more sense to design extensive generalized tables of classification into which the legal systems of different countries can be slipped, and it is likely that no additional customized country classification schedules will be developed. Finally, there may be an object lesson in the fact that law libraries were able to cope with a more informal classification scheme for hundreds of years.

The first edition of this book tripped alarm bells about the potential disruptions if complete retrospective cataloging under Class K became a reality: It was feared that materials bearing on the law, legislation, or governmental processes of *any* subject would be removed from their original subject classifications and reclassified in the appropriate subclass of K and shelved with the law books. It now appears that this will not come to pass. The Library of Congress has done no retrospective cataloging of this kind, preferring instead to concentrate its limited resources on retrospective cataloging of the legal volumes already in the custody of the Law Library. It is true, though, that subsequent editions of books formerly classified under political science (JK), for example, will be given a K number and shelved with the legal collections when new editions of those books come into the Library. This change will lead to some confusion for a time, but such adjustments should occur gradually and thus be more easily assimilated.

A National Law Center

The Law Library has been at the center of another interesting debate in the last few years: Should it be integrated to a greater degree with the other scholarly disciplines in the Library of Congress or should it pursue its "separate" status and break away from the Library altogether to create a national law center?

A little background will help. When the present Librarian of Congress, Daniel J. Boorstin, was appointed to his post in 1975, he came with a background as a distinguished American historian *and* as a lawyer. His position on the role of law and the social sciences was clear: He saw them not as separate but as complementary disciplines. He had spent a lifetime weaving them together into a common theme; he had no reason to change his philosophical approach upon coming to the Library.

At the same time, there was a general trend among university and academic libraries in the 1970s to try to bring the law libraries on the campuses under more direct control of the university library systems. The independent law libraries resisted. The American Association of Law Libraries took a stand in opposition to this trend, seeing it as a denigration of their status.

The Librarian's 1976 Task Force on Goals, Organization, and Planning looked at the whole issue of the Law Library and its services and appointed an outside Law Advisory Group to advise it on the matter. The advisory group's report (the Neal report) essentially stressed what could be called "missed opportunities" on the part of the Law Library.

The group felt that the Law Library wasn't doing badly as it was but also felt that with more money and a change in direction, it could do so much more.

Specifically the Neal report recommended that the Law Library assume a role of national leadership in the creation of a computerized data base covering publications in law and related fields and in coordinating the acquisition of legal materials (so that certain law libraries would assume direct responsibility for collecting in specific fields of law). The advisory group identified a whole range of services that the Law Library could provide to law libraries around the country (from a more expeditious processing of law books to the development of internships) and pleaded that the Law Library's information and publications programs be upgraded. Finally, the advisory group considered the identity of the Law Library: Should it be a convenient reading room for the area's law students or a serious center for legal scholarship? (A reader survey conducted in 1976 while the task force study was being conducted turned up the fact that 42 percent of the users of the reading room were Washington-area law students.) The advisory group came down hard in support of the latter option.

The advisory group failed to face up to the question of integration versus separation, other than to say it did not feel equipped to make judgments in that area and to recommend that "a comprehensive survey of the Law Library be commissioned." The task force also ultimately recommended that there be a study of "the organization and future direction of the Law Library."

After a year and a half of further study and discussion, the Library's Office of Planning and Development bit the bullet in August 1977 and proposed that the Law Library become one of three branches of a new "super reference department" reporting to an Assistant Librarian for Research Services. That proposal was only a single piece of a complicated plan that represented the first major overhaul of the Library's administrative structure in thirty years. But there is no denying that it got the most attention.

The Librarian clearly saw the proposal as an opportunity to "recognize the important role of the law in our society and take account of the increasing application of the natural sciences and the social sciences to the major legal questions of the day"—as a chance to bring law and the sciences together, beginning with an administrative change. The Law Library, and law libraries across the country, saw the proposal as a threat to their traditional and statutory autonomy.

The Congress (i.e., the Joint Committee on the Library) called for hearings on the proposed reorganization, and not surprisingly, the only questions asked related to the Law Library. A Law Library employees' association, individual staff members of the Law Library, and other law librarians testified against the proposed change. Library management contended that it should be free to structure the Library in the manner it deemed to be most efficient and effective.

In the best traditions of the political process, a compromise was struck: The rest of the proposed reorganization would proceed as scheduled, but the Law Library would be left untouched for the moment. At the same time, the Library of Congress would hire an outside consulting firm to undertake a major study of the operations, activities, and future direction of the Law Library.

The Arthur D. Little firm made the successful bid on the contract and, in 1979 (for $150,000), began the task of studying the overall operations of the Law Library. The firm submitted its final report in 1980 and staked out a middle ground. Although acknowledging that the collections of the Law Library were unparalleled and that Congress was well pleased with the service it received, the Little report noted that "as an organization the Law Library has not met the demands for national leadership put forward by law librarians and the American Association of Law Libraries."

Unlike the Law Advisory Group that worked with the Librarian's Task Force on Goals, Organization, and Planning, the consulting firm *was* charged with the task of looking into the organizational placement of the Law Library, and it recommended that the Law Library should remain a part of the Library of Congress, but as a separate entity reporting directly to the Librarian. The report also argued for enlarged responsibilities for the Law Librarian (to assert leadership both within LC and among law libraries in general and to pursue the question of the processing of law materials); for improved service to government and scholarly users; for additional resources for the Law Library (raising the issue of the possibility of charging fees for certain services); and for a further integration of the activities of the Law Library into social science research.

What are the next steps? The debate that has been swirling around the status of the Law Library is apparently finished; it is time to move on to something else. It seems unlikely, though, in a period of fiscal conservatism, that vast new sums will be poured into the Law Library to pursue the challenges and opportunities spelled out in the Neal and Little reports.

On the other hand, some changes are inevitable. The Law Library has moved from the old "main building" to the new James Madison Memorial Building. It has a magnificent reading room overlooking the atrium from the second floor, with space for 75,000 volumes and 176 readers, and it has separate rare-book and microtext facilities that would

Specially designed compact shelving—which glides together when not being used—was installed in the subbasement of the Madison Building to hold the bulk of the Law Library's 1.6-million-volume collection.

be the envy of any research library. The move allowed the consolidation (in Class K order) of the collections of the five language/area divisions on electronically controlled compact shelving in the subbasement (more than sixty miles of it). The Law Library is now reasonably well equipped to serve readers and to seek out some new directions. Its essential services to the Congress will probably remain unchanged. Whether the Law Library is also able to reach out and provide new, innovative services to some of its other client groups remains to be seen.

9

SERVICES TO THE BLIND AND PHYSICALLY HANDICAPPED

"I have been the beneficiary of the Library of Congress program, and I cannot begin to say how extremely helpful this has been. . . . These days the federal government comes in for much criticism. It is good to give high praise where it is due!" "It has been my pleasure to be associated with the State of Arizona Talking Book Library since 1972. They could not be more well-managed, nor could they provide better service to users than they do." These unsolicited words of praise are typical of the many hundreds of letters the National Library Service for the Blind and Physically Handicapped (NLS) of the Library of Congress receives each year. They are paying tribute to a unique service that brings reading materials right into the homes of the blind and physically handicapped persons who cannot read standard printed books.

How this reading service began at the Library of Congress and how it has developed and expanded over the years in a distinctly nonbureaucratic fashion is the intriguing story we plan to tell in this chapter.

The Early Years

John Russell Young became Librarian of Congress in July 1897, just as the Library was preparing to move from its overcrowded quarters in the Capitol to its new building on the other side of First Street. He had been in office only six weeks when he sent identical memos to his two principal assistants, Ainsworth Spofford (the former Librarian) and David Hutcheson, proposing that there should be special accommodations for the blind in the new building.

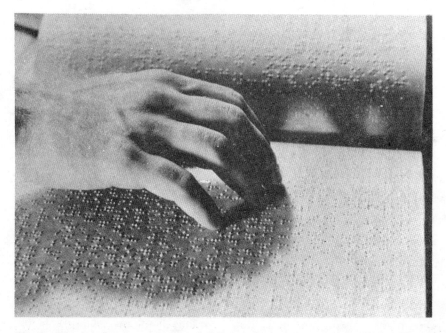

The braille alphabet is made up of different arrangements of six dots within a single braille cell. Each cell represents a letter or a number or a contracted form of a word.

Under the operations of the copyright law, we must have on our shelves a large number of publications especially printed for the blind. These might be kept together and attendants deputed to give them special care. If the present reading room would be inconvenient, a room could be set aside in another part of the building. The idea is somewhat [nebulous] and there may be practical obstacles with which I am not familiar. At the same time, a special service for the blind would go far towards the complete idea of a national library. I respectfully submit it to you for consideration—with the view as to a practical way of realizing the best that can be done for those who in their infirmity rest under the hands of God.

Spofford had no trouble containing his enthusiasm for the project. He agreed that it might be a good idea at some time in the future but felt that "at present it is not probable that any such readers (or if any, exceedingly few) would come nor are there in our collection more than a hundred books in raised letters." (Recall, Spofford lost his job as Librarian to Young because Spofford had expended all of his energies on getting and storing materials and had been much less concerned about finding and using them!) When it became clear that Librarian Young was not to be denied (perhaps because the idea was inspired by Mrs. Young's concern for handicapped persons), Spofford came up with some specific suggestions as to how Young might proceed. Spofford advised Young to write to the American Printing House for the Blind in Louisville, Kentucky, to get a list of their publications and to the Perkins Institution for the Blind in Boston to solicit their ideas. Young did so. He soon had a catalog from the Perkins Institution, which he asked David Hutcheson to compare with the Library's holdings. The American Printing House did not immediately reply, but Librarian Young went ahead anyway, though he did wonder to Spofford why the American Printing House shouldn't make some return to the Library since they received "an appropriation from the Government." Young then moved on to the question of securing and furnishing a suitable room for the use of blind patrons, a task he delegated to Hutcheson.

So it was that when the new Library opened to the public in November 1897, it had a Department for the Blind with some 200 books in raised characters on the shelves, the first of its kind in the United States. Pursuing her interest, Mrs. John Russell Young organized a reading hour when "ladies and gentlemen of Washington" would read aloud to the blind patrons of the Library. And the service was born. Within four months, libraries in Philadelphia, Chicago, and New York had established similar reading rooms for blind users.

The federal government had become involved in providing direct assistance to the blind as early as 1879 when Congress had established a trust fund, the income from which went to the American Printing House for the Blind to enable them to supply textbooks for blind children. The production of embossed books (those with raised characters) was an expensive and cumbersome process. Louis Braille had invented a shorthand kind of system for blind readers, based on a raised six-dot cell, when he was only a fifteen-year-old student in a French school for the blind in 1824. But his alphabet and series of contractions were not officially adopted in the United States until 1916, and it was 1932 before braille was approved for the whole English-speaking world. Consequently, reading materials for the blind were produced using many different systems of embossed characters. By 1929, for example, the reading room for the blind in the Library of Congress contained several thousand volumes in six different forms of raised type, most of them produced by hand for individuals and then donated to the collection. Other books resulted from a 1913 amendment to the 1879 law that provided funds to the American Printing House for the Blind and required that one copy of each of the books manufactured by the Printing house be deposited with the Library of Congress (finally resolving former Librarian Young's frustration in trying to get copies of those expensive volumes for his own reading room for the blind).

But it was clear that the available private facilities could not assure the production of an adequate supply of reading materials without some help from the government. A study requested by the American Library Association in 1928 was undertaken by the American Foundation for the Blind in New York City, and it was estimated that there were 10,000 library patrons out of a population of 100,000 blind people nationwide. The difficulties in producing, storing, and shipping large-sized volumes in small quantities made production by private enterprise unprofitable. Service-oriented nonprofit and volunteer groups could undertake embossed book production, but only in limited amounts.

Pressure for more books for the blind increased until Congress held hearings on the subject in 1930. Witnesses testified that "only about fifteen libraries, most of them located in the northeastern section of the country," provided adequate service to blind readers, and they noted that there was "a dearth of books for the adult blind which the libraries may purchase, even when they are established." A twenty-two-volume edition of the Bible was displayed as evidence that the size and cost of embossed books essentially limited their purchase to libraries. And sheer bulk precluded any one library from developing a very extensive collection of books for blind readers.

These efforts led to the passage of the Pratt-Smoot Act of 1931, which authorized a nationwide library service, administered by the Library of Congress, for blind adults. The law also provided that "the Librarian of Congress may arrange with such libraries as he may judge appropriate to serve as local or regional centers for the circulation of such books." The initial appropriation for the program was $100,000 for fiscal year 1932, which began on July 1, 1931.

"Project, Books for the Adult Blind" (as it was designated within the Library of Congress) was administratively separate from the Library's long-standing service to blind readers during its first years of operation. The project was directed by Herman H. B. Meyer, head of the Legislative Reference Service at the Library (and former president of the American Library Association). Seventy-two books on different subjects were chosen to be produced in embossed characters in fiscal 1932. Circulation of the books once they were available was handled by nineteen libraries around the country, which were selected on the basis of suggestions received from the ALA and the American Foundation for the Blind. Titles such as *The Magic of the Stars* (Maurice Maeterlinck), *Keeping Mentally Fit* (Joseph Jastrow), *Aunt Sammy's Radio Recipes, Revised* (U.S. Department of Agriculture), *The United States in World Affairs, 1931* (Walter Lippmann), *The Frontier in American History* (Frederick Jackson Turner), and *The Scarlet Letter* (Nathaniel Hawthorne) were chosen for the program. The basic operating premise of the project was that the presses would produce the books that would receive the widest use while volunteer organizations would continue to transcribe those titles for which there was limited demand. That the best mix of titles was not achieved during the project's first year of operation was clear from the letters received from librarians around the country asking for more popular fiction. A letter from Saginaw, Michigan, is typical: "Many of the books . . . have been enjoyed and appreciated by our patrons. Those, however, of purely educational value have been read but little by our readers."

The basic purpose of the books for the adult blind program has not really changed in the past fifty years. Technology has greatly expanded the ways in which reading materials can be provided to blind and handicapped individuals, and the law has been amended to include blind children and physically handicapped persons who cannot read standard print and to provide music instructional materials and scores as well as books and magazines. Although there was an effort in the mid-1950s to transfer the service to blind readers from the Library of Congress to the Department of Health, Education and Welfare, it was killed when the Joint Committee on the Library agreed with incoming Librarian J. Quincy Mumford's arguments that the program was above all else a *library* service and that it was properly housed in and administered by the Library of Congress.

Today, the National Library Service for the Blind and Physically Handicapped, operating out of a separate building several miles from the main Library complex on Capitol Hill, directs a multimillion-dollar enterprise ($34.5 million in 1980) that involves technological innovations in the recording and electronics fields. It coordinates the distribution of braille and "talking books" to a readership of some 800,000 users through a network of multistate centers and cooperating regional and subregional libraries. Let's take a look at just how this complicated service network is managed.

NLS: The Operational Side

Network is the key word in describing how the National Library Service for the Blind and Physically Handicapped works. Although the selection of titles, the setting of production standards, the development of machines, and the publication of informational materials and catalogs are carried out at NLS in Washington, D.C., the actual provision of reading materials to blind and physically handicapped individuals is the business of a network of some 160 state and local libraries around the country. The Library of Congress, in fact, has not provided direct general service to blind readers since 1973 when the new Special Services

Division of the Martin Luther King Library in the District of Columbia was designated the regional library for blind and physically handicapped users in Washington. Thus ended an era that had begun seventy-six years before with Mrs. Young's reading hours for the blind in the new Library building.

NLS is divided into two basic divisions based on function: (1) the Materials Development Division decides which titles will be produced for the reading program and what kinds of playback equipment are needed; and (2) the Network Division provides guidance and assistance to the libraries, machine-lending agencies, and volunteer organizations that work with NLS in providing reading materials to users. An administrative section handles personnel and fiscal matters, publications, and shipping and receiving.

The director of the National Library Service has overall responsibility for the allocation of funds and for plans and policies for the whole reading service. Although the budget of NLS is the largest of any other single program at the Library of Congress—a fact that arouses some sensitivities within LC at appropriations time—it should be noted that about 85 percent of the $34.5 million budget for fiscal year 1980 was spent on books (braille, cassette, and disc) and audio playback equipment. Books and equipment are made available, free of charge, to all eligible users for as long as they wish to use Library reading materials. Thus, a participant in the program will receive not only a loan copy of *Murder in the White House* by Margaret Truman (on a four-track cassette), but also a specially designed machine on which to play it. Or, if the user prefers, a talking-book machine that can accommodate both hard and flexible discs. In 1980, federal funds were used to purchase 85,000 playback machines (35,000 talking-book, 50,000 cassette-book), 100,000 headphones, 100,000 replacement phonograph needles, 11,400 braille mailing containers, and 20,000 blank cassettes. In addition, states and localities contributed another $16 million which, with $3.8 million in other federal moneys, brought the total budget for the program to approximately $54.3 million.

Who is an eligible user? Basically anyone, child or adult, who cannot read a standard printed book, whether because of blindness, other physical handicap, or severe organic dysfunction. Readers must be residents of the United States or its possessions or American citizens living abroad.

Materials Development Division

The Materials Development Division has the responsibility within NLS of deciding on the content of the reading program. It selects, distributes, and oversees bibliographic control of the reading materials

An easy-to-operate cassette book machine is provided free of charge to participants in the NLS program. If they prefer, patrons may have talking book machines that accommodate both hard and flexible discs.

and develops, tests, and evaluates related equipment. Within the Materials Development Division, there are the Collection Development Section, the Bibliographic Control Section, the Production Control Section, the Quality Assurance Section, and the Engineering Section.

The Collection Development Section decides which of the more than 45,000 titles published in the United States each year will be included in the NLS collection. The staff members make their selections on the basis of literary reviews, reader requests, and the recommendations of network and consumer advisory committees. There is no question that their choices meet with greater reader satisfaction than those made back in 1932! Approximately 2,500 new and established titles are chosen each year to satisfy the reading interests of people of all ages and backgrounds. About half of the books selected will be classics, and the remainder will be divided between fiction and nonfiction. Best-sellers, biographies, and how-to-do-it books are the most popular. Additional titles are produced by volunteers working in cooperation with the regional libraries, and they added a total of 996 titles to the program in 1980—795 in braille and 201 on cassettes.

Once a title is selected, the publisher is contacted for copyright permission, and the section decides whether the book will be recorded or brailled (or both) and in what format. The overwhelming use of the reading materials in the program is in recorded form—either on discs or cassettes. In 1980, a readership of almost 436,000 (55 percent) asked for books on discs, and 332,510 (41.9 percent) wanted books on cassettes.

Braille books come in two forms: press braille (mass produced by large machines) and limited production braille (hand-copied by volunteers). The titles produced in limited production braille (by definition, those for which NLS expects less demand) are then copied on thermoform machines and distributed, one copy each, to the four multistate centers around the country. (Even the thermoform copies are produced by volunteers under NLS guidance, many of them by groups of prisoners who donate their time.) For example, Eric Ambler's *Send No More Roses* was produced in press braille (four volumes), although *Kalki: A Novel* by Gore Vidal (six volumes) is available only in hand-copied form. Only about 3 percent of the total readership participating in the national reading program requests materials in braille, but it remains a vitally important component of the program. Nationwide, one out of five visually handicapped individuals can use braille. Braille users generally have been blind for most of their lives—and consequently, learned to use braille at an early age—and tend to make up a disproportionate share of the younger and more active users of the program. Braille reading, like sight reading, is an active process, and for those people who are proficient, it is very fast and efficient. Older participants in the reading program whose vision has deteriorated late in life and physically handicapped persons usually ask for their reading materials in cassette or talking-book form.

NLS also produces magazines (seventy-six different titles, recorded or in braille) for its readership, and users may receive free personal subscriptions upon request. Titles in braille include *Better Homes and Gardens, Fortune,* and *Popular Mechanics,* and *American Heritage, Atlantic,* and *U.S. News* can be obtained on flexible discs. The *National Geographic* and the *New York Times Large Type Weekly* are produced both in braille and on discs.

The Bibliographic Control Section catalogs new titles and enters them in the NLS computer-produced microfiche catalog, which is distributed quarterly to each network library. The catalog also lists books produced in local network areas, which are available on interlibrary loan, plus holdings of other organizations. The ultimate goal is to create a national union catalog of books in special formats for blind and physically handicapped persons. Such a catalog will be the realization of Librarian John Russell Young's long-ago dream for "a catalogue of all the embossed books in existence." Today's reading program takes that dream one step further with the development of a mechanism (cooperating libraries and free mailing privileges) that means copies of the desired books can actually be obtained without ever having to leave home!

The assignment of books to various contractors for production in the determined format is the job of the Production Control Section. This section also oversees the NLS Recording Studio, which provides guidance to manufacturers and volunteers. A limited number of books, no more than 5 percent a year, are narrated in the service's own Recording Studio. The rest are provided on contract and are done by professional narrators, primarily in the studios of the American Printing House for the Blind and the American Foundation for the Blind. Some of the narrators have been recording talking books for years and find it one of the most satisfying things they do. Alexander Scourby, an actor and television narrator who has been working with the program for forty years, is so popular that readers will request "anything narrated by Scourby." Pearl Bailey, Art Buchwald, William F. Buckley, and Desi Arnaz are a few of the authors who have narrated their own books for the reading program.

The Quality Assurance Section tests control copies of every cassette, disc, and braille publication before final production to ensure that they conform to established standards and specifications. This section also periodically reviews contractors' facilities. The Engineering Section helps to develop the state-of-the-art equipment used in the program. Engineers and technicians prepare detailed technical specifications for the production of equipment and braille and recorded books and work with consumer review panels to determine whether the products actually meet the consumers'/readers' needs.

Network Division

The principal responsibility of the Network Division is to see that the braille and recorded books reach the users in the most efficient manner possible. What is this mysterious "network" we keep referring to? A brief description will help.

At the apex of the network is the National Library Service (NLS) in Washington, D.C. Then the country is divided into four regions—North, South, West, and Midlands—each served by a multistate center. These four centers are NLS agencies that serve as warehouses and distribution points for the regional libraries in their areas. The centers store and lend to the network libraries extra copies of reading-program materials. They also have available backup supplies of sound reproduction equipment, publications, forms, and other materials the network libraries might need.

The regional libraries make up the next level, a total of 56 libraries in 1981. These libraries usually act as the state library agency, with responsibilities that include book circulation, outreach, publicity, tape duplication, equipment assignment, publications distribution, reader advisory service, reference, and production of local interest materials.

Finally, direct service to the user is provided by the subregional libraries—usually local public libraries—designated by the regional library with NLS approval. Their collections generally include only current recorded books; braille readers request their titles directly from the regional library closest to them. The subregional libraries provide book services, publicity, and reader assistance; they also enlist public and volunteer support for their programs.

Another component of the network is the machine-lending agency, the entity designated by NLS to receive, issue, and control the federally owned and supplied equipment that is part of the program (specially designed talking-book machines, cassette players, and accessories). Usually the regional library is also the machine-lending agency, but in some states this service is provided by other executive agencies that deal with the disabled. Finally, deposit collections may be set up to serve individual institutions—such as nursing homes, convalescent centers, hospitals, and public libraries with walk-in services—and demonstration collections are used for display and information purposes, as well as to provide emergency service to readers.

The purpose of the Network Division is to guide and direct the many components of the network system—keeping in mind that the whole objective of the program is to get reading materials into the hands of eligible users. The division is made up of a Braille Codes Section, a Consumer Relations Section, a Music Section, a Network Services Section, and a Reference Section.

The Braille Codes Section prepares guides to and teaching manuals for all braille codes. Volunteers can take transcribing courses, which lead to official LC certification in literary, music, and math braille. These courses are usually offered through local volunteer groups or network libraries. The Consumer Relations Section helps the network agencies develop volunteer programs and maintains a liaison with patrons and with organized groups representing blind and physically handicapped individuals. This section is also responsible for circulating books to users who live abroad and for handling international interlibrary loans.

Since 1962, the development of music materials for blind, partially sighted, and physically handicapped musicians has been part of the national program. The Music Section develops, maintains, and promotes this aspect of direct library service for NLS patrons. The music collection of NLS now consists of more than 30,000 titles, including large-print and braille music scores and books about music, and recorded self-instructional courses on cassettes and discs. This section's staff also provides direct reference assistance in all areas of music to eligible musicians.

The Network Services Section has direct responsibility for helping the network libraries carry out their day-to-day activities. Section staff consultants visit the libraries to review their operations and offer guidance, and they work closely with the multistate centers to assure proper inventory and handling of NLS materials. The section also provides guidance and training to recording studios operated by network libraries and volunteers. This section is particularly concerned with the efficient distribution of materials around the country and has initiated a program to coordinate the redistribution of excess copies of books among the network libraries.

The Reference Section provides general reference and referral services on the national reading program itself as well as on various aspects of handicapping conditions. The section assists NLS and LC staff, network agencies, and, of course, the public.

NLS and the Library of Congress

The National Library Service for the Blind and Physically Handicapped operates relatively autonomously within the Library of Congress's organizational structure. It puts together its own budget, with general guidance from the Librarian and the Associate Librarian for National Programs, and it sets its own priorities within the overall framework of Library of Congress policy. Its goals and objectives are clearly spelled out in the 1931 Pratt-Smoot Act as it has been amended over the years, and the Library has given the program a good deal of operational flexibility. In times of shrinking budgets, however, the director of NLS may be reminded that the program is indeed part of the Library of Congress and that it must march to a similar beat. NLS cannot exercise the same degree of independence as the CRS or the Copyright Office—but its constituency is, if anything, even more vocal than the Congress and the creative community. The NLS reading program really *matters* to hundreds of thousands of people, and they have never been hesitant to express that fact to the Librarian and to the Congress when necessary.

The Gadgetry

One of the most intriguing aspects of the national reading service is the gadgetry—the machines—that have been developed specifically to suit the needs of the users. The machines must be simple to use, compact, and durable, and at the same time, they must embody the latest in technological innovations.

Talking books, or books recorded on discs, became part of the National Library Service in 1933. Within a year, the first titles had been selected (among them the Bible, the Declaration of Independence, the Constitution, and a number of Shakespeare's plays), and production of machines and recordings had begun at the American Foundation for the Blind. Research and technical improvements have shaped the course of the program ever since. The standard long-playing record, which runs at 33-1/3 revolutions per minute (rpm), was in fact developed just for the talking-book program by an electrical engineer working under the auspices of the American Foundation for the Blind in 1934; it was not commercially available until fourteen years later.

Discs

The technological breakthroughs did not come easily. Playing time for the standard 33-1/3 rpm disc was increased to thirty minutes by adding more grooves, and then, after World War II, the Library began to investigate the applications of the latest advances made in the recording and electronics industries. In 1958, research and development efforts led to the recording of two 16-2/3 rpm prototype books with a maximum playing time of one hour and thirty minutes per disc. By 1963, all books were recorded on ten-inch 16-2/3 rpm discs. New milestones were reached in 1968 with the conversion of magazines to 8-1/3 rpm discs, the production of a flexible-disc edition of *Talking Book Topics* (the NLS publication that lists new talking books), and the field testing of cassettes and cassette players for use in the program. The 8-1/3 rpm disc became the standard for all talking books in 1973 and remains so today. At that speed, it hardly seems to turn, and it increases playing time to almost three hours for a ten-inch rigid disc and two hours for a nine-inch flexible disc. The change obviously means that each book requires fewer discs, which results in added savings and less storage space. *The Second Lady*, for example, a 1980 book by Irving Wallace recorded on seven flexible discs, takes fourteen hours to "read."

The use of flexible discs has been expanded since 1973. In 1976, Alex Haley's *Roots* was produced and distributed on flexible discs shortly after the television series aired, and now many of the monthly magazines are produced on flexible discs. The discs are relatively inexpensive to make, so this format is used for all new best-sellers, for which a large and immediate demand is anticipated.

Cassettes

Development of cassette machines and tapes has led to increases in their playing time as well. In 1969, the first cassette machines played two-track tapes at 1-7/8 inches per second (ips), one hour and thirty minutes playing time per cassette. The cassettes produced today run at 15/16 ips, on four tracks, resulting in a playing time of nearly six hours a cassette—the equivalent of 200 pages of print. The program has relied more and more on the cassette format since 1977, not only because the cassettes are compact, lightweight, and long-playing, but also because they are easy to duplicate when additional copies are needed.

The Playback Machines

In the early years of the program, only the recordings were provided by the Library of Congress, not the equipment to play them on. The machines, costing thirty-five to forty dollars apiece, had to be bought by the readers themselves or supplied by community groups. Under the Works Progress Administration, federal funds were made available to construct the talking-book machines for needy individuals from 1935 to 1942, but with the onset of World War II, this project was halted like so many others because it was not essential to the war effort. However, Congress provided some additional funds to the Library during the war period so that it could purchase machines produced by the American Foundation for the Blind. And in 1947, for the first time, the Library purchased commercially manufactured machines built to its own specifications.

Research and consumer testing have also improved the playback machines over the years. Today's talking-book machine plays both hard and flexible discs at speeds of 33-1/3, 16-2/3, and 8-1/3 rpm. The cassette-book machine operates at speeds of 1-7/8 ips (the speed of commercial cassette tapes) and 15/16 ips, with two- and four-track capability. A cassette-disc machine has been developed that will accommodate both cassette tapes and discs, and work is under way on an easy-to-operate cassette-book machine for use by newly handicapped individuals who have trouble using the ten operation-control settings on the current machines.

Other accessories have been developed to make the machines more convenient to use: headphones, pillowspeakers (for bedridden users), amplifiers (to boost the sound through the headphones for persons with significant hearing disabilities), a tone-arm clip for the talking-book machine (for users who have difficulty grasping the tone arm), and an extension lever for the cassette-book machines (to allow easier operation by people with low finger-pressure control). New model cassette-book machines will allow a tape to be played faster than its normal speed and still be intelligible, which means that a reader can get through a cassette book more quickly without having to put up with the "Singing Chipmunks" effect of a speeded-up tape.

Braille

Advances in technology are helping braille production, too. New computer programs can accept input from typewriter terminals to produce output as contracted braille forms. The common Grade-2 braille is not a character-for-character transposition into six-dot braille cells but a shorthand form with many standard contractions to reduce bulk and to facilitate reading. However, computer-produced contracted (Grade-2) braille still must be proofread by expert braillists, because many of the contractions depend on the context in which they are used.

The use of machine-readable compositor's tapes to produce braille editions of books is another promising application of computer technology. *Helen and Teacher*, a book by Joseph Lash, was ready for circulation in braille just a month later than the print publication date of May 1980. It was prepared by using the compositor's tapes for the printed book (the storage medium used to drive the phototypesetting equipment to print the book), which were provided by the publisher prior to publication, in interaction with the braille plate-embossing machines at a braille printing house. Unfortunately, the process is not as simple as using the tape from one machine to drive the other; a certain amount of human intervention is necessary to make the braille version come out right. But the process does offer promise for faster and more efficient production of braille books. The Lash book was the first attempt to produce a full-length book using compositor's tapes, but the process had already been used for two years to produce the *National Geographic* magazine.

In addition to being cumbersome to produce, braille books are bulky. *Helen and Teacher*, for example, fills eight braille volumes. NLS is now testing a cassette-braille (also called paperless-braille) machine, a device the size of a cassette-book machine, on which a line of braille cells has its dots created "dynamically" by the rising and falling of pins within the sets of six holes per cell. The pins are driven electronically by magnetic-encoded data on a cassette or by computer printer output (for terminal-like machines). The book can be "read" as the cassette creates the dots on a six-inch-long plastic belt that runs along the top of the machine. A 150- to 200-page book can be stored on a braille cassette, obviously a huge savings over the multivolume paper braille books commonly used today.

The Library of Congress has one Kurzweil Reading Machine available for use by the public. It scans an ordinary printed page, translates the print elements into basic sound elements, and then joins the elements into a synthesized form of speech. The machine literally reads the page aloud.

Machines That Talk

The Kurzweil Reading Machine can scan a printed page and translate the basic print elements into basic sound elements and then join them into synthesized speech. Although it will never be mistaken for Alexander Scourby, the machine is understandable once you have taken a few minutes to adjust to its speech patterns. Kurzweil Computer Products, with NLS support, is in the process of modifying the machine for print-to-braille translation as well. The beauty of the machine is that it permits independent reading of any printed product, and thus the machine opens up a whole world of information because it doesn't first have to be transposed into a special format for the handicapped user. A Kurzweil machine is available in one of the general reading rooms of the Library of Congress for readers to use there.

The Future

The silicon chip and the microprocessor (an integrated circuit consisting of the complete central-processing unit of a computer on a single silicon chip) hold many possibilities for further improvements in the machines used in the national reading program. They will undoubtedly become smaller, more reliable, and easier to use as new applications of these technologies are developed.

Volunteers

No discussion of the national reading program coordinated by NLS is complete without a few paragraphs about its volunteers. Very simply, the program could not operate at its current level of service without the thousands of volunteers who donate their time every year. They are an integral and necessary part of the program—a unique feature of the NLS that makes it different from any other federal service program.

Volunteers around the country produce reading materials—in a great variety of formats and languages—to supplement the titles that NLS provides. A seventy-four-page directory published by NLS gives names, addresses, and phone numbers of organizations and individuals to contact if you, as a blind or physically handicapped reader, need particular printed matter transcribed or recorded in a format you can use. The service is free except for the cost of the materials. Braille transcribing courses are offered through network libraries under the guidance of NLS, and all transcribers who work in the program must be certified by the Library of Congress. Volunteers also produce recorded cassette books, and they must meet the same standards as those required for the commercially prepared volumes. One example: in 1980, 144 persons volunteered their services as narrators, and only 24 of them were accepted.

Thermoform copies of limited production braille books are made by volunteers, one page at a time. The thermoform machine, using heat, requires five seconds a page to imprint the braille characters on another piece of paper. Many of these copies are produced by groups such as the Baltimore Braille Association and the Nashville PIRATES

(Prison Inmates Recording and Transcribing Educational Materials for the Sightless)—both groups of prisoners who volunteer their time to the program. They have been praised for the high quality and quantity of their work and take pride in their efforts. One of the Baltimore prison volunteers undoubtedly spoke for many of them when he said, "The idea of helping someone adds meaning and purpose to my life and makes living here so much easier."

Even the machines distributed to readers are repaired by volunteers, the Telephone Pioneers of America. These senior and retired telephone-industry employees donate their time to repair and service the talking-book and cassette players used in the program. Active nationwide, about 3,000 Pioneers now repair approximately 45,000 machines every year. The Pioneers also repair damaged cassettes, help cooperating libraries inspect cassettes before they are loaned out, and monitor the narration of books and magazines for individual libraries. They often act as ambassadors of the reading program, visiting readers in their homes to explain how the equipment works or to service a broken-down machine.

Publications

NLS keeps in touch with its far-flung complex of cooperating libraries, volunteers, and users in part by means of a variety of publications and newsletters. *Braille Book Review* and *Talking Book Topics*, published every two months, let users know what new titles are available. Other magazines excerpt articles from printed magazines that deal with the popular and classical musical scenes. Newsletters keep individuals and organizations informed about NLS program developments and the activities of the many volunteers involved with the program. Subject bibliographies list all the titles available, by format—for example, best-sellers, books on science or health, or books suitable for children.

The National Library Service for the Blind and Physically Handi-capped is at first blush a rather unlikely program to be administered by the Library of Congress. But with an understanding of its origins—and an appreciation for its daily importance to hundreds of thousands of people—it is apparent why the service is a very appropriate extension of the Library of Congress. And the program probably wins the Library of Congress higher praise and greater endorsement than anything else it does.

10

THE LIBRARY OF CONGRESS AND THE PERFORMING ARTS

The final area that we view has glamour. Not only do the materials sparkle with the riches of the fine and the lively arts, but many of their users seem to have come out of the Sunday supplements as well. The man at the Steenbeck viewer there is Gregory Peck, the gentleman in the next listening booth is Leonard Bernstein, the lady in the headphones across the table is Joan Baez, and that was Yehudi Menuhin talking to Maxine Kumin in the elevator.

The Library of Congress preserves culture in ink, wax, and silver salts. It has music, etchings, poetry, lithographs, motion pictures, photographs, and phonograph records. So do many libraries, but what is different about the Library of Congress is that it not only collects and preserves these products of the creative spirit, but it also generates, sponsors, and even underwrites the treasures it collects. Furthermore, although the material is fragile, incredibly valuable, and often unique, no portion of the Library is so involved in hard day-to-day use of its materials as the divisions to be described here. For want of a better way to proceed, let's take them one bureaucratic unit at a time and, within each unit, work from the prosaic to the sublime.

Music

In 1980, the music collection reached 6 million items. In that year, the Library's five Stradivari instruments and its one Guarnerius were played in fifty free concerts, which were rebroadcast over dozens of "good music" stations in North America and Europe. In that same year, the Music Division added to its vaults original manuscripts from the hands of George Gershwin, Luigi Dallapiccola, Leo Delibes, and Ernest Bloch; it also put 16,543 new books and pieces of music on the shelves.

The Julliard String Quartet plays regularly in the Coolidge Auditorium, using the Library's Stradivari instruments.

How Do You Organize Musical Material
So You Can Find It?

If you, as a user, walk into the Music Division, you will find yourself facing four separate catalogs. The first is a typical dictionary catalog of books about music; the second has nothing in it but material on music theory and teaching; the third indexes the Library's huge collection of opera librettos; but it is the fourth that is the most unusual, for although the first three involve words, the last—and largest—catalog is limited to *music* (as in notes)—sheet music, collections, and full scores. The music catalog is in turn divided into three quite different parts. One part is filed by composer; the second, by title; and the third (which in a typical book catalog would be by subject) is filed by call number. It is what is called a classed catalog.

A great deal of use in a library of music is for kinds of music: carols; harpsichord solos; harpsichord, flute, and cello trios; Indian temple music; sea chanteys; singing television commercials; Moog transcriptions. To accommodate this kind of access, the cards for the thousands upon thousands of individual pieces of music are sorted into their classification numbers to permit browsing by "class," just as you would browse books on shelves by subject. To look at some samples at random: M 298 Drum and bagpipe music; M 1958.D87 Songs and music of

Duke University; M 1682-3 Mexican music; M 1507 Piano-vocal excerpts from motion picture musical comedies; M 1527 Music for silent films in general; M 176 Accompaniments to silent motion pictures in specific. But even these varied points of access will not get you to every item in the collection. Given its size, it is virtually impossible to catalog individually every single piece in the division's collections. The music reference librarian is on hand to bridge that gap.

Working with this display of musical knowledge, you can make your own selections, and you will find that the actual shape your choices come in may turn out to be as varied as penciled manuscript sheets, printed scores, player-piano rolls, phonograph records, or reel or cassette tapes. To get the pieces delivered to you in the division's reading room, you fill out a request slip, and the deck attendant disappears into the stacks to collect the goods. The attendant faces a lively challenge because the materials themselves are housed in remarkable ways. Most sheet music is unbound, so it is kept flat in cardboard boxes, which are stacked high on metal shelves. A few of the most frequently used pieces will be in thin cardboard covers, and the thickest scores are likely to be bound in buckram like oversized books. Where the piece is actually located will be determined by its format or where it came from. If it came from the copyright deposit, the attendant will have to paw through cartons of loose sheets arranged only by their copyright number. If it is on a phonograph record, it will be filed by manufacturer and then by serial number. (The Library owns almost 765,000 records, all of which are stored vertically, so there are literally hundreds of yards of discs disappearing down aisles like cut stone courses in endless walls.) If your requested item happens to have been a part of one of a hundred special collections, it could be in one of a hundred different places arranged by the original owner (such as the cluster of 12,500 opera librettos collected by a single railroad man).

Ultimately, having assembled the pieces you want, the attendant will bring them to you and you can go into a soundproof room and either play them on the piano provided or listen to them via the appropriate audio apparatus. Qualified violinists can use the Library's Amati violin.

What Do You Use a Music Library For?

On one typical day, the following situations arose and were resolved:

1. A producer wanted to show a classic silent film entitled *Broken Blossoms* and asked the Music Division if it could find the original score that accompanied it when it was first released in 1919.

2. An author writing a biography of John Philip Sousa was continuing his study of everything Sousa wrote (the Library has virtually all of

Sousa's manuscripts as well as his published works) and was searching for duplication. The problem: Sousa would write a march for some special occasion and then throw the copies in a drawer after it had been played; years later, when he needed something new, he would take a trio from one and an introduction or a coda from another and write in a new body. Similarly, if some major piece he had written went particularly well in some parts but nobody whistled the rest, he would simply take the good parts, paste them to the good parts of another piece, and come up with a better whole. The author was trying to trace all the permutations.

3. Another author wanted a list of all the operas written by black composers.

4. A professor was preparing a lecture on Igor Stravinsky and the process he went through to write his music. He asked for color slides of a number of pieces of Stravinsky's work from the extensive collection of Stravinsky music manuscripts so that he could illustrate how Stravinsky would first write his musical notations in pencil and then go back to correct or modify them using a different color of ink.

The majority of the Music Division's reference questions come from people living outside of Washington, D.C. The librarians will answer any legitimate musical query, and they rely heavily on photoduplication to provide copies of the original music, score, or libretto to the correspondent. (The copies are charged for at the Library's regular photoduplication rates.) The division is staffed by twenty-five people—seven in the administrative unit and eighteen in the public reference section.

The Rarities

The Music Division's treasure vaults are filled with such an astonishing array of incredibly valuable material that the professional musicologist tends to be as awed as the "reader in the street." In the past eighty-five years, a series of aggressive, imaginative heads of the division have amassed original manuscripts from essentially all of the great composers of Western music—from Bach to composers of musical shows.

Some of the manuscript collections are simply "representative," with examples of particular kinds of works (as in the cases of Bizet, Tchaikovsky, and Sibelius), and others are "comprehensive." The latter contain extensive holdings of most of a composer's musical production. (Recall, we are referring here to the scribbled worksheets and half-done rejected efforts, as well as the finished on-the-way-to-the-printer manuscripts, all in the composer's hand—not to the printed versions that resulted.)

The works of American composers fall into the "comprehensive" holdings, and thus there are thousands of manuscript pages from Samuel Barber, Leonard Bernstein, Elliott Carter, Aaron Copland, Howard Hanson, Victor Herbert, Frederick Loewe, Edward MacDowell, Walter Piston, Sigmund Romberg, and William Schuman. All of the scores of the great Richard Rodger's musicals sit side by side on a shelf, each bound in rich, red leather. Inside their slipcases (on common dime-store music composition paper) the notes are in pencil, neatly marching along single staffs with the Hammerstein words jotted below. *Oklahoma!*, *South Pacific*, and *The Sound of Music* are written in simple arrangements that even a beginning pianist could play. The manuscripts of Gershwin's *Porgy and Bess* and his *An American in Paris*, on the other hand, are in ink, also neatly drawn but fully orchestrated so a single chord can appear in twenty stacked staffs, each tagged to the proper instrument to which Gershwin assigned it.

The international "modern" scene appears in quantity. The Library owns the manuscripts of Bartok's Concerto for Orchestra, Benjamin Britten's opera *Peter Grimes*, Honegger's Fifth Symphony, Villa-Lobos's *Madona*, Ginastera's "Bomarzo Cantata," and hundreds more.

The great masters of classical music are richly represented, and their manuscripts have come from three sources. Some were given to "the Library and the nation" by the composer or his family, some came as gifts from organizations such as the Beethoven Association of New York, and some were purchased from foundation funds (of which more later). The first major block arrived as far back as 1921, when the family of Leo Delibes presented the full scores of *Lakmé, La Source,* and *Sylvia*. Others followed. Herbert Witherspoon gave the full manuscript score of Leoncavallo's *Pagliacci,* and Fritz Kreisler presented the manuscript of Brahms's Violin Concerto in D Major (this is in ink and is a fearful mishmash of scribbled notes, fully orchestrated, almost unreadable to an amateur). On the other hand, the manuscripts of Robert Schumann's First Symphony *(Spring)* and Mendelssohn's String Octet op. 20 are neat, precise, and easily read by any pianist. The original manuscript of Beethoven's Piano Sonata in E Major op. 109 is hurried and cluttered, but the ink chords and notations are thin and spidery, like snippets of black thread thrown on the page. Brahms's pages look like what one imagines Beethoven's should be—thick notes, spattered bars, and generally black all over.

This exercise in name-dropping could go on for pages without adding to the point, but the yards of precious stuff so impress us we can't resist just a few more lines. The Library owns great masses of Stravinsky material given by the composer himself; it has the Haydn's Piano Sonata no. 52; the Coolidge collection has stacks of manuscripts, including Copland's *Appalachian Spring,* Prokofiev's String Quartet op.

50, Ravel's "Chansons Madecasses," and Respighi's *Trittico Botticelliano*. The Whittall collection contains Schoenberg's *Verklaerte Nacht*, Brahms's Third Symphony, Haydn's Sympony no. 90 in C Major, and the andante movement of Haydn's Symphony no. 94 *(Surprise Symphony)*. Sergei Rachmaninoff's wife donated an enormous collection of rare musical material (letters, phonograph records—many unreleased—and general memorabilia of the great man), among which are the manuscripts of the composer's *Rhapsody on a Theme by Paganini*, the score of his Third Symphony, and the two-piano transcription of his Prelude in C Sharp Minor. Other great collections provide similar riches: the Heifetz collection, the lifetime correspondence of Arnold Schoenberg, the Geraldine Farrar collection, the Liszt-Rosenthal collection, and the gifts of Mrs. Gisella Selden-Goth, which include manuscripts of Liszt, Mendelssohn, Brahms, Schubert, and Paganini.

What Use Are They to Anybody?

The cynic might well ask why the Library should bother with all these manuscripts when music of any worth is available in printed form and much easier to use than the scribbled originals. Aside from the simple archival, historical, sense-of-presence justification, the treasure materials are heavily used in basic musical research for the following reasons.

1. Much of it was never published, and the unfinished and rejected manuscripts frequently tell more about the development of a composer than the final, polished products.

2. Even as many of the pages are nearly illegible to us, thanks to the work habits of the composers, they were almost as illegible to their contemporary publishers, and in many instances, research has shown that accepted versions of the classics simply are not what the composer intended them to be. The engravers, working under pressure, misread many of the notations, and once the pieces appeared in print, the printed version became the authorized one. (The discrepancy need not apply only to details. Examination of the Library's manuscript of Mozart's famous *Serenade for Thirteen Wind Instruments* reveals that Mozart had scored it for twelve wind instruments and a bass viol.)

3. Both musical editors and conductors have felt free to embellish or modify passages to improve them. Oddly enough, some of these changes or additions were accepted by the composers, but more often, the composers were casual proofreaders or not consulted at all. In such cases, the manuscripts provide the only means of returning to the purity of the original.

Folk Music

Not all of the Music Division's collections are as drenched with dignity and concert hall hush as the above would imply. In 1928, four private citizens each gave the Library $1,000 to start the Archive of American Folk Song (later renamed the Archive of Folk Culture). With that money as a base, three Library of Congress employees, Robert W. Gordon and later John and Alan Lomax, began threading their way from jail to jail, up narrow Appalachian valleys, and onto the docks of fishing villages trying to capture authentic American folk music while it was still close to its antecedents. The music was picked up via wax cuttings, then wire, and ultimately recording tape and brought back to the Library's Recording Laboratory (established in 1940 with Carnegie Foundation money), where it was converted to formal pressings for public sale at cost.

The archive now boasts over 250,000 specimens of songs, instrumental tunes, spoken tales, and other lore from all over the world. The Library offers some eighty-odd long-playing records of this music, much of which has become the primary source material for basic research in the field. (Celebrated American performers, such as Harry Belafonte, have spent hours listening to unreleased recordings to find authentic material for their own programs.)

The accumulation of the original sounds has not slackened, but it is now done differently. Whereas in the archive's early days very few individuals had the tools to do what LC managed to do with its mobile truck equipment, nowadays, thanks to the ubiquitous tape recorder, anyone with the inclination can capture sound anywhere. This has resulted in less fieldwork for the Library but more reproduction and distribution, and more drawing on the skills of trained folklorists around the country.

In 1980, for example, the archive acquired its 20,000th field recording (excluding early cylinders): a recording of blues musicians "Little Dickie" Rodgers and Chuck Smith, made by Peter Lowry. The archive also copied the entire tape collection of Lowry's record company, Trix Records, which added more than 200 hours of recordings of living blues musicians to its collections. Other musical and folk materials captured by the archive during the year included 18 hours in stereo with African kora player Bai Konte, recorded in Gambia by Mark and Susan Pevar; 60 hours of all kinds of folk music recorded at the 1972 National Folk Festival; an interview in Spanish with Mexican-American singer and guitarist Lydia Mendoza, conducted by James Griffith (and later transcribed and translated); 2 hours of folklike songs relating to President John F. Kennedy and John Glenn; and a collection of books, serials, and LP recordings of the Molokan religious community in San Francisco, given to the Library by the Highgate Road Social Science Research Station.

Once the North American antecedents were reasonably well developed, the archive began to broaden its scope, and now, the musical traditions of Latin America and the Caribbean have been covered in detail. Coverage of the African scene is being perfected, building on the already developed holdings from the west coast south of the Sahara, the Congo basin, and Morocco. The collection of the music of the Far and Near East is similarly growing, and the Library is presently strong in the Korean, Japanese, Iranian, and Iraqi areas.

In 1976, an American Folklife Center was created in the Library, with a separate board of trustees, for the purpose of preserving and presenting American folklife through programs of research, documentation, exhibition, and publication. In 1978, the Folklife Center and the Archive of Folk Song joined together to provide a single focus for folklife research at the Library of Congress. The center acts as a clearinghouse both to generate and to support research in the varied folk and ethnic traditions found in the United States, and the archive carries out the more traditional "library" functions of acquiring material, organizing it for use, and providing reference and research assistance to scholars and other users. Thus, the data generated by the American Folklife Center eventually ends up in the collections of the archive or in the custody of other appropriate units in the Library (pictures, for example, would go to the Prints and Photographs Division).

To carry out its program, the American Folklife Center (with the Archive of Folk Culture) proceeds on a number of different fronts. It publishes directories, such as *Arizona Folklife Survey, Maritime Folklife Resources,* and *Ethnic Broadcasting in the United States,* which are based on comprehensive surveys it has directed. It carries out research in the field—one two-year study culminated in an exhibit at the Smithsonian Institution called "Buckaroos in Paradise: Cowboy Life in Northern Nevada" and produced a great deal of original data on the subject as well as the center's first film—and it assists other institutions and agencies in organizing projects to look into unique folk traditions in their own areas. Finally, the center loans professional recording equipment to other institutions and individuals for documentation projects. In 1980, the center's equipment was used to study the interaction between French witchcraft and voodoo in southern Louisiana, to document Orthodox church songs performed in native languages in Alaska, and to make recordings of some of Oregon's oral traditions.

Not long after its creation, the American Folklife Center, at the suggestion of Daniel Boorstin, initiated a series of outdoor folk concerts

The American Folklife Center works in a number of different ways to generate and support research in the varied folk and ethnic traditions found in the United States. A demonstration of Ukrainian egg decorating is always popular at Eastertime.

during the summer on the front steps of the Library's Jefferson Building. They have proved enormously popular with the lunchtime crowd on Capitol Hill—in 1980, those who attended were treated to performances by groups as varied as country guitarist Don Stover; Caribbean musicians Las Estrellas del Son; and Laotian, Vietnamese, and Hmong artists playing traditional Southeast Asian instruments. These informal concerts, in fact, have done more to humanize the Library of Congress than anything else it has attempted in recent years.

The Library as Patron and Impresario

The Library of Congress and the nation's audience for fine music are deeply in debt to two strong-willed women whose impact on the Library went far beyond their own areas of cultural interest. The first was Mrs. Elizabeth Sprague Coolidge (the "Sprague" was that of the Sprague-Warner Corporation; her father was the noted Chicago busi-

Under the auspices of the American Folklife Center, a number of folk concerts are held during the noon hour on Neptune Plaza in front of the Library from May through October. Here Missouri fiddler Joe Politte entertains the lunchtime audience.

nessman). Mrs. Coolidge had been trained as a concert pianist, gave critically acclaimed performances at the time of World War I, and thereafter became immersed in a long career of musical philanthropy. In 1918, she founded the Berkshire Music Festival for chamber music and awarded her first Berkshire Prize for an original composition. In 1924, she approached the Library of Congress with an offer to build an auditorium in one of the courtyards of the Jefferson Building and then give the Library an endowment with which to promote "the study and appreciation of music in America."

The Library, being a government agency, had no right to accept money and keep it in the bottom drawer, so Herbert Putnam turned to the Congress for help. The Joint Committee on the Library thereupon sponsored legislation that would permit the establishment of a Library of Congress Trust Fund, and after its passage on March 3, 1925, the Library could "accept, hold, and invest moneys" via a trust fund board. The U.S. Treasury was directed to pay 4 percent on all gifts so deposited— in perpetuity. The Elizabeth Sprague Coolidge Foundation became the first private monetary donations to be accepted by the Library, but, thanks to the device her philanthropy created, private support of the

Library's cultural activities has become possible throughout all its divisions. By 1980, there were no fewer than 108 of these gift and trust funds, bringing in income "available for obligation" (cash to be spent) of some $10.5 million a year. There is scarcely a department in the Library that does not now receive some service or acquisition support from these nonappropriated funds.

But to return to Mrs. Coolidge, she did finance a 500-seat auditorium, which proved to have almost flawless acoustics. She began a lavish tradition of free chamber music concerts played by the leading artists of our time, and she commissioned a seemingly endless series of new musical compositions by "unknown but promising" as well as by established composers. She stated her purpose as:

> to make possible, through the Library of Congress, the composition and performance of music in ways which might otherwise be considered too unique or too expensive to be ordinarily undertaken. Not this alone, of course, nor with a view to extravagance for its own sake; but as an occasional possibility of giving precedence to considerations of quality over those of quantity; to artistic rather than to economic values; and to opportunity rather than to expediency.

Mrs. Coolidge lived to be eighty-nine, active to the end, and the proceeds from her original investments continue to flow in.

Mrs. Gertrude Clarke Whittall of Worcester, Massachusetts, came to the Library in 1935 and quickly joined Mrs. Coolidge in the role of patroness. Mrs. Whittall began by giving the Library five splendid Stradivari instruments (the Betts violin made in 1704; the Castelbarco violin, 1699; the Ward violin, 1700; the Cassavetti viola, 1727; and the Castelbarco violoncello made in 1697). She accompanied the original gift with a Tourte bow for each instrument. As important as the Strads themselves were her explicit instructions that the violins must not become museum pieces but were to be played regularly for the sake of maintaining their tone and general well-being. To this end, Mrs. Whittall established the Gertrude Clarke Whittall Foundation to pay for free chamber music concerts to be held throughout the year. The instruments cannot leave the building, so the public and the performers must come to the Library. Under such rules, the Music Division has now staged a rich series of concerts running from October to May every year for half a century. Longtime Washington music critic Paul Hume wrote: "There is always a special, welcome feeling when the Library of Congress concerts resume each fall. For nearly 60 years, Coolidge Auditorium has been one of the world's notable centers of chamber music."

The Budapest String Quartet acted as artists in residence for many seasons, and since 1962, the Juilliard String Quartet has carried on the role. As the tradition has developed, the Library has varied the concerts between chamber groups and individual performers. It has offered with pride such artists as Menuhin, Serkin, Francescatti, Rubinstein, Bernstein, Arrau, and Schuller. Mrs. Whittal lived to be ninety-seven and never missed a concert season until her death in 1965. Both the Coolidge and Whittall foundations continue to prosper and expand.

In 1949, the famous conductor Serge Koussevitzky established a foundation in his name to commission new works for the Library; in 1968, Mr. and Mrs. Walter Louchheim created a fund so that all the Library's musical performances could be made available for little or no cost (via audio and video tape) to educational and good music stations around the country; and in 1970, Mrs. W. Duncan McKim left to the Library a portfolio of securities to support the composition and performance of chamber music for violin and piano and to undertake other projects (lectures, publications) of value to students of the violin. (Under her maiden name, Leonora Jackson, Mrs. McKim had enjoyed a short, but successful, career as a concert violinist herself.)

The end product of these private, nonappropriated funds has been the sponsoring—and creating—of music in great quantity. Through its foundations, the Library has commissioned, paid for, and produced such works as George Crumb's *Ancient Voices of Children*, Britten's *Spring Symphony*, Menotti's *The Unicorn, the Gorgon, and the Manticore*, Stravinsky's *Apollon-Musagète*, Hindemith's *Hérodiade*, Barber's "Hermit Songs," and Schoenberg's Third and Fourth String Quartets.

In 1980, more than fifty concerts were staged in the Coolidge Auditorium, and the Library commissioned new compositions from Ned Rorem, Ralph Shapey, and David Baker. How many of the resultant works will prove to be of enduring quality and how many will fade into obscurity in unopened boxes in the back stacks is, of course, the nature of the game—but that unknown is what makes the game so fascinating.

The Performing Arts Library

At the Kennedy Center

The great strength of the Library of Congress is the breadth and depth of its collections—and in no area is this more true than in performing arts. The Library's wealth of materials in music, film, sound recordings, posters, photographs, correspondence—as well as books and magazines—make it a kind of "one-stop shopping place" for serious researchers in this field. With this fact in mind, the Library of Congress

The Performing Arts Library at the John F. Kennedy Center for the Performing Arts is a cooperative venture between the Library of Congress and the Kennedy Center. Staffed by regular Library of Congress personnel, it houses a small reference collection dealing with all aspects of theater and the performing arts and provides direct links (via computer terminal and audio hookup) with the more extensive materials at the main Library.

and the John F. Kennedy Center for the Performing Arts joined forces in 1979 to create a Performing Arts Library in the Kennedy Center.

Located on the second floor of the Kennedy Center, the Performing Arts Library is staffed by Library of Congress specialists in music, dance, and theater arts and is open to the public five days a week. The library can accommodate forty-four readers and houses a working reference collection of 3,000 volumes around its walls. It also provides separate viewing and listening facilities for readers as well as exhibit space to showcase selected items from the Library's collections and the Kennedy Center's archives. Most important, though, there are direct links via computer terminal and audio hookup to the main collections in the Library of Congress, and thus visitors, performers, designers, and musical artists working at the Kennedy Center can have quick access to that huge body of material in the performing arts. Both Dr. Boorstin and Roger Stevens, chairman of the Board of Trustees of the Kennedy Center, have expressed the hope that the Performing Arts Library will encourage "new talent and new works . . . by making readily available the creative resources and materials so necessary to these efforts."

On Capitol Hill

The addition of the Madison Building to the Library of Congress provides another opportunity to bring together—at least from the users' point of view—the performing arts materials in the Library. The individual units of the Library of Congress "grew up" as separate pieces of a puzzle—music, motion pictures, manuscripts, photographs—and each was started as a separate collection simply for the sake of convenience: different formats required different kinds of handling and arrangement. To pursue a single subject across the arbitrary lines drawn by the divisions between formats (the career of a singer who recorded extensively and appeared in Broadway shows and motion pictures, for example) requires a certain amount of persistence, not to mention legwork.

Library managers, trying to resolve this age-old dilemma, offered an innovative proposal in 1978: the creation of a Performing Arts Reading Room where the user could have access to music manuscripts, television videotapes, recorded discs and cassettes, and even videodiscs, all in the same facility. The old custodial divisions would remain the same, but reference specialists in music, dance, film, television, broadcasting, and theater arts would be on duty in the reading room to assist users and to direct them to other sources if necessary. The reading room would be stocked with a basic reference collection in all of the performing arts; separate viewing, listening, and playing areas would be provided; and all audio and visual materials would be operated from a remote facility one floor below. It would be a veritable Nirvana for the poor harassed researcher who had been putting up with insufficient space and inadequate viewing facilities in the Library's Music, Motion Picture, and Prints and Photographs divisions for years!

The budget realities of the early 1980s may contract this ideal a bit, but the involved divisions are pressing determinedly ahead. At this writing, a room on the first floor of the Madison Building is being readied for occupancy in late 1982, the machines are standing waiting in their shipping cartons, and even the logo has been applied to the glass door. There is no doubt that the reading room will open and provide assistance to readers as planned; what is less sure is how many people the divisions will be able to hire to staff the room and what level of service they will be able to provide. In any case, the cooperation among the different administrative units and the potential payoff to the users cannot help but bring huge dividends in the future.

The Poetry Consultant

There is a splendid suite of rooms that sits across the brow of the Library of Congress overlooking the Capitol Plaza. The rooms are carpeted, comfortable, and furnished with antiques, overstuffed sofas, and casual chairs. If you pass through the French doors, you will find yourself on a high balcony looking down on the Capitol steps to the west (pictures of presidential inaugurations have been taken from here for eighty years). The Supreme Court, Senate office buildings, and Union Station march in dazzling marble to the north. The view is one of the finest in Washington, and the rooms might be expected to belong to the Librarian himself—but they don't. The Librarian occupies a glowing baroque chapel buried in one of the Library's courtyards without a view of any kind. The peaceful rooms with the splendid view belong to the Library's Poetry Consultant. Since 1929, the Library has accumulated no fewer than sixteen consultantships and honorary chairs (aeronautics, American history, Slavic studies, historical cartography, et cetera), but like Abou ben Adhem, the one that leads all the rest in visibility and prestige is that of the Consultant in Poetry in English.

This unlikely office (the local press always refers to the incumbent as the American Poet Laureate) was created in 1937 by Herbert Putnam. By then, Putnam had already established half a dozen chairs, and in 1937, an anonymous donor, who later proved to be Archer M. Huntington, gave enough money to support yet another one. Thus Joseph Auslander, the poetry editor of the *North American Review*, became the first Consultant in Poetry. He served for four years, during which time he compiled a catalog of all the American and English poetry in the Library, begged a substantial number of original poetry manuscripts for the Library, and gave innumerable lectures before poetry societies and university audiences.

In 1943, Auslander was followed by the eminent poet and critic Allen Tate, and from that time on, the Chair of Poetry (according to Archibald MacLeish) would "be filled for annual periods by distinguished American poets whose interest in bibliographical and critical problems may be of service to the Library in the development of its collections." Auslander, Tate, and their successors, some of whom served for more than one year, make up a truly breathtaking roster of the finest names in American belles lettres:

THE CONSULTANTS IN POETRY IN ENGLISH

Joseph Auslander	1937–1941	Robert Penn Warren	1944–1945
Allen Tate	1943–1944	Louise Bogan	1945–1946

Karl Shapiro	1946-1947	Stephen Spender	1965-1966
Robert Lowell	1947-1948	James Dickey	1966-1968
Leonie Adams	1948-1949	William Jay Smith	1968-1970
Elizabeth Bishop	1949-1950	William E. Stafford	1970-1971
Conrad Aiken	1950-1952	Josephine Jacobsen	1971-1973
Randall Jarrell	1956-1958	Daniel Hoffman	1973-1974
Robert Frost	1958-1959	Stanley Kunitz	1974-1976
Richard Eberhart	1959-1961	Robert Hayden	1976-1978
Louis Untermeyer	1961-1963	William Meredith	1978-1980
Howard Nemerov	1963-1964	Maxine Kumin	1980-1982
Reed Whittemore	1964-1965	Anthony Hecht	1982-

Howard Nemerov, whose stint fell in the mid-1960s, was wont to say with a sad smile, "The Consultant in Poetry is a very busy man, chiefly because he spends so much time talking with people who want to know what the Consultant in Poetry does."

What Does a Poetry Consultant Do?

De jure, pretty much what he or she wants to. Like the typical college, which has just snared the latest Nobel Prize winner to be its Something in Residence, the Library tends to be so awed by and grateful for the poets' presence that the poets can play their role in almost any way they see fit. De facto, however, each seems to struggle to do everything his predecessor tried to do, as well as to add a few innovations of his own. The result is that the consultant's one- or two-year sabbatical becomes a frenzied attempt to keep up. Stanley Kunitz observed at the conclusion of his second year at the Library, "In the beginning of my consultantship I wondered what I was supposed to do; in my second term I fretted whether I would have the time to do it."

For example, Robert Penn Warren started an ambitious recording program, using the Music Division's Recording Laboratory, and during his tenure drew thirteen poets and three novelists into the Library to read their own works so that posterity might know how *they* heard and interpreted their writings themselves. The resultant long-playing records are available for sale by the Library. Louise Bogan compiled a checklist of 1,000 belles lettres published in England during and after World War II, which the Library published for the use of scholars. Miss Bogan expanded Warren's recording program, secured money from the Bollingen Foundation to broaden the selections, and prepared five albums of contemporary American poetry read by the poets themselves. She produced additional recordings by W. H. Auden and got T. S. Eliot to read enough of his works to fill an album of his own.

The succeeding consultants became involved in staging regular seasons of poetry readings in the Coolidge Auditorium. Free programs, underwritten by Agnes and Eugene Meyer of the *Washington Post*, were by Carl Sandburg, Robert Frost, Robinson Jeffers, and Stephen Vincent Benét, and the programs became a major part of the Washington cultural scene. Mrs. Whittall gave money to outfit the Poetry Consultant's rooms, to expand the readings from poetry to literary criticism, and to support the staging of free drama productions.

Robert Frost embraced the growing obligations of the consultants by recruiting readers for the recorded series, planning programs for the Coolidge performances, and inaugurating an innovation of his own by teaching a year-long seminar for graduate students and professors from the five local universities. At the end of his stay, he declared:

> I have had a fine time, a whale of a good time, as Poetry Consultant; there hasn't been a boring minute. Of the talks in the Hall [the Coolidge Auditorium] at the Library, I have liked them all. The high school children were fine and I liked the Library group very much. These times when I had a chance to talk to people about poetry are the ones I recall first.

Richard Eberhart added the voices of some ninety poets to the Library's growing Archive of Recorded Poetry and Literature and continued the seminars for local students. He also worked closely with the Voice of America, conducting interviews for overseas broadcasts and preparing a short history of American poetry for the U.S. Information Agency. Louis Untermeyer staged a National Poetry Festival at the Library, bringing together some thirty-five of the nation's leading poets for three days of discussions on technique and purpose. (The festival was underwritten by the Bollingen Foundation and resulted in a 367-page *Proceedings*, published by the Library.)

The National Poetry Festival proved so successful that Reed Whittemore staged an even larger event in April of 1965—the Symposium on American Literature. A hundred editors of literary magazines and many writers from abroad took part in this two-day conference (financed by the Carnegie Corporation), and by this time, the accumulated "voluntary" activities had reached such density that when Whittemore turned in his final report, he noted having given "about three dozen" poetry readings, thirteen radio programs for the Voice of America, a television show on poetry for children, and "innumerable lectures." He had held informal meetings with government officials on "the useful arts," had written a pamphlet for distribution at the Jefferson Memorial at the request of the National Park Service, and had participated in a University of Texas conference on "What To Do with the New Government Foundation for the Arts and Humanities." His Library of

Congress lecture, "Ways of Misunderstanding Poetry," is still one of the Library's best-sellers.

Consultant Stephen Spender worried about the problem of translating poetry from one language to another, and his concern stimulated a 1970 conference of translators and the translated, under the leadership of Consultant William Jay Smith. James Dickey of *Deliverance* fame increased the consultants' television activities and introduced two of his own variations to the expected role: combined poetry readings and guitar concerts for children and the inauguration of three-man reading programs in the Coolidge—two guest poets reading their works, moderated (or baited) by a third.

Josephine Jacobsen reached out to black poets, who she felt had been too long overlooked, and during her second term, held an enormously successful Conference on Teaching Creative Writing. Daniel Hoffman, who, like many of the consultants, saw himself as a liaison between the Library and the literary community, helped to establish three substantial poetry/literature awards funded by the Copernicus Society of America, and Stanley Kunitz staged a Conference on the Publication of Poetry and Fiction (funded by the Whittall Poetry and Literature Fund and a grant from the National Endowment for the Arts), which 250 writers, publishers, and magazine editors attended.

Robert Hayden was the first black poet to be appointed to the consultantship, and he was a bit uncomfortable with the hoopla that accompanied his selection. "I did not want any of this, for it had little to do with me as an artist and far too much to do with me as a member of an ethnic minority." He initiated informal Thursday afternoon coffees for "poets and friends of poets," which evolved into a series of Thursday afternoon lectures and poetry readings. Dedicated to his craft, he agonized over giving a full measure of work to the Library and still finding the time and energy to continue to write. Hayden's tenure was capped with a gala evening of poetry reading in which he and twelve former Poetry Consultants took part. Noted Hayden, "For most of us this was the literary event of a lifetime."

William Meredith worked with the International Communications Agency to bring foreign writers to the Library of Congress and also encouraged greater ties with "nonestablishment" American writers and poets. And Maxine Kumin reached out to women poets. She started a series of "bag lunch" poetry workshops in the Poetry Office, at which the work of fledgling women poets was critiqued, and feeling that women had been underrepresented in the poetry series at the Library, she invited a number of women poets to read from their work during her first term.

In short, the tradition continues and accretes, enabling the Library of Congress to fan the flames of contemporary poetry with both hands. The "Monday nights in the Coolidge" are not only bringing a lively stream of the spoken word to Washington audiences, but, via the tapes distributed through the National Public Radio network, the Library's programs of poetry, literary criticism, drama readings, and festival discussions are becoming increasingly familiar throughout the country.

The Poetry Office operates with three people: the incumbent Poetry Consultant; the Special Assistant in Poetry, who runs the office and manages the public programs; and the Poetry Assistant, who is a research assistant and secretary for the enterprise

Prints and Photographs, Motion Pictures

We come now to the last two Library of Congress units that we shall describe, and the fact that this final piece of the picture comes at the end, more by accident than design, projects an irresistible irony. Historians tell us that man's first written communications were the pictures drawn on cave walls and that the printed word came long after. Thanks to educational films, television tapes, and the whole trend in image processing, every sign seems to point to a future that says that the world of the printed word is fading and reliance on the picture or a pictured page is coming around again. The laser/videodisc seems to be passing in front of Gutenberg's press, and if this eclipse is as real as the futurists are trying to get us to believe, the two divisions we are about to see may yet end up as the central core of the Library— with all the books simply an adjunct in some peripheral annex down some as yet unknown street.

From the very beginning, one of the Library's major obligations was to preserve the experience of the nation. It was to store the story of our peoples, our national successes and failures, and the sense of our daily lives. During the early years, this function was primarily fulfilled via the printed word; then our social history began to be captured by the daguerreotypes, the Brady wet plates, and the strips of jerky motion picture news films; then came the wirephotos and the picture magazines; and now television tapes. There seems little doubt that our mental images of the past come from written descriptions for the first 100 years but from frozen pictorial descriptions for the second. The Prints and Photographs Division reflects this trend, and the videotape and videodiscs of the Motion Picture, Broadcasting, and Recorded Sound Division will carry the images into the next generation.

When the Prints and Photographs Division was established, its collection was properly a part of "culture" as evinced by the fine arts, and it began with Rembrandt and Dürer. It then began to include "culture" as in the lively arts (theatrical history and the motion picture era), and it now is overwhelmingly immersed in "culture" as in social culture, the record of the here and now.

When this book was first written in the late sixties, the Library and the division had just inherited 1.25 million news photographs from the *New York World-Telegram and Sun.* Since then, the Library has received the entire photographic archives of *Look* magazine (some 5 million images covering a forty-year span), recordings of speeches by world leaders made at the National Press Club in Washington since 1952, and scores of prime time television programs. The *one* division at the Library responsible for preserving the nation's history through the pictorial image has become *two*—in recognition of the ever-growing role of television and film in capturing our society's cultural values.

The Prints

The Library got into the picture business because of the featheredge between art and printing. The art museums on the Mall seemed appropriate for painting and sculpture, but the reproduced drawings of the printing press seemed to belong to the national library. The copyright deposit thus brought in the first art prints in the nineteenth century, and at the beginning of the twentieth, Mrs. Gardiner Green Hubbard donated her husband's splendid collection of Dürers, Mantegnas, and Rembrandts and pressed the Library to buy prints to reinforce the Hubbard holdings. Although printmaking had long been a strong sideline for American artists (Benjamin West, the Peales, Whistler, and Winslow Homer are well represented by their engravings and etchings), twentieth-century limners Frank Duveneck and Joseph Pennell built international reputations on their printed lines. When Pennell reached artistic stardom, he discovered to his surprise how very strong gifts and the copyright deposit had made the Library of Congress in his field, and he resolved to use the existing holdings as a base on which to build a collection by contemporary printmakers. Thus in the 1930s, the Library got Pennell's own collection of nineteenth- and twentieth-century masters, together with a substantial endowment "for the continuing purchase of prints of the highest quality, executed in the last hundred years by artists of all nationalities."

According to Pennell's will, the Library was to create a committee composed of a leading etcher, a recognized lithographer, and the chief of the Prints and Photographs Division. These three were to recommend prints for the Library's permanent collection, and they have been doing so for nearly fifty years now. The Library wanted to be certain that its collections did not merely reflect the names of those who had achieved artistic popularity, but that it would find and recognize the young and the unknown, those with potential and promise. For thirty-four years, the Library sponsored an open competition, the National Exhibition of Prints, judged by distinguished artists and curators, which was circulated to museums throughout the United States after its initial showing in Washington. From these prints, a number were selected for purchase by the Library.

Although the National Exhibition of Prints is no longer used as a device to ensure a wide range of prints from which to choose, the three-member committee still meets—usually twice a year—to select fine prints for the Library's collection under the terms of Pennell's will. The committee aims for comprehensiveness in American material and will look at a great many very recent works before making their final choices. Artists and dealers often submit slides or photographs of works they wish to have the committee consider, and the committee sometimes meets in other cities to view some of the prints firsthand. The committee also keeps an eye out for older works to fill gaps in the collection (Pennell funds may be used to purchase any prints produced after 1825) and tries to use alternate meetings to accomplish that objective. Unfortunately, the Pennell funds do not stretch as far as they used to. In 1980, only twelve prints could be purchased (albeit one was a Matisse and others dated from the early twentieth century), and in 1981, probably only twenty-five to thirty prints will be added to the collections through this means.

Posters

Posters, a dramatic art form, constitute a bridge between art for art's sake and art that captures time and events. The Library has one of the largest, most diverse collections of public posters in the world. They range from nearly 3,000 nineteenth-century theatrical billboards (Jenny Lind, P. T. Barnum, *H.M.S. Pinafore*, *The Great Train Robbery*) through art nouveau to shattering sheets of al-Fatah recruiting posters and the self-styled "revolutionary challenge" of the student uprising in Paris. A collection of 3,000 political propaganda posters from all over the world, published from 1965 to 1978, was given to the Library in the mid-1970s by collector Gary Yanker—what more appropriate characterization of the last two decades? In 1980, such unlikely additions as the best Swiss posters of 1978 and a twenty-four-sheet lithographic poster by the Morgan Company depicting Rosa Bonheur's *Horse Fair* were slipped into the division's long, flat drawers.

Photography and the Social Scene

The early librarians of the division immediately recognized the camera's potential for preserving social history, and a catechism of their contributions serves as a sampling of the kinds of materials we now take for granted when we approach the division's files. Jeffrey Parsons headed the unit from 1899 to 1911 and loaded its drawers with rows of pictures from the Klondike gold rush, cartoons of the Russo-Japanese War, and rare views of Liberia and West Africa taken by the American Colonization Society in the nineteenth century. The rage for stereoscopic views sent photographers around the world, and Parsons carefully preserved their double-view cards, which he received in vast quantity through the copyright device. Parsons made prints of 2,000 portraits, built a collection on the development of equestrian statues, and scooped up political cartoons from any place he could find them.

He was followed by Richard A. Rice, who was sixty-six when he took the job and stayed with it until he was eighty! Rice acquired the Civil War drawings of Forbes and Ward, the Mathew Brady daguerreotypes, and such uncommon hoards as a huge collection of British railway posters.

Division Chief L. B. Holland, who managed the unit from 1929 to 1943, was a trained architect, and in 1931, he instituted the Pictorial Archives of Early American Architecture. This archive started as a collection of photographic negatives and prints but quickly grew into a library of drawings and data sheets, and it now includes the photographs of the Historic American Buildings Survey. The survey became real through the joint efforts of the Library of Congress, the National Park Service, and the American Institute of Architects and now contains 30,000 measured drawings and 40,000 photographs of over 13,000 buildings.

Holland also began what he called the Cabinet of American Illustration, a collection of thousands of original drawings used to illustrate books and magazines in the 1880s and 1890s. (Their modern counterparts are the thousands of original New Yorker cartoons that have been given to the Library during the past half century.) Holland was one of the first to collect and publish Currier and Ives prints, and as far back as 1931, he was having special exhibitions of the original copyright copies to draw attention to the remarkable social history those prints contain. Interestingly, the prints, cartoons, and advertising signs in the graphic art collection are valuable not only for what they depict (the clothes, activities, customs of a particular age), but also for the medium used to produce them. As documents in themselves, they are often useful in demonstrating the development of graphic design or technology.

During the 1930s and the Depression, photographic social history became a near-art form in itself. The Library has all of the famous Farm Security Administration photographs of the Dust Bowl and other depressed areas made during that time of economic despair. The nation's memory of those desperate years is increasingly built on images caught by the cameras of Walker Evans and Dorothea Lange.

Indeed, much of the national memory is preserved in the division's Master American Photographers collection. The pictures that have become an essential part of American publishing are drawn (and duplicated) from the division's files. The beginnings of photography itself—the calotypes of Henry Fox Talbot, the Brady Lincoln portraits, the Civil War pictures of George N. Barnard—are all there, as well as Roger Fenton's photographs of the Crimean War. The early pictures of the West—the Grand Canyon, Yellowstone, Yosemite—as seen through the lenses of William Henry Jackson and Timothy O'Sullivan are well represented and available for copying by anyone who needs them. The Library takes particular pride in its collections of the Photo-Secession Group represented by Alfred Stieglitz, Edward Steichen, Clarence H. White, and others. These records of the work of individual photographer-artists are still eagerly sought and acquired. The Library has rejoiced in its receipt of the photographic files of Ansel Adams, Brett Weston, and Toni Frissell. Miss Frissell's magnificent collection of portraits of the great (de Gaulle, Churchill, Adenauer, Pius XII) and of the American society scene (Astors, Vanderbilts, Whitneys, and Mellons) runs to 40,000 color transparencies and over 270,000 black-and-white negatives.

A huge collection of photographs of country courthouses in the United States (11,000 black-and-white negatives, 8,000 reference prints, 2,500 master prints) is the most recent large addition to the photographic collections. Commissioned by Joseph E. Seagram and Sons to mark the American bicentennial, twenty-four photographers fanned out across the country between 1974 and 1976 to record these unique elements of grass roots democracy. They managed to capture the style and feel of county courthouses, from the simplest white frame building to the most elegant monument of glass and steel. The company presented the whole superb collection to the Library in 1980.

Film and Television

The Library's motion picture collection began, quite literally, with a sneeze. In 1894, the moving picture *Edison Kinetoscopic Record of a Sneeze*, better known as "Fred Ott's Sneeze," was deposited for copyright. Because the copyright law did not provide protection for moving pictures until 1912, this and other early films were deposited as photographs printed on rolls of paper (now called the Paper Print collection). Even after the law was modified, the Library did not collect the films themselves because of the extremely flammable nature of the nitrate film in use at the time. By 1942, motion pictures had become such an important aspect of everyday cultural life that the Library reversed its earlier decision and decided to take the films anyway. The film and television collection today contains over 75,000 titles, with several thousand more being added each year through copyright deposit, purchase, gift, or exchange.

Museums and film archives have long been concerned with how to preserve the fragile medium of film. Nitrate film was subject to deterioration and spontaneous combustion; the colors of modern films are likely to fade over time and lose their original vibrancy. In the last thirty years, though, advances in technology have restored films once regarded as hopeless, and they offer promise for the preservation of films far into the future.

Item: In 1948, the Academy of Motion Picture Arts and Sciences and the Library of Congress embarked on a cooperative project to salvage the early motion pictures surviving only in the Library's Paper Print collection by transferring the images to acetate film. The old paper rolls were brittle and twisted, making viewing impossible. But a re-photographing technique was perfected, and by 1964, the project was completed. Researchers can now view films that did not exist in any usable form for decades.

Item: In the 1960s, the Library began a similar restoration/preservation effort for the old nitrate films. In collaboration with the American Film Institute (AFI), the Library established a sophisticated conversion laboratory in which old nitrate film is cleaned by an ultrasonic process, repaired, and transferred to acetate stock. All of this work is now being carried out in the Library's newly expanded laboratory facility on the grounds of Wright-Patterson Air Force Base in Dayton, Ohio. Recent fires involving nitrate film (the National Archives lost a good deal of nitrate film stored in a warehouse near the Library's vaults in Suitland, Maryland) underscore the importance of continuing the nitrate film conversion program if the content of those old films is to be saved at all.

Item: For many years, professional photographers have stored their unused film in refrigerators to keep it fresh. This same technique is now being applied to the finished product as well. The Library currently stores some 36,000 reels of film in refrigerated storage rooms in the Washington suburbs to keep the images from deteriorating (master prints of black-and-white films are kept at fifty-five degrees; color films, at thirty-five degrees).

Item: New technologies—research on the archival possibilities of videotape and the new laser videodiscs—offer even more hope for longer-lasting images and increased storage capacity.

Oddly enough, films considered lost to the ages keep turning up, sometimes in the strangest places. (Over half of the films produced prior to 1930 are not known to still exist!) One of the best stories is the find in Dawson City in Canada's Yukon Territory, where 510 reels of film (produced from 1903 to 1929) were dug up in the late 1970s at the site of an old hockey rink. All nitrate, the films had been stored in a library basement before they were used to fill in a swimming pool so that the hockey rink could be stabilized on top of it. The frigid basement and the frozen ground had preserved the films to a certain extent, although all of them suffered water damage. Many of them, in fact, are still jellied into a solid mass, awaiting new techniques of restoration. Amazingly, at least 425 of the reels are salvageable in whole or in part, and work on them is progressing at the National Film Archives of Canada and the Library of Congress under the AFI archives program.

The ubiquitous television screen projects the image of today. The Library has been collecting radio broadcasts since the 1920s as an aspect of recorded sound, and television programs have been coming in (first as films and then as programs in their own right) through the copyright deposit. Under the copyright law revision, an American Television and Radio Archives was created in the Library of Congress in 1978 to allow the Library to tape programs directly off the air without regard to copyright restrictions. New recording facilities in the Madison Building will allow the division to expand its television materials by taping additional programs (presidential press conferences or the coverage of special events, for example) for the collections.

Who Cares and Why?

Short of the comfort of knowing you have several million pictures stored in the attic, what good is all this vast collection to anyone, and who uses it anyway?

The audience is intriguingly varied. The television world is plowing through the hoard daily—compilers of documentaries, costumers for period dramas, set designers. Museum curators use the fine and historical prints and secure duplicates of photographs for their own collections. Novelists spend hours browsing, looking for local-color detail, and historians and book designers select pictures to elaborate and adorn their texts.

Oddly enough, the Historic American Buildings Survey material is one of the most heavily used single collections in the whole Library, and the stream of visitors who use this collection range from trained architects restoring major national shrines to "ordinary householders" repairing their private but historic homes.

All told, the reference assistants in the Prints and Photographs Division dealt with almost 8,000 readers in 1980 and responded to a total of more than 60,000 questions. The reference staff in the Motion Picture, Broadcasting, and Recorded Sound Division fielded more than 27,000 queries during the course of the year.

How Are the Collections Arranged?

How does a publisher or a media person find the pictures he or she needs? There are various ways, of course, the major approaches being:

1. Certain rare items are cataloged individually, just like books, and these appear in the division's card catalog. Examples: the original plate of Paul Revere's Boston Massacre scene, Bellows's *Dempsey and Firpo*, and single posters like Jacques Villon's "Guinguette Fleurie."

2. There are book catalogs of the various individual collections. The Johns Hopkins University Press published a splendid, illustrated 568-page *American Prints in the Library of Congress*, and the Government Printing Office put out a more summary *Guide to the Special Collections of Prints and Photographs in the Library of Congress*. The latter volume describes some 800 individual groupings, such as the 18,500 photographs in forty-seven albums that belonged to Field Marshal Hermann Goering— his private, chronologically arranged snapshot albums!—and the Detroit Publishing Company's 20,000 prints and 30,000 glass negatives of stores, town squares, courthouses, factories, and what have yous that the company rented for picture postcards and advertisements. (Speaking of advertisements, thanks to the copyright deposit, the Library's nineteenth-century collection of soap wrappers, cigar box covers, beer signs, cigarette packs, and playing card designs is without peer.)

3. The third approach is via browsing files—the Farm Security Administration and Office of War Information glossy prints are in this form—wherein all the pictures are pasted on cardboard, sorted by subject, and filed in upright file drawers so the user can simply flip and look.

4. Over the years, a specific-subject index has been developed to direct the user to particular items that are good representations of objects, topics, or activities. Glancing down the rows of drawers, your eye bounces from advertising to chimney sweeps to McCarthyism to whales and whaling. This very useful index now contains some 65,000 entries and is the largest index in the division.

5. Many thousands of pictures have already been published from the division's collections, so there is a continual demand for "the original of _____" or "a big, copiable print of so-and-so picture of yours I saw in _____."

6. In the areas of film and television, the researcher can rely on the division's extensive card catalogs, which are arranged by title of

the work. The Library has published catalogs of specific parts of the collection, such as *The George Kleine Collection of Early Motion Pictures in the Library of Congress* (films produced between 1898 and 1926), to provide additional help.

The Product

Unless an item is still so recent it is covered by copyright or some special instruction from its living photographer, anything in the collection can be duplicated, and the Prints and Photographs Division will have the copies made in whatever form is most useful to the requester: slides, color prints, glossy prints, matte prints, blueprints, photostats, or what have you.

The operation runs with a staff of twenty-two people, who divide their time among acquisitions (trying to determine what is needed), researching and cataloging (so the user can be certain about what he actually has as well as identifying it so he can conveniently find it), and preservation (a major task when dealing with everything from cigar bands to Win With Willkie campaign billboards, not to mention restoring the mildewed, water-soaked, stuck-together cavalryman's pictures of Kiowa chiefs at Medicine Lodge—or of Lincoln at City Point).

The staff of the Motion Picture, Broadcasting, and Recorded Sound Division—numbering about seventy—finds itself faced with the same mix of activities and having the same goals in mind. In addition, its twenty-person recording laboratory makes listening copies for research use and records the many chamber concerts, literary programs, and special events that are held at the Library during the year. And twelve of the division's staff members work at the nitrate film conversion lab in Dayton, Ohio.

And thus we end our hurried, obviously superficial glance at a few of the many libraries that make up the Library of Congress. Not only could whole books be written about a single room—or drawer or item of the Library—but whole books *have* been so written!

For our present purposes, the best we could hope to do was provide a general idea of the kinds of things the Library keeps and the kinds of things the Library does with them. We now turn to a more difficult matter. So far, everything we've seen has been bathed in the pleasant glow of stained glass and an operational Elysium. Experience tells us that even the best of man's creations have hairline cracks, and candor (and the publisher) require that we step a little closer to this institution and check out the glaze. We therefore proceed to the stresses and strains of administration: to competing customers, conflicting missions, difficult choices—the Library of Congress under stress.

Part Three

THE LIBRARY
UNDER STRESS:
RELATIONSHIPS WITH
THE SPECIAL ELITES

11

THE LIBRARY OF CONGRESS AND CONGRESS: THE CONGRESSIONAL RESEARCH SERVICE

Thus far in this book, we have tried to examine two things: how the Library of Congress came to be and how it works when it is working well. We turn now to its troubles. "Troubles," here, may not conjure quite the image we seek, because at this time in its institutional life, the Library of Congress is a cheerful agency, well respected, and carrying out its mission with professionalism and reasonable satisfaction for all concerned. But there are frictions: points of heat, drags, and stresses, which presage a very difficult time ahead.

The Library of Congress is essentially a service agency. It secures and preserves great collections of written, audible, and visual records, which are secured and preserved for use *by someone else*. It has little need of its great collections for its own ends. The materials are there for use by three outside groups: the Congress, the library profession, and the scholarly research world. The three groups barely tolerate each other at best, and at worst, they resent each other bitterly.

They should not be blamed. From their point of view, such selfishness is quite valid and legitimate. Congress, the parent elite, says firmly that the Library is *Congress's* library. Congress built it, funded it, and the sole reason for its existence was to give the legislature the information it needed to run the country. Congress quite properly feels that the Library of Congress should concentrate on serving Congress fully and adequately, and not until it has completely satisfied this purpose dare it consider the luxury of helping other customers.

Congress has been remarkably civil about the complaints of the other users, but beneath such debate rests the ultimate congressional

The Congressional Research Service was the first unit of the Library to move into the new James Madison Memorial Building in December 1979.

argument, which has never been better expressed than when Representative Wayne Hays spoke on the 1972 Library budget before the House Appropriations Committee. As the newly appointed Chairman of the Joint Committee on the Library, Congressman Hays said: "I have had conversations with Mr. Mumford before because I have been on the House Administration Committee and had been ranking member. He told me quite candidly this is not really a Library of Congress; it is a national library. I quite candidly said, 'Why don't you get your money someplace else?' That sort of ended the conversation."

Thus the congressional position. But both the federal librarians and the librarians of the nation's public, college, and research libraries can make a strong case for the Library's attention. They say with perfect validity: We are in the business of providing information to the various parts of the public with the public's money. We are all buying and storing and retrieving information from essentially the same sources. We owe it to the public to buy materials at the lowest cost and to organize them for use with the greatest efficiency. Since we are all using essentially the same materials, "someone" should act as the central agent for purchasing, cataloging, record keeping, reducing duplication, and providing leadership, and since the Library of Congress is the biggest and richest library and is run with the public's own money, it is clearly the library that should do these things.

And the third group, the scholarly research world, has a dozen ways to express a single theme. The scientists, for example, are also concerned with duplication, but for them, the pivotal problem is the reinvention of the wheel. Their distress concerns the vast amount of public and private money being spent for research that could be done so much faster and so much more efficiently if "someone" would do a faster, better job of analyzing and retrieving technical literature and disseminating the reports of solved problems throughout the interested research community. The "someone" would be both a storage unit and a switching or crossover point for the receipt and dissemination of scientific data. Thanks to its hundred-year-old Smithsonian Deposit and its ties to government research reporting, the Library of Congress is already the largest scientific library in the world and accumulates more technical data every day than any other institution anywhere. Ergo, it is the obvious candidate to be the "someone." Similar cases can be (and are being) made by the historical community, the Latin American scholars, the motion picture scholars, the geographers and mapmakers, et cetera, et cetera.

To add to the philosophical conflicts, each of these competing elites has points of stress and friction in its day-to-day relationships with the Library as a service institution. In several rather threatening instances, the customers have "given up on LC" and solved their own problems on their own, frequently starting services and solutions that not only could ultimately leave the Library isolated and out of the mainstream, but could actually eat away at what the Library has done for almost 200 years.

These, then, are the contending positions. Now where are the trouble spots? How does the Library relate to its three customers? Let's start with the elite that has the prior claim: the Congress.

The Library of Congress Versus the Congressional Research Service

When Congress looks at the Library, most of the members and their staffs see two quite separate and independent institutions: the CRS *and* the National Library, the Congressional Research Service *and* the Library of Congress. Intellectually, even as a member knows that the Federal Bureau of Investigation is really a part of the Department of Justice and that the Internal Revenue Service is really a part of the Treasury Department, Congress knows that the CRS is one of the departments of the Library. But emotionally, the legislative establishment assumes two parallel, almost independent units. There was a time in the fifties and mid-sixties that this dichotomy had threatening overtones. Supporters of Congress's Legislative Reference Service were fearful that some activist Librarian of Congress—such as Luther Evans or Archibald MacLeish—might use the LRS to propagandize the Congress. They feared that when the Library wanted legislation passed that would serve its own ends—copyright revision, aid to local libraries, postage rates for books, import exceptions on overseas publishing—it might force the LRS to slant its analyses or to alter its statistics.

To protect the Legislative Reference Service from such potential pressure, Congress wrote into the Legislative Reorganization Act of 1970 the following instructions:

> It is the policy of Congress that—
>
>   1. the Librarian of Congress shall, in every possible way, encourage, assist, and promote the Congressional Research Service in—
>   A. rendering to Congress the most effective and efficient service,
>   B. responding most expeditiously, effectively, and efficiently to the special needs of Congress, and
>   C. discharging its responsibilities to Congress; and
>   2. the Librarian of Congress shall grant and accord to the Congressional Research Service complete research independence and the maximum practicable administrative independence consistent with these objectives.

It was the "maximum practicable administrative independence" phrase that created the crack between the CRS and the Library. Since the implementation of the act, three successive CRS directors have felt obligated to see that this separation was meticulously observed. From it has come the practice of the CRS budget's being prepared independently by the CRS and left unchallenged by the Library and the practice of the CRS director's defending his budget before the appropriations committees as a separate line item that is completely independent of the Library. The phrase also fathered the practice of an annual half a million dollars' worth of CRS contracts being let without Library approval, and so forth.

The reorganization act and the larger, more explicit role of the congressional support agencies have led the CRS to drop its traditional cover—indeed, to change how it thinks about itself. Up to 1970, the LRS played the role of a faceless congressional staff member who, like the administrative assistant or the backroom caseworker, existed only as "the Congressman" or "the Senator." Since the 1970 act, the CRS reports have been increasingly referred to in the press as "The Congressional Research Service says . . ." or "According to a Congressional Research Service study . . ." in contrast to sixty years of "A newly released publication of the Library of Congress reveals . . ." Similarly, the media increasingly tie the CRS to the Congress and the other support agencies instead of to the Library: "According to a speaker at the CRS-GAO seminar . . ." or "The Congressional Budget Office and the Congressional Research Service estimate the energy shortfall at an excess of . . ." A decade ago, "the Library of Congress" would have been used instead of "the CRS," and the difference has led to a sense of independence on the part of the one and resentment from the other. Within the Library itself, the CRS has not hesitated to take full advantage of "Service to Congress first, service to everybody else second."

By the mid-seventies, the CRS versus the national library contention was generating bitter resentment that was barely below the surface. The CRS got the best space, had first claim on the computer, got perpetually larger funds with minor effort—until Librarian Boorstin arrived. Boorstin's interest was in the national intellectual community, and as he developed and publicized the national library role, Congress's affections and attention began to shift. It was soon accepting the legitimacy of the idea of a national library and gradually embracing it with considerable pride. The recognition that the two institutions were not in a hierarchical relationship but of equal legitimacy reached a climax when the Reagan budgetary reductions began and the chairman of the Senate Appropriations Subcommittee on the Legislative Branch said:

> we are going to have to make further cuts in the Congressional Research Service. . . . possibly if we have to apply the surgeon's knife further, let's put it really where it is going to hurt most, let's put it to our own benefit and our service and let the Nation at large retain that service as much as we can.

That statement raises two questions: the old, Is it Congress's library or the nation's? and the newer one, How does the Congress view "its" part of the Library (the CRS) now? We'll return to the ownership matter later. At this point, let's look at a few of the problems of the Congress-CRS relationship.

Confidentiality

From the creation of the LRS, Congress has decreed that every query placed on the Library shall be completely confidential: No member of Congress may find out what questions other members have placed, and no CRS answer can be revealed to another member without the original requester's explicit permission. In the first fifty years of the service, the overwhelming majority of the question-answer, request-study relationships were on a me-and-thee basis. The replies were tailored precisely to the questioner, the response was written to answer each specific inquiry, and the dialogue was similar to that in an attorney-client relationship.

But the volume of queries rose year after year, first into hundreds

Calls from congressional offices are received in a central inquiry unit, typed into a minicomputer, and transmitted to one of the divisions within CRS for response.

then thousands and now hundreds of thousands of requests, and it became impossible to reply on a one-to-one basis every time. Instead, basic, prefabricated parts of reports, Issue Briefs, and research guides have been created, stockpiled, and used as needed. Similarly, in the early days, a Library researcher did all the work—all the "looking-up" of the answer. As volume rose, it became reasonable (and possible) to put many of the answers into the computer and to place a computer terminal in each congressional office so that congressional staff members could do much of the "looking-up" themselves. This change had a logic to it, but a dramatic by-product developed from this progression.

The basic CRS Reports became vastly valuable legislative material for state legislatures and university classes. The CRS computer programs, produced at the taxpayers' expense and therefore unprotected by copyright, contained rich mines of bibliographic material, almost hourly updated briefings on national problems, and in general, much of the data that state legislative reference services and executive departments were spending tax dollars to gather themselves. The not too surprising result of this accumulation of information was that there were increasing demands for the Library to make these CRS Reports publicly available and the computer data generally accessible. Problems developed immediately.

The first requests were for the basic printed reports of CRS policy analyses. The Council of State Governments pointed out that it was sending two copies of all its studies to the Library of Congress for its collections and asked if it might have copies of the CRS Reports in return. The CRS asked its oversight committees for permission; the committees said no, the studies were confidential. Various state legislatures pointed out that they were sending their legislative journals to the Library, might they have the CRS Reports? Congress said no.

As the computer programs became more useful, the various university computer networks and federal agencies like the Department of Agriculture and the National Institutes of Health asked for access to the bibliographic data bases. The Library worked out an at-cost method by which the material could be placed on-line and paid for at hourly rates. The plan was taken to the congressional oversight committees, and the Library was told no, the material must be limited to Congress only. In each case, the supplicant was left resentful, and the question, Why should we give our products to you free if you won't make your products available to us, even for money? was raised. Conflict between Library customers. The position of the state legislators, the executive departments, and the college libraries is obvious, but how can Congress's apparently arbitrary refusal be justified? Congress would say the answer is "purpose."

Congress uses the Congressional Research Service as its own, in-house group of experts. They focus on *legislative* responses; their replies should be tight, action-oriented statements that are related to ongoing legislative activities. Congress believes that if the CRS researchers knew that their responses were to be read by "everybody," they would soften the edges, being careful not to say something that might irritate a foreign government (if the study were a foreign policy analysis), being careful not to antagonize an executive agency (thereby limiting future requests), and being certain to convey the depth of their knowledge by throwing in a full load of footnotes, qualifications, and peripheral theories. The product would no longer be a legislative researcher replying to a member of the legislature on a matter of legislative action; indeed, in no time, it would become a series of scholarly papers designed to help the author reach the next step on his or her career ladder.

Congress is also concerned about opening its data banks to lobby groups and foreign governments. If all of its materials are available in any public or college library, skillful retrieval would easily reveal the kinds of options the committees are pursuing, along with the probable thrust of coming treaties and international agreements—all this just from analyzing the kinds of questions the members and committees were asking. Rather than encouraging a greater use of specialized knowledge, the likely result would simply be that Congress would stop using the Congressional Research Service for anything of a substantive nature and another window would close on the legislative process.

Members Versus Committees

There are conflicts even in Congress's use of the service. Who can use the CRS? Individual members of Congress and senators, committee staffs, staffs of individual members. Until the Legislative Reorganization Act of 1970, individual members had first call on the CRS, and staff members followed shortly thereafter, but the act changed that order of priority. The CRS was instructed to give priority to committee support; work assisting individual members and their staffs should be limited to preprepared written materials. Major analytical and long-term studies should be initiated for committees only. The justification for this primacy was simple: It is in the committees that the actual laws are written, the real action choices are made, and the legislative programs are detailed. The CRS is, above all, oriented to legislative issues, and the committee work is the payoff of legislative activity. Concentrate on the committee work. Logical, essentially a truism.

But at the end of ten years' experience, it would seem that the assumption is barely half true, if that. First, criticism developed because the same 1970 act had greatly increased the personnel of the committee staffs themselves, which yielded a situation in which the CRS experts were assisting the units that themselves had specialized experts. The individual members' offices are primarily dedicated to serving their constituents, and they have neither space nor funds for specialists in all the matters on which the members are expected to vote. If anyone should have access to congressional specialists, they argued, it should be the individual senators and members of Congress.

Second, it was discovered that some of the most innovative solutions to difficult problems were coming from individual members who were frequently not even on a subject committee but who were being pressured by constituents to do new things, or from individuals who, although on the "outside" of the power structure, had unusual solutions— solutions that were later proved to be right. Increasingly, individual members felt that the CRS should be at least equally available to these non-committee-oriented individuals.

The result of this tug of war is that the CRS has somewhat receded from its committee-first instruction. In fact, it is splitting the member-versus-committee investment of time and resources about equally, but no one on any side of the argument is happy with the situation.

What the CRS Won't Do

An odd point of stress has developed from the dignifying of the CRS following the 1970 act. It was clear that the CRS could not do all the work of the Congress, so the oversight committees attempted to define what the CRS could do best and force the members' staffs to do the rest themselves. Among the steps taken, the CRS would (1) spend less time helping the members answer queries from their constituents, (2) firmly refuse to write speeches for the members, and (3) no longer offer translating services and photoduplication facilities. Each of those tasks, on its face, was an inappropriate use of objective subject specialists.

But paradoxically, the side effects of the cure have generated new problems. Since most of the questions constituents ask members of Congress relate to national affairs or current legislation, the CRS could respond to them with speed and minimum effort. Now that the congressional offices are required to answer the questions themselves, or wait long weeks while the CRS finishes the "members' requests" first, the offices are spending far longer on each letter than if the CRS had answered it in the first place.

Speech-writing is a corollary. Before the 1970 act, the CRS would prepare speeches on current legislation (a senator would say, "I am in favor of S.22. Please prepare me a speech explaining it and giving the favorable case for presentation to the Rotary Club in so-and-so town"). The speech would be written rather quickly by a subject specialist in the field and would have several unusual characteristics: The facts would be sound; the statistics, accurate; the partisan rhetoric, absent; and frequently, the senator would learn aspects of the problem he had not known before. Under the current law, the present practice is to send briefing materials to the office and, in effect, tell the senator (in fact his staff) to write the speech himself. The product almost always takes longer, the argument is usually more partisan, and the senator or staffer is taken away from floor presence, committee activities, or legislative work that only he can do. The solution of "tell the senator to refuse to give the speech" is not as meaningful as it appears either. One of the major constructive roles any elected official plays is to explain to constituents at home what is going on in Washington, and the speeches made to service clubs and ethnic associations are frequently the best opportunities that official will have to explain what the real issues are in a political solution and to tell the constituents what is being planned to ameliorate the problem—and they, in turn, can tell him what he has perhaps failed to consider.

The third solution noted above, less translating and less photo-

The CRS has prepared a number of "audio issue briefs" on tape cassettes for use by members in their offices, at home, or in their cars. Each tape gives the background of a specific legislative issue, some discussion of the main arguments, and an up-to-date summary of congressional action to date.

duplication, has an obvious disadvantage: It saves money, but it makes the Library's materials less useful to Congress.

What Really Matters

The above examples are simply expressions of the trouble that has developed from success. With 40,000 bills introduced in each Congress, and 20,000 people working on them, trying to provide accurate, incisive analysis means that there must be less and less person-to-person assistance by the CRS and more mass seminars, impersonal videotape training programs, prewritten and stockpiled answers. Those changes permit a maximum use of expensive staff but force the service into an ever more distant, Olympian relationship, which seriously detracts from the effectiveness of its work. In earlier years, the most triumphant successes of the service came when a subject specialist sat knee to knee with a member of Congress and they argued back and forth over "What can we do about the problem?" The CRS specialist would produce legitimate options, the legislator would talk about political realities, and slowly the two sides would hammer out answers that, when they appeared as legislation, have stood the test of time. Either returning to that point or creating its moral equivalent would seem to be a major challenge for the CRS in the coming years: Without doing so, the service is going to drift into the gray world of remote, faceless, and increasingly irrelevant bureaucracy.

But Is the Idea Even Real?

We come finally to the biggest paradox, and possibly the hardest dilemma, of them all: Does the CRS idea really work? Is there such a thing as policy analysis? Here is an agency that costs $30 million a year—the equivalent of an Oberlin College or a William and Mary—and operates at an almost hysterical pace to answer over 1,500 inquiries a day, yet no one is absolutely certain that the most substantive part of its activities is real.

Consider: What is the CRS supposed to do? Three things: provide information when requested, train new staff, and provide in-depth policy analysis on public issues. Experience has proved that the CRS provides information superbly. The replies are accurate, and people in Washington believe that the CRS produces answers faster than any other agency in the city.

Training? This is a new skill of the service; it is doing it adequately now, and it is getting steadily better at it. The congressional staff involvement is increasing, and early participants keep coming back for more training as the programs progress in difficulty and sophistication.

But the record on policy analysis, the keystone of the CRS idea, is not so clear. Note some of the questions that are still unanswered: What knowledge goes into a real legislative solution? How much of a committee's created law is the result of specialized intelligence and sophisticated ratiocination? What difference can "objective research" really make in a political environment? Can there really be such a thing as action-oriented research if the researcher sits in a library and reads printed words instead of going out in the field and seeing the real people affected? Can there even be "objective researchers" when they are the products of modern campuses and single-issue activism? Isn't anybody who really cares about a topic committed to an answer long before he or she gets to the CRS? Of all these questions, the CRS can answer with conviction only the one concerning objective researchers.

To dispose of that unknown quickly, the answer is yes, objectivity in staff and analysis is quite possible. Over its almost seventy-year history, the service has gotten very skilled at identifying the specialist who genuinely loves his field, who wants to share his knowledge about it, who recognizes that there is no single truth about any public issue. Similarly, the CRS has gotten skilled at identifying the advocates, the firmly committed, and (even more unusual) at firing them. The fact that CRS researchers are accepted and used by all sides of the political spectrum would appear to be proof of the researchers' professional detachment. The staff is perceived as being eager to solve problems, without personal axes to grind. Detachment is possible, but how about the rest of the questions?

End results should be some kind of a valid test. The CRS has done social security analysis for years, having worked closely with the appropriate congressional committees since 1948. Unfortunately, at the time of this writing, social security seems to be in more trouble than any other major government program. Did the CRS analyses warn the members of coming troubles and did Congress ignore the CRS projections? No, apparently what went wrong was that past experience could not predict future action, since what occurred had never happened before in the 180 years of U.S. history. Never before had the cost of food and shelter gone up as employment went down. Never before had interest rates climbed so high; indexing had never worked the way it did between 1972 and 1982. Thus, what actually happened was impossible to predict, since nothing in the nation's experience suggested it was possible.

Similarly, the CRS has been deeply involved in educational legislation, playing a major part in providing the data on which the 1960 education acts were based and the 1970 funding was distributed. But education, on the federal level, is in severe disarray. Likewise government's involvement in housing. Could more skilled expertise or knowledge have anticipated the failures of public housing and the current problems of private construction? The CRS has produced an uninterrupted stream of background papers on housing for thirty-five years. If the data had been properly applied, could the difficulties have been prevented? Should we ask for such triumphs from mere factual research? (The questions, incidentally, need not be raised in connection with social problems alone. The CRS produced data on Vietnam, Iran, Angola, and Lebanon that would have led to the same actions as those that resulted from the conventional wisdom of the time.)

The effectiveness of more data and more expert understanding is very difficult to trace. The CRS can point to hundreds of instances in which legislation appears to have been made more humane and more effective as a result of the CRS's involvement, and it can identify government solutions that stemmed from insights and data that the CRS initiated, but it is impossible, of course, to know what would have happened had the CRS not been involved. In the wonderland of government, a weaker bill might have done more good; an ineffective agency might have forced a better solution.

But not to believe that more knowledge will make government wiser becomes as unthinkable as the thought that war is inevitable and that men will always prey on each other in the cities. It is just that in nearly half a century of experimentation, the answer should have been clearer by now.

12

THE LIBRARY OF CONGRESS
AND CONGRESS:
THE NATIONAL LIBRARY

Is the Library of Congress Congress's library or the nation's? Such a question was never even considereed when the Library of Congress was in the Capitol Building. Up to 1897, it was clearly Congress's library to which the nation's scholars were given access. Since 1897, however, the answer has swung back and forth like a pendulum. In Librarian Mumford's time—especially during the 1960s—the argument reached the point where a senator on the Joint Committee on the Library sponsored an extensive study by the associate director of the Harvard University Library, which recommended the displacement of the Library to the executive branch where it would be split into at least three separate parts and maybe five. By Librarian Boorstin's time (and the Reagan shrinkage of the executive branch), librarians within the Library of Congress and in the profession outside were hoping that no one in Congress even remembered that previous apostasy, and all now rejoice at the wisdom, the support, and the protection Congress has given the institution throughout years of sensitive care. We have noted a few anomalies in Congress's ties to the CRS; let us now consider how Congress relates to the national library.

Congress–Library Relations

Library of Congress–Congress relations center on two areas: where the money comes from and who tells the Library what to do. Appropriations and oversight. There are very specific committees in charge of these responsibilities, so let us first note the formal, organizational links.

The formal dedication of the Madison Building, after more than twenty years of planning, jockeying, and construction, took place on April 15, 1980. Helping to cut the ribbon are Representative Lucien Nedzi, Joint Committee on the Library; Senator Harry F. Byrd, Senior Senator from Virginia; Representative John Rhodes, Minority Leader in the House; Senator Frank Cannon, Joint Committee on the Library; Representative Thomas O'Neill, Speaker of the House; Daniel J. Boorstin, Librarian of Congress; and George White, Architect of the Capitol.

The Appropriations Committees

There are two appropriations committees—one in the House and one in the Senate—and it is they who really run the Library. They rarely say, "We want you to do this, we don't want you to do that," but they either provide money to staff an activity or they do not. These signals from the appropriations committees—plus tradition, protocol, and common sense—provide the Librarian with his instructions.

There are some unusual elements in the Library's funding process. To begin with, unlike the typical obstacle course that an executive program agency must run, there is no annual "authorization committee" to convince. When the Department of Housing and Urban Development wants to float a new housing program, it must sell it first to the House Banking and Currency Committee and then to the Senate Banking, Housing, and Urban Affairs Committee. Once those committees approve and agree on the purpose, magnitude, and necessary funding, the idea must be presented and defended all over again before the House and Senate Appropriations Committees.

Not so the Library of Congress. It has no authorization committees whatsoever. The Librarian goes directly to the House Appropriations Committee's Subcommittee on the Legislative Branch, and after enumerating the Library's ongoing services and requesting continuation of enough money to sustain them at a viable level, he presents whatever new services or expanded programs he desires and requests the committee's approval by appropriate funding. He repeats the procedure before the equivalent committee in the Senate (the two bodies operate as if they have scarcely heard of each other), and representatives from the two committees meet in a conference session where they decide how much of the program they want to buy. Their decision is announced some two or three months after the hearings, the two houses then vote the money with little demur, and that ends the process for the year.

The fact that the Library is a legislative agency asking the legislature for funds is only partially in its favor. There are now so many legislative agencies competing over a relatively small segment of the budget that success is always fragmentary. The legislative pie must be divided among the Government Printing Office, the General Accounting Office, the Office of Technology Assessment, the Congressional Budget Office, the Architect of the Capitol, the Botanic Garden, et cetera, et cetera— and the Library of Congress. In modern times, the Library has suffered reductions in base on only three occasions (fifty-two jobs eliminated in one year is the worst loss so far), and its requests are always cut back at hearing time.

But by and large, the Library has fared very well. Each year, the Library describes new programs and services it would like to offer the public or the library profession, and each year the Congress denies them. The library profession is annually outraged over the "niggardliness of the legislature," but in literal fact, the budget has risen steadily through the tenures of the last two Librarians, both of whom have had the personal confidence of the Congress. Mumford's conservative administration and impeccable professionalism took the annual appropriation from $9,561,000 to $96,696,000, and Boorstin's success in awakening the nation to the Library and in opening the Library to the world (plus cost-of-living adjustments) carried the appropriation to $179,517,000 for fiscal year 1980.

More important than dollars and staff, though, has been Congress's willingness to permit and underwrite significant advances that would have been easy to brush off as too much trouble, not appropriate, or "let's wait and see." Starting with the great acquisitions of the Gutenberg Bible and the Renaissance rarities, the Congress has supported the purchase of treasures and masterworks. It underwrote a massive program of international acquisition and governmental exchange in the 1960s, and it passed the new wide-ranging, vastly innovative Copyright Act in 1976. It allowed the construction of the Adams Library and permitted the Madison Memorial Library to be placed on scarce Capitol Hill land (the act of closing off two whole city blocks for the Madison directly on the squares set aside for congressional office buildings nearly a century ago was the near-equivalent of replacing the Rockefeller Center Skating Rink in New York City with a neighborhood lending library). The current, costly rehabilitation of the 1897 Jefferson Building to its original appearance is further evidence of Congress's genuine affection and respect for the institution. Indeed, speaking of near miracles, the Library has dwelt beside the center of swirling politics for over eighty-three years now, yet there has never been an instance of patronage pressure placed on the Library's personnel office nor of censorship of its holdings. This is a remarkable tribute to the members' respect for professionalism.

Returning to the appropriations process, the House subcommittee is composed of nine members, and the Senate's Legislative Appropriations Subcommittee has five. In recent times, the five senators have tended to be among the most powerful men on Capitol Hill, while the House representatives have usually been first or second termers. However, the latter have more than made up for their lack of seniority by an intense interest in what the Library was doing. The House subcommittee members have brought with them a personal familiarity with new computer applications and with library problems at the state level. There is no telling from year to year which side will turn out to be sympathetic and which critical. Over the long pull, the House side has tended to be more probing and somewhat more distant, treating the Library more as a "stranger" executive agency, which is slightly suspect and not to be trusted too far. The Senate usually approaches the hearings with an "Are you giving us our money's worth?" attitude, but with the assumption that the Library's function is at least that of an accepted congressional support body.

The Librarian's annual appearance before the two groups is always an occasion for a mixture of hope, delight, and despair, and it has produced an endless series of anecdotes. Among our own favorites is one occasioned by a committee chairman's being called to the telephone in the midst of the Librarian's presentation. When the chairman returned, he apologized profusely for the interruption and said, "Now let's see, you were explaining why you wanted the additional eight hundred million." The Librarian corrected him, "Eight hundred *thousand*, sir," and went on with his presentation. The chairman also served on several committees dealing with the executive branch.

The Joint Committee on the Library

The Joint Committee on the Library has long been LC's friend at court. With only an occasional exception, its chairman has taken great pride in the Library's activities and collections and has frequently attended its public events. In this relationship, the Joint Committee and the appropriations committees are analogous to the government bodies traditionally concerned with a public or university library. The Joint Committee is much like a library board or library committee that assists a librarian with his problems and confers with him about how and where he invests his library's resources. The appropriations committees are the counterpart of the mayor or the college president. Eager as they may be to support and expand, they must divide their resources among many competing customers, and they play the part of the no-sayers. It is the Joint Committee on the Library that tends to be the mediator when conflicts arise.

The Joint Committee was established in 1800 at the same time and by the same legislation as the Library of Congress itself. Through the years, it has conveyed Congress's needs to successive Librarians, and it has urged adequate and enlarged support for the Library from fellow members of Congress. The Joint Committee is composed of ten members, all of whom are drawn from the two legislative supervisory committees: the Committee on House Administration and the Senate Committee on Rules and Administration. The chairmen of the two administration committees act as the rotating chairmen of the Joint Committee on the Library. The House chairman serves during the two years of odd-numbered Congresses, and the Senate chairman sits during the even-numbered. The remaining eight members are selected from the two administrative committees, four from each, and equally divided between the two parties. The fact that there are three separate and independent committees but with one made from parts of the other two has an interesting result. Although the Joint Committee on the Library is the parent oversight committee, if there is disagreement between the representatives of the two houses within the Joint Committee, its members can "go home" and with full authority instruct the Library in the role of their *Administration* Committee membership! Any one of the three groups has the authority to send the Library directives or even hold critical hearings or investigations as an independent administrative body.

There are a number of anomalies built into the Joint Committee's relationship to the Library, with the "ill-definition" usually found in British parliamentary practices: The Joint Committee has no authority to consider or report legislation that affects the Library; it has no relationship to the money that is appropriated for the Library; the Librarian is appointed by the President, and confirmation is recommended by the Senate Committee on Rules and Administration. On the other hand, by "custom and tradition," the Joint Committee is deeply involved in the ways the Library spends its money, in the kinds of programs it supports, and in the Library's public image. (And the Joint Committee on the Library does have full legal responsibility for the Botanic Garden and the monuments in the Capitol's Statuary Hall!)

The Administrative Committees

Most legislation relating to the Library (other than appropriations) is sent, not to the Joint Committee on the Library or to the appropriations committees, but to the Committee on House Administration and the Senate Committee on Rules and Administration. Thus, those bodies are in the strongest position to modify the long-term objectives of the Library by changing the Library's statutory charter.

If the plan so often suggested by the nation's librarians—moving the Library of Congress into the Department of Education—were to materialize, it presumably would be first considered by these two committees. Legislation permitting the Center for the Book and the American Folklife Center, as well as action concerning the Library of Congress Trust Fund Board, was handled by the two administration committees.

In addition, on the House side, the all-powerful Rules Committee has had a particular interest in congressional reform. Thus, it was the committee that handled the detailed development of the Legislative Reorganization Act, which had such an effect on the Congressional Research Service.

And Many Others

In addition to the above, there are many congressional committees that are concerned with specific activities of the Library. Thus in a typical year, the Librarian may testify before such committees as the two Judiciary committees (copyright matters), Foreign Relations (UNESCO, ratification of treaties re the exchange of books and documents), Ways and Means (tax deductions for charitable contributions to libraries), Agriculture (foreign book funds obtained under the Public Law 480 program of agricultural exchange), Public Works (expansion of the Library plant), Post Office and Civil Service (postage rates for materials to the blind and physically handicapped and LC staff "supergrades"), Science and Astronautics (Library support for technology assessment), and so on.

Who decides what the Library shall do? Who resolves differences between conflicting aims? All of these committees, individually and in concert. The resulting problem is self-evident.

Congress's Library or the Nation's?

While we are looking at the question of how Congress relates to the Library of Congress, it is appropriate to ask the question, Should the nation's library belong to the Congress at all? Traditionally, the Congress has created programs and funded them, and the executive branch has carried out the services so offered. Obviously, the Library of Congress started as Congress's own library, but the materials it accumulated to serve its own needs became a treasure for the whole nation. Should the treasure be transferred to the executive branch to join the National Gallery of Art, the National Library of Medicine, and the National Zoological Park? The question arises with such remorseless regularity that it should be discussed at this point in our examination of the institution.

Who cares? Oddly enough, many people. Each of the three elite groups who use the Library have at some time in the past twenty years wanted to uproot the status quo. Let's look at the case each of the three has made.

The Scholarly Position

The scholarly world and "the public" have been the most vocal. They resent competing with the governmental world in general, and with Congress in particular, for the books, space, and resources that would give them a Bibliothèque Nationale or a British Museum, or an American National Library. They point to the fact that although the great collections of the Library of Congress are without peer in the Western world, all the administrative fiddlings of the different reading rooms and the refined access rules will be meaningless so long as the "national library" is considered a by-product of Congress's working legislative collection. It is competition with *government* that is causing the trouble, the scholars hold. Competition for acquisitions, space, staff, and service is dragging the great research resource toward mediocrity and aborting its purpose. If LC is to recover its thrust toward scholarly excellence—especially in the broad areas of applied social science and in the role of "keeper of the American heritage"—there must be a change in ownership. Jurisdiction over real estate, staff, and mission must shift.

The scholars usually offer one of two solutions: One, split off the portions of the present Library needed to serve applied government, leave those portions with Congress, and then declare the rest an independent national library in the executive branch. Or, two, call the present library the National Library, give it to the President, and build a more precisely focused congressional library from scratch. With the Congress-only library comes the assumptions that the departmental libraries in the executive would assume responsibility for information support around the Mall and the Supreme Court Library would be expanded to support the courts system. Congress's library would be a strictly legislative operation.

Some years ago, an Australian visitor became frustrated with the competition in LC's reading rooms and wrote a protest that filled five columns in the *Washington Post*, in which the public's solution was crisply stated:

> Is there no body of librarians and legislators who will advocate the radical but real solution: Establishing a National Library, independent of Congress and its demands, along the lines of the flourishing Smithsonian, operating under executive jurisdiction and advised by a council of scholars? . . . Is this country not sufficiently wealthy and sufficiently concerned with the nation's heritage to afford two libraries, as other nations do, one for Congressmen, their aides and other privileged borrowers, and another which functions as repository for the nation's recorded culture, making its collection democratically available to all?

The Australian's proposal—an independent executive agency library—is the solution most often suggested by the public, but proposals occasionally appear in which the national library would become a subunit of the Smithsonian, like the Air and Space Museum or the Kennedy Center, or a subunit of the National Archives and Records Service, like the Franklin D. Roosevelt Library at Hyde Park or the Lyndon B. Johnson Library in Austin. Regardless of which administrative structure is selected, the proponents of this solution insist that independent status would permit the Library to be more flexible and sensitive to the public's needs, would permit it to concentrate on collecting and processing those materials that the scholars require, and would leave the satisfying of the needs of the government and the library world to some other agency.

The Congressional Position

Members of Congress are equally irritable about lack of attention and LC's diversion of purpose. It is their library; they thought it up and have nursed it along through all these years, and simply because they graciously permitted "outsiders" to use its facilities, it now develops that the outsiders want to walk off with it. The whole matter has gotten completely out of hand.

When critics deplore the "dreadful cost" of the legislature, one of the most popular proofs is to divide the Library of Congress's annual appropriation by the number of senators and congressmen and thus charge each member with $300,000 worth of personal library services each year. An offended Congress asks if this is the thanks it gets for broadening the Library's collections for the nation.

Although such arithmetic frequently puts Congress on the defensive and increases the Librarian's difficulties at budget time, Congress's real concern comes from a more serious source: a longtime fear that LC will become so distracted with other obligations that it will fail to fulfill its purpose as a legislative library.

That concern can be demonstrated in a rather bizarre fashion. Librarian Mumford's predecessor was Dr. Luther Evans, a political scientist, scholar, internationalist, and ultimately a distinguished director general of UNESCO. Evans had resigned from LC to take the UNESCO post, and when Mumford was nominated, his first "official" act was to appear before the Senate Committee on Rules and Administration for confirmation hearings. Instead of exploring his professional background, as is somewhat more usual, the committee began by presenting Mumford with a series of rhetorical questions that added up to a catechism of what they expected him to do through the coming years. The questions, albeit of vintage 1954, have a timelessness about them:

1. "What about the public services? Do you think they have been expanded to the detriment of the services rendered the Congress itself? . . . If you found that the Library of Congress was neglecting its primary duty—that for which it was established—that of service to Congress, and was going into other fields to the detriment of Congress, you would be willing to correct that situation?"

2. "Since the primary purpose of the Library is for the use of Congress, just how far should it go in the maintenance of bibliographical materials for the executive branches and agencies? Do not other agencies have their own libraries?"

3. "[Are your] intentions to devote full time and attention to the work of the Library?" [This question stemmed from Congress's earlier distress with MacLeish's public role in general and Evans's interest in international scholarship in particular.]

4. "Would [you] act as a censor?" [The confirmation hearings occurred in the middle of the so-called McCarthy era, and the committee chairman's elaboration on this query made it clear the Librarian was to have books on all sides of every issue. Congress did not want sanitized selections.]
5. "We would like you to discuss the methods which might be put into force which would increase the services to the Congress even at the expense of services to the public. . . . The committee would have your comment on the means that you may have decided upon which would halt and perhaps decrease the ever-growing load of public demands, both locally and nationally, upon the Library's facilities."

The chairman noted parenthetically that in "the present problem of arrearages in the processing of accessions . . . there should be some survey made of what is necessarily obsolete, for junking purposes." He could not understand why Congress kept giving the Library ever more catalogers, who never seemed to catch up, and he summarized by saying, "The Librarian exercises enormous powers and assumes the right to put the Library in the many activities for which there exists no clear authority."

Those questions were asked in the fifties. We can move much closer to our own time and find that in the seventies, the political scientists and the fathers of the congressional reform movement came up with an even more radical device for keeping the Library focused on Congress's needs. The reformers were by then members of the Joint Committee on the Organization of Congress, and they pressed for a solution that would break the Congressional Research Service out of LC as an administrative unit and move it, geographically and administratively, into Congress itself. They analogized the CRS to the administrative mode used for the Architect of the Capitol or to the services of the Joint Committee on Printing. They would have had it overseen by a joint committee, paid from the House or Senate Disbursing Office, housed in the Capitol or one of the congressional office buildings, and given the highest-priority access to LC's collections. High-priority access would have been a temporary arrangement until the CRS accumulated a current, governmentally centered research collection of materials tied directly to national issues. Once such a collection was organized, it was believed that further reliance on LC holdings would drop to a fraction of the total CRS work load.

The outsiders' (noncongressional) solutions to the problem embraced a corollary position. They, too, urged that the CRS be detached and given a smaller, more focused collection with more responsive acquisition and classification procedures, but they based their argument on different analogies. The Council of State Governments had surveyed the history and effectiveness of the state legislative reference services and found that an overwhelming majority had started as adjuncts of the state libraries but had been forced to become independent because of the incompatibility of the two missions. The state library was dedicated to long-term, archival, historical collections of the state's history and traditions, and the legislative reference service was organized for the day-to-day pursuit of state and local issues requiring immediate response. Various specialists in comparative government pointed to the Canadian and Australian divorcements of their legislative reference services from their national libraries and underlined the traditions of independence and self-sufficiency in the House of Commons Library and the parliamentary libraries in Bonn, Tokyo, and Stockholm. (The solution proposed by the Australian scholar quoted above referred to the result of an unfortunate experience that the Australian parliamentary service had had while functioning as a part of the National Library, which had led to a successful separation of the two.)

The Position of the Library Profession

The library world proposes an equally self-evident solution—but a different one, of course. For years, librarians have been urging that the Library of Congress be put into the Department of Education and be run in the same way that Howard University and Gallaudet College are overseen by that agency. In the days of the great HEW grants for higher education, library matching funds, and the original $6 million annual grants for LC's National Program for Acquisitions and Cataloging (it was originally funded by the Office of Education), the HEW affiliation was appealing. However, as grant money has dropped away and the future of the Department of Education has become clouded, many library groups have swung toward the idea of a separate executive unit similar to the Smithsonian. In that position, the Library's fortunes would not be so tied to generalized feelings for or against education, and it would eliminate the bureaucratic competition and infighting found among many subunits competing for a limited amount of departmental funds.

One library group was represented by the Bryant Memorandum, a formal recommendation for a de jure national library, vintage 1962. Douglas W. Bryant was associate director of the Harvard University Library, and he headed a study that was sponsored by Senator Claiborne Pell of the Joint Committee on the Library. Bryant and his supporters maintained that although they preferred an independent library in the executive branch, they would tolerate a legislative location if effective control could lie in a national library advisory board. The board would include "leaders in research, scholar-administrators such as university presidents and deans, librarians of major research libraries, members of the Congress, and other distinguished citizens." The Bryant recommendation included a formal description of what was to be sought in new Librarians:

> The Librarian of Congress must be a man who can administer an extremely diversified and organically complex institution; in addition, he must make important decisions on technological innovations in bibliography profoundly affecting the access of scholars to information, supervise the building up of enormous research collections, exercise imaginative leadership nationally, and take advantage of the Library's unique opportunities for contributing to American cultural life.

(There was talk at the time that if future Librarians could be found to fit those specifications, after a respectable term in office they might be considered for the presidency of the United States.)

As a rule, what the library world really wants is not so much a great national storehouse as a central library that would act as the hub of a national library wheel or (different image) a powerhouse at the center of a voltage grid. Properly named the National Library, this central library could more effectively achieve uniformity of cataloging, more appropriately develop shared computer ties, and more efficiently eliminate acquisition duplication. It could concentrate on serving the national library community full time rather than trying to keep Congress and the visiting scholars happy at the front door, while surreptitiously serving the librarians at the back door. Again, international models are cited. Britain, Canada, and Sweden all have highly centralized library systems, which process materials more cheaply than we do, flash loans back and forth more efficiently, provide better service to the constituent units, and reduce duplication everywhere.

The three insurgent positions could be enlarged on and various authorities quoted, but the essential positions are clear. Indeed, they all sound quite logical and appealing: better division of labor, better focusing of energies and resources, more responsive service. What possible case could be made for the status quo?

The Other Side

The opposition, consisting of equally distinguished scholars and analysts, says the above solutions are meretricious. The Hoover Commissions on federal reorganization studied the problem and recommended leaving everything just as it was. A growing body of public and library administrators conclude that in spite of minor tensions, the present mix of a governmental/national library tied to Congress is the best of this possible world. To embrace any of the radical moves could result in throwing the baby out with the bathwater. These advocates work from the following premises.

Funding

The reformers have always believed that the Library of Congress would have access to larger sums of money with less stress if it were a part of the executive branch. They point to the fact that although it is difficult to get an agency established, once in being, it will run indefinitely and Congress will tend to fund it adequately to accomplish its purpose. They hold that if the national library were established as a national treasure, just as in the case of our great museums and cultural monuments, Congress would see to it that it could serve its audiences as required. Furthermore, they contend that when the appropriations committees deal with the executive agencies, they distribute moneys by the hundreds of millions, leaving it up to the agencies to use them effectively. They believe that since LC is immediately under Congress's eye, it tends to be nickled and dimed into mediocrity.

The conservators maintain that that theory is quite at variance with the facts. They hold that year in and year out, Congress has done marvelously well by the Library. Although some institutions like the Smithsonian and the national parks are frequently in favor, in just as many instances they are ignored for years at a time. Furthermore, being a part of the executive branch would subject the Library to all the fluctuations of presidential freezes, grade reductions, and denials of budget increases to which all administrative agencies are subject.

The conservators maintain that over the long pull, the Library has consistently been the darling of the Congress, that the legislature has always had a paternal feeling for its library, and that many congressional leaders have taken great pride in the fact that in this democracy, the people's representatives have been the patrons of the cultural heritage.

(This argument brings out some of LC's most intriguing stories—for example, the one about the time that Putnam asked Congress for $1.5 million to buy ten cases of incunabula, which included the Gutenberg Bible. No one was more surprised than Putnam when the money was appropriated with scarcely a demur. On the way back to the Library, still shaking his head in amazement, Putnam met an arch-conservative congressman from an agrarian district who had voted in favor of the money. Putnam thanked him and then asked timidly, "Why?" He was told: "Mr. Putnam, we are a young country. We have no monuments. If we know where they are and can be got we ought to get 'em.")

Two Librarians of Congress—L. Quincy Mumford and Archibald MacLeish—stand on ·the third-floor balcony of the Jefferson Building in 1956, overlooking the Capitol dome to the west.

The conservators' point has been that with rare exceptions, Congress has supported its own Library. If Congress would be equally sympathetic to "just another federal agency" could well be a dangerous "if" to test.

Leadership and Efficiency

Those people who have embraced the conservative side of the argument maintain that many of the words used by the library profession to describe its stand sound very well but the ideas they express simply would not work. They believe that the repeated cry that LC should "lead" or be the "center of a great library system" ignores the very delicate balance that presently exists between LC and the nation's libraries—a balance that if replaced by statutory leadership would quickly move toward "government interference." Now LC and the library world get along reasonably well because each needs the other and each has to be civil to achieve its own purposes. If the arrangement became de jure, the natural corrosion of even the best bureaucracy would begin to erode the common aims. Strong leadership and an aggressive national board would soon lead to firmer demands for uniformity for efficiency's sake. Once the official manner of operation was established for the good of all, demands for "better communication" would follow. Better communication would lead to a growing stream of memorandums, bulletins, official programs, orders, and then firm dicta with sanctions against the constituent who failed to play the what's-best-for-everybody game. The conservators would have us believe that it is almost impossible to think of a more independent, heterogeneous group than the nation's libraries, which reflect different audiences, incredibly diverse sources of funds and resources, and various purposes, traditions, and means of responding to their immediate clienteles. They believe that strong leadership at the center of a great system would shatter this fragile system and soon bring on either open warfare or withdrawal—or, most likely, domination by the largest elements in the system.

The conservators challenge the idea of efficiency on many levels. They question it in macrocosm under the above charge. They question it within the Library itself or with Congress under a different rationale. The idea of separate elements—a congressional library, a scholar's library, or a governmental library—being able to serve their special audiences better is equally unreal, they say. One librarian compares the present missions of LC to the Ballantine Ale trademark of interlocking rings. He claims that the three rings symbolize the congressional/scholarly/library-world programs and audiences but that the overlapping center is the processing aspect. He believes that LC has developed the fastest, cheapest, and most comprehensive processing techniques of any unit in the library world. He claims that because of LC's multifaceted acquisition systems, it can serve any constituency better than that constituency could serve itself. Although any library could handle the

"easy ones," the marginal, ephemeral, fugitive materials can be found
and processed more quickly by a large, centralized processing unit than
by fragmented, specialized ones. Thus, he says, any detachments or
splits off the present whole would weaken the then independent parts.

The CRS Should Be Closer to Congress

The conservators believe that the idea of getting the CRS closer to
the congressional establishment and right into congressional halls is a
two-edged sword that would cut into the very area that the reformers
want to secure: more independent, unpressured analysis. They note
that since the CRS is housed in its present gray temple—psychologically
detached from the cut and thrust of politics while physically connected
to the intellectual, Olympian Library of Congress—it can examine volatile
issues with minimal fear of partisan reprisal. It involves itself in
congressional committee activities and the legislative process by going
to that audience daily or weekly and then symbolically withdrawing
to do its analysis. If CRS were placed in the very halls of Congress,
it would find itself caught between the pressures of patronage and
direction by strong chairmen or by the leadership itself. Its involvement
in and evaluation of day-to-day issues, all of which matter deeply to
someone, would make it a sitting target for the defeated, who would
blame the CRS for their loss and retaliate. Moving into the partisan
area in order to be more receptive to needs might well cost the CRS
its image of a detached, objective, uninvolved source of accurate, honest
data.

And the Intangibles

The conservators underscore the dangers of tampering with a good
thing. They claim there are an unknown number of delicate balances
in the present arrangement, which were probably achieved by accident,
and it would be shocking if our generation were the one to destroy
them.

The conservators point to the almost miraculous sequence of able,
honest men who have been Librarians of Congress for the past 100
years. The conservators wonder how much of this is luck and how
much reflects the pressures of the multiple elites and the demands
placed on the job, all of which act as a process of natural selection.
Specifically, if the Library of Congress were solely a governmental or
legislative library, would the Librarianship have been a routine
plum with which to reward partisan supporters or an easy place to put
the current éminence grise? If LC were solely a national library, would
the office have become a battleground for representatives of the great

research libraries, the public libraries, the school libraries, or possibly even the publishing world?

How much of the Library's preeminence in the intellectual world stems from the unusual crossing of presidential selection, congressional funding and oversight, and scholarly, professional standards and demands for excellence? If the institution the nation seems to have muddled into were broken up or relocated to increase efficiency and response, might we reduce it to being "just another government agency" and destroy the tensions that were in fact the very source of its energies and drives to excellence?

The conservators want to be certain that some drastic administrative changes do not derive from resentment against a temporary incumbent, from the personality of someone seeking professional attention, from a search for better things simply for the sake of the search, or from the reflection of a passing administrative fad that revisionists will loudly challenge when the next generation of graduate students comes along.

Query

So where do we come out in this quite fundamental argument? We have tried to reflect the mixture of emotion and substance in the conflict, and we hope we have also reflected the dangers of a casual decision. There was a time when the argument could be passed off with a simple, "Ah, it's academic anyway. Congress would never give up the Library no matter what anyone says." That assumption may no longer be true. To the continued astonishment of longtime Capitol Hill watchers, Congress seems to be increasingly short-tempered with obligations that are mixed blessings on the way to becoming more trouble than they are worth.

Who would have believed that the legislature would write off the entire postal service with its limitless opportunities for rewards of political support? But all the postmasters, all the rural routes, all the new post offices are now selected and set by nameless civil servants in a barely governmental operation. Equally astonishing is the fact that Congress would give away its two-centuries-old control over government salaries. The dreadful impact these sums have on budget balances plus the splendid opportunities to court gratitude in election years would seem to have kept this high on Congress's priority list. But Congress has now passed the job over to the President and all but washed its hands of the whole subject.

So Congress's relations with the Library cannot be taken for granted. At the present time, satisfaction with the incumbent Librarian is high, the CRS is well received, and the oversight committees are filled with members who sympathize with the Library's purposes. But if any of those elements change, the situation could reverse very quickly. Care must be taken to ensure that Congress continues to receive benefits and that accumulated aggravations do not find the Library unloaded in a fit of pique. It is a serious matter.

13

THE LIBRARY OF CONGRESS AND THE LIBRARY WORLD: CARDS AND THE NATIONAL BIBLIOGRAPHY

We have found that the relationship between the primary elite, Congress, and the Library of Congress is a complicated one with threads running in many directions. How about the second elite—the library world? Here there is no confusion about what is wanted. As Samuel Gompers said about labor's aims, what the librarians want is "more!"

The "more" relates to three areas of great importance to the librarians: cataloging; their grip on the world's publishing ("bibliographic control," they call it); and innovative technological leadership (automation, preservation, uniform technical standards). When generalized, these areas of interrerst sound dull. In reality and in detail, they relate to some remarkable activities involving tens of thousands of professional librarians and tens of millions of dollars every year.

The Printed Catalog Card

Let's start with cataloging. This whole area of LC activity began with the simple, printed Library of Congress (LC) card. It was the first benefit the profession wanted from its "national library," and it has proved to be not only the most popular service the Library has ever rendered the profession, but the foundation on which a dozen other services have been built.

For twenty-five years before Herbert Putnam took over the Library in 1899, the nation's librarians had been pleading for a single source of cataloging so every library in a thousand different institutions need not process the identical same books, each performing precisely the

A statue of James Madison, sculpted by Walter K. Hancock, dominates the Madison Memorial Hall.

same exercise as its neighbor and nine times out of ten coming up with the identical answer. Solution: Let the largest library do the work. Let everybody buy copies of the largest library's cards and spend the money they saved (by employing fewer catalogers) on purchasing more books. Putnam was one of the most ardent of the recommenders, so it was appropriate that when he became Librarian of Congress he should start the card service at once, an act that he justified in four ways.

First Premise. The service would cut down on duplication of effort. In this respect, Putnam was right, and the concept was embraced by the library world beyond his wildest dreams. In 1902, there were 212 subscribers with cash sales of $3,785. By 1968, there were 25,000 subscribers, who bought in that one year alone 79 million cards for $7 million. For the benefit of the statistically minded, 79 million cards would produce a single deck of cards fifteen miles high. One year's sales! Of these subscribers, 2,500 were foreign libraries, many of whom not only bought LC cards for their American books but used them for books that had been printed in their own countries.

Second Premise. Since LC was going to have to make the cards for itself anyway, running some extras for sale would be next to automatic and have little impact on the Library. Mr. Putnam was wrong on this one. From the very beginning, the card service has been operated primarily for "outside" subscribers and through the years has actually told LC what to put on its cards and even what books to keep in order to get cards made. (Until fairly recently, the choice of which congressional documents were to be retained and bound was based on which titles were most likely to generate the most card orders!) Modern librarians will identify with Mr. Putnam's November 30, 1901, circular to his brand new subscribers. In it, he explained why the cards they had ordered were so late in coming, but he assured them that a number of useful new things would soon be added to the cards for the subscribers' benefit.

LC has been adding elements to the cards ever since, elements that are of little use to the Library of Congress itself. At the present time, an LC card carries: the Dewey Decimal number for the benefit of libraries not using the LC classification system; children's subject headings for special juvenile collections; audiovisual information to serve public libraries with collections of film strips, educational motion pictures, and phonograph recordings; the Superintendent of Documents classification number for depository and other libraries filing by those numbers; and the International Standard Book Number for institutions using that bibliographic device.

Although those elements are of limited use to readers working in the Library of Congress itself, many other improvements incorporated at the library profession's request have been of vast benefit to LC readers as well. The cards began with only the author, title, publisher, and date on them. The following year, the Library added some "collation"—description of pages, plates, maps, and multiple parts. In the 1920s, uniform subject headings were included, each one prepared in accordance with the American Library Association's cataloging rules. In the 1940s, more detailed biographical information was added, plus more descriptive notes. In the 1960s, the contents of the cards were put on computer tapes, and the tapes were made available to subscribing libraries. In the 1970s, the card service began to carry the cards of Canada, Japan, Germany, and the United Kingdom, which are prepared by the national bibliographers of those countries.

Third Premise. LC would get all of the books that smaller libraries would want cards for, so it would automatically have a card for every book any library would want. Mr. Putnam was wrong on this one too. By the mid-1960s, the presses of the United States had become so fertile that LC was cataloging barely half the books kept by all the "smaller libraries." Further, the huge research libraries had taken to buying so much abroad that they could find LC cards for barely half of the foreign books that they were purchasing but that LC was not. (In 1965, for example, LC created some 100,000 cards for books on the way to its own shelves, but in the same period, the card subscribers were acquiring over 200,000 *more* titles that LC did not have, had no intention of getting, and for which LC had therefore prepared no cards to sell. The outside libraries had to catalog these books themselves.)

Fourth Premise. Mr. Putnam's final justification was, in his own words, "to place in each center of research as complete as possible a statement of the contents of the national collections in Washington." His hopes here have been dramatically fulfilled. In his lifetime, it was done by passing out depository sets of every card printed. In the 1950s, enormous book catalogs were produced of every LC card arranged by author and by subject, and over 2,500 libraries acquired these complete indexes to the LC collections for their own reference room shelves. And with the shift to digital tapes in the 1970s, the contents of LC became a part of the six great computer utilities distributed around the nation.

But Now the Bad News

Unfortunately, those accomplishments are the good news. By the mid-1960s, the LC card program had become so all-pervasive that in libraries from the Japanese Diet to the Vatican, one could pull out a card tray and find that all the cards looked exactly the same, for the printed LC card was purchased and used everywhere. (The late Verner Clapp used to say the LC card was a triumph of international stand-ardization. Precisely 75 by 125 mm, not only were the cards ubiquitous but they made catalog drawers and library furniture, the very symbols of librarianship, uniform on five continents!)

But if you look at the statistics for the card sales, they show a startling trend:

1971	74,474,002	1976	39,821,876
1972	72,002,908	1977	30,799,708
1973	73,599,751	1978	23,318,278
1974	58,379,911	1979	22,555,290
1975	44,860,670	1980	19,536,019

Although in any normal setting, sales of 19 million anything is not to be treated casually, it is still a far cry from the nearly 80 million cards sold not too many years before. What happened? The story involves the following elements.

How it Worked. For nearly sixty years, the sequence ran thus: A library received a book. It took an order slip, noted the author and title on it, and sent it to the Library of Congress, requesting a "set" of cards for its catalogs. The Library of Congress went to its warehouse where millions of cards were stored in chronological order, and eight cards were drawn, packaged, and sent back to the requesting library. The eight cards for each title represented a standard set, which normally would be used to make a shelflist inventory card, an author card, a title card, a card for each of the subjects and "added entries," and a few cards for branch library or bookmobile records as well. The requesting library was charged around twenty-five cents per set on a frequently changing rate schedule because the original 1902 statute required Putnam to charge "a price which will cover their cost and ten per centum added." All proceeds went directly to the Treasury.

The plan worked very well for a long time. Various devices were invented to speed up the turnaround between the receipt of a book in a local library and the time when it could be put on a shelf, fully cataloged, with the call number and all the cards in place. Soon each book was given a discrete LC book number, and the requesting library did not need to fill out the author and title data but could simply request the cards by book number. Publishers began to publish the number on the back of the title page of their newly issued volumes or on the jackets of their recordings. *Publishers Weekly* began to publish the numbers before the books were actually printed so libraries could preorder the cards and have them waiting when the books themselves actually arrived.

Then the Library got smug, arrogant, and distracted. During the great foreign acquisition programs of the 1960s, the numbers of books coming into the Library flooded the system, and a simple U.S. best-seller got caught in a stream of thousands of East European provincial reports. The Library took longer and longer to catalog books published in the United States, it took longer to print the resultant cards, and (since the total cost of making the cards had to be divided by the total number of cards created) the cost of the set for the U.S. best-seller began to climb to pay for the cards for works such as a Bulgarian highway department report (for which there was less demand). The lag in response time grew to be so great that it became profitable for private publishing firms to print and distribute cards for U.S. commercial titles more cheaply and much faster than LC. U.S. public libraries turned to the private services in droves. In no time at all, over 75 percent of the cards purchased in the United States were bought from private sellers who used LC copy! Those problems were only the beginning. The Library was by now so embarrassed over the delays (and so overwhelmed with tens of thousands of cards pouring out of the system each month) that it acceded to a longtime request by the library profession and agreed to what became known as the Cataloging in Publication (CIP) program.

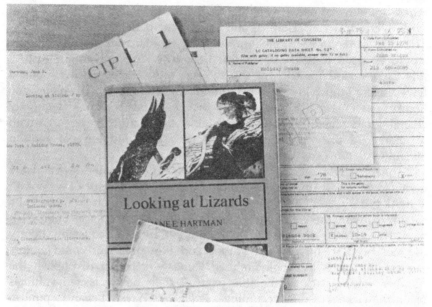

Through the Cataloging in Publication (CIP) program, which is a cooperative effort by the Library and more than 2,000 American publishers, cataloging data is prepared for books from publishers' galleys prior to publication.

CIP was an obvious service to the users of LC bibliographic data, but it did the Library itself no good at all. The way it worked was that publishers would send galley proofs of forthcoming books to the Library, and while the author was making final corrections, the Library would use the proofs to catalog the book. LC would then tell the publisher (within ten days of receipt of the galleys) what the card for that book would look like when it was cataloged as a published, bound book. The publisher would then print this information on the copyright page, so when a local library bought a copy of the book, it could simply look on the verso page and either copy the data or, in some instances, actually machine copy the miniature card. CIP began in 1971, and by 1980, 180,000 U.S. books carried CIP data. Currently, 71 percent of all books published in the United States have "cataloging in publication" data in them when they appear (needless to say, this book does too, as do all Westview publications).

The Cataloging in Publication program eliminated the need for buying catalog cards for bookstore kinds of books, but the cards represented less than 5 percent of what was being added to the Library of Congress and the great research libraries around the world. The difference was quickly covered by the computer.

In the late sixties, the Library of Congress began putting all its roman-letter cataloging (all English language materials and everything from Western Europe and South America) onto computer tapes. The Ohio College Library Center (later Online Computer Library Center or OCLC) computer network developed programs by which any library belonging to its system could bring up an entry on a CRT terminal, check to see if it matched the book the cataloger had in hand, and if it did, could order printed cards designed to match that library's catalogs— even to having the symbols of a particular campus's libraries in place. The idea worked so well that as the other computer networks were created, variations on the theme were developed, and another 20 million to 30 million LC card orders disappeared!

In fact, as this book is being written, the slope on the graph is all too clear. The only libraries that really need the vaunted LC card order system are either the very small libraries—such as private law libraries, scientific corporation libraries, trade associations—or the very large libraries that have large collections of nonroman holdings (Chinese, Japanese, Hebraic, Arabic, Indonesian). Although some institutions are solving the latter problem by transliterating the titles of those holdings, those who wish the data in the original script now order cards from LC, where the cards are printed one at a time using high-speed laser printers. That device is awesome to watch, because the original card images (matching the ones in the reading rooms of the Library) are held on optical digital disks. When needed, Cataloging Distribution Service (CDS) personnel simply punch in the LC card number on a computer switchboard, and the minicomputer finds the image on the optical disk, prints eight cards with breathtaking speed and precision, packages them automatically, and bills the account in a single instant. The millions of stored cards have all been trucked away and sold for 100 percent rag pulp.

Philosophically, the life story of the card service could produce endless homilies. The service was originally offered (sold?) to the library profession; the product was accepted beyond the inventor's wildest dreams; preoccupation set in, and the users' needs were increasingly ignored and ultimately forgotten. By the time the Library realized what was happening, it was too late. On the one hand, it can be said that "private initiative and enterprise" is filling the need and therefore government shouldn't have been providing the service in the first place. On the other hand—an entirely different aspect—what happened to the card service can be used as a model of what can happen to any part of a library's activities, even something so different as the use of the books a library holds.

The Library as Wholesaler

But important point: The content of those disappearing cards is just as vital and just as popular as ever, and the intellectual world still relies on the Library of Congress to provide the standardized cataloging of each volume. The only difference is that libraries get the information off a page provided by a publisher or off a tape made available by a network; the publisher or the network gets the data from LC. The *information* is still the same Library of Congress processing product it was in 1901 (with embellishments).

But the library world complains about two aspects of LC support in cataloging the world's publishing. The great research libraries are reasonably happy with the quarter million titles LC catalogs each year, but the public libraries and the special libraries are not. The public libraries say that LC's elitism (snobbishness?) ignores a great many of the materials kept in even small public libraries, much less those in major metropolitan centers. LC itself generally does not keep (and therefore does not catalog) paperbacks, even though an ever-growing proportion of U.S. publishing appears only in paperback form. LC also does not catalog reports of industries, frequently the local payroll source in a community. The Library does not pursue local historical materials or books and government reports about the communities the public libraries serve, nor does it seek out material concerning the product technology or the local agricultural crops and skills the libraries' patrons expect their libraries to provide.

The special libraries also complain. Industrial libraries, commercial libraries, and advertising, insurance, and trade associations live on offset and xerography reports, doctoral dissertations, microfiche services, and scientific series. LC keeps very few of those materials and therefore simply does not prepare catalog cards on much of what the specialized libraries keep and want. The overseas acquisitions that delight college research libraries are viewed as useless distractions by the public and private libraries.

The divergent views of the research versus the public versus the special libraries bring to mind similar arguments over how LC should catalog its materials. Both the large *and* the small institutions object to the Library's subject headings. A substantial number of those institutions claim that LC's tens of thousands of terms have simply grown through the years and that it is time to do a complete reexamination and restatement of them. And while the Library is at it, these institutions suggest that LC ought to eliminate the sexist terms it has carried along since Victorian days and delete some of the traditional headings from past generations that are now recognized as racist and culturally inappropriate. For instance, the Ukrainian community wants the Ukraine to be recognized as a separate nation and insists that Ukrainian materials should be segregated from the Soviet headings.

Superimposed on these problems are the impassioned pleas from the small, underfunded libraries that the Library of Congress is constantly changing and generally "messing with" its subject heading list, and that this inconstancy is frightfully expensive for small libraries, which must seek out each changed catalog card, erase, retype, shift *see* and *see-also* tracings, and in general, look backward to earlier acquisitions when they ought to be working with newly arrived materials for which patrons are impatiently waiting. The change of a single subject heading can require the reprocessing of hundreds of cards, even in small library systems.

Hanging over the whole debate is the traditional demand of the research libraries for more subject headings for every book, so there are more retrieval points, versus the distress of the public libraries that say LC is loading their catalogs with such complexities that the public can't use them, the libraries can't afford the furniture and space required to house the cards, and the libraries can't pay the staff needed to file the cards. Although all the participants in all the arguments are very properly convinced of the righteousness of their position, LC's attempts to find a single path that will do the most good (or the least harm) is not easy.

Totality and the American National Bibliography

You recall that Mr. Putnam's final justification for a card service was "to place in each center of research as complete as possible a statement of the contents of the national collections in Washington." Putnam intended to accomplish this aim by sending complete sets of every LC card to the major research libraries around the country. This was actually done for forty years, until the libraries became so buried in proof slips they found they were devoting more staff time and floor space to preserving the record than their clients' use could ever justify. So, the Association of Research Libraries attacked the problem and convinced the private publishing firm of Edwards Brothers in Ann Arbor, Michigan, to make pages of LC cards laid top to bottom, shrink their size so that thirty could fit on a page approximately the size of a page of the *Encyclopaedia Britannica*, and sell the resultant set as a profit-making venture. LC organized and provided the cards free, and the first two printings were enormously successful. They contained only author entries and covered the years from August 1898 through December

1947. Tiny as the miniature entries were, it required 229 huge volumes to print the original series.

The success of this approach—space-saving book catalogs—was so convincing to the scholarly and bibliographic world that a whole series of these catalogs is now published regularly. Without taking time to described how each index came to be (or what particular scholarly group pressed for its creation), we note in passing that a research library can now buy the following: *Music, Books on Music, and Sound Recordings* (the cumulated catalog of all these, issued twice a year); *National Union Catalog of Manuscript Collections* (the contents of some 2,000 different collections housed throughout the United States); *New Serial Titles* (the serial holdings of more than 800 libraries in the United States and Canada); and the towering *National Union Catalog* itself.

The National Union Catalog

The *National Union Catalog (NUC)* is essentially the great, total index to the world's publishing that Putnam and the Association of Research Libraries dreamed about, and many people believe it to be the most valuable service the Library renders the scholarly and library world. It is an enormous author index to practically every book printed anywhere! It contains column after column of LC cards, each reduced to half size. Each year's catalog lists the quarter of a million titles that LC adds to its collection annually—but that is literally only half of the venture. Eighteen of the nation's major libraries—2 from each geographic/ bibliographic area (Cornell, UCLA, University of Texas, University of Chicago, and so on)—report to LC essentially everything they add to their own shelves. In addition, 1,100 more U.S. and Canadian libraries report their unusual volumes, most of their foreign-language works, and essentially all of their local publishing. When these hundreds of thousands of cards come in, the outside "locations" are added to the LC cards. If LC does not have the volume, a special card is made up and filed into the proper alphabetic place with the symbol of the reporting library on it. The result is that there are another 250,000-plus titles included beyond those for which LC creates cards. This bibliographic tour de force comes very close to organizing the monographic publishing of the world. It sells for $1,275 a year, runs to some fifteen volumes annually, and is bought by 2,440 libraries in the United States and abroad. Its impact on scholarship and librarianship can scarcely be overstated.

More Trouble

But, regrettably, the best days of the *National Union Catalog* are behind it as it has been overtaken, like so many other aspects of traditional librarianship, by the computer. Libraries use the great union catalogs for three things: (1) to find out what books exist; (2) to find out where copies of these books are located, so they may be borrowed by interlibrary loan; and (3) (if they have acquired the volume for their own collections) to catalog them quickly and accurately so they can be made available for library patrons with the proper call numbers, subject headings, and consistent "authorized" author descriptions appropriate for their local catalogs. Unfortunately, all of these things can be done better and faster by computer tape and distribution through the library utilities than by very slow, very expensive book production. The days of the printed NUC are certainly numbered, and its replacement by on-line CRTs or videodiscs or computer tapes is inevitable—and within very few years. The data the NUC contains will continue to be produced, but it will come from many sources, and it will be stored and retrieved in dramatically different ways.

14

THE LIBRARY OF CONGRESS AND THE LIBRARY WORLD: COMPUTERS

It seems no matter what door we open in our story, it reveals a situation either changed or changing because of and affected or dominated by the computer. It is time to describe the growth of the computer in the Library of Congress. LC's experience with the computer so closely parallels that of most U.S. libraries, it might well serve as the stock plot for the drama. Its computerized synopsis could well read: LC avoided computerization as long as possible, was intimidated into exploration, suddenly realized the potential, became fascinated and wildly hopeful, received the icy shock of reality, and is now grimly trying to make it work among those day-to-day procedures for which it seems to be genuinely appropriate. The automation of LC has taken longer and cost more than even its worst enemy ever predicted, but it is finally in place and doing *most* of what was promised, reasonably reliably.

In a nutshell, the story runs thus: In 1961, using money from the Council on Library Resources, the Library hired an outside computer group to do a feasibility study to see if LC's operations were appropriate for automation. In 1963, to no one's surprise, the report said they were. The report concluded that the process would be reasonably simple in terms of procedures but something of a problem because of size. However, since each item (the equivalent of a catalog card) was a tiny, finite block, each could be loaded into the computer and then controlled, added to, and recalled without trouble. The study pictured a system in which one of these tiny binary "documents" would be created when a book was ordered, expanded as it was cataloged, annotated as the book was charged in and out or sent for rebinding, and in general,

Storage racks hold the "MARC tapes" that carry over a thousand bibliographic records each week to some sixty major networks and computer facilities.

manipulated so as to reflect everything that happened to the book during its lifetime in a library.

The survey (done by a team under Gilbert W. King and therefore referred to as the King report) pictured LC's great reading room cleared of bulky card catalog cases, and in their place, dozens of desk-sized computer terminals at which readers would sit and ask questions. What is the call number for such and such a book? Answer appears on the terminal's television tube: Z 733 W38. How many books do you have on thus and such a subject? Answer: 150. Let me see those written in English, printed after 1950, that contain a bibliography. The tube shows a catalog card for each, one at a time, at the reader's command, and if the reader wants to retain the citation, he presses a button and a copy of the card slides out the side of the machine for him to take with him. The King report recommended a timetable that would bring all these magical visions to reality by 1972.

The system would clearly permit great flexibility and economy for the Library of Congress, but it would have an even greater impact on American librarianship in general. The computer would hold in its memory not only the equivalent of the LC catalog but the entire National Union Catalog as well, so the computer would indeed have a record of almost every item held in every library anywhere in North America. Thus, a library in Phoenix or Bangor would only have to tell LC to add its symbol to the LC "card" for every book it got, and Phoenix and Bangor could throw away their catalogs, too. An Arizonian would ask the Phoenix computer terminal, What books do you have on thus and such, written in English, printed after 1950, with the symbol for the Phoenix Public Library on it? and the machine would work as well in Phoenix as in Washington, D.C. The cost of a rented telephone line would be appreciably less than all the catalogers' salaries that could be eliminated. Assured by the computer specialists that the system was feasible, LC went to work.

Work began with the building of the tiny block that represented a catalog card in the computer's memory. Recognizing that if the King report were right, this block or document would someday be the basis for a worldwide bibliographic network, the Library designed it in close cooperation with all the major library groups. Months of meetings involving representatives of the American Library Association, the Special Libraries Association, the Association of Research Libraries, the Committee on Scientific and Technical Information, the British National Bibliography, the International Atomic Energy Agency, the National Library of Medicine, and the National Agricultural Library produced a "format" known as MARC (pronounced "mark" and standing for MAchine-Readable Cataloging).

With MARC established, LC began producing computer tapes containing all the English-language books cataloged by LC and made these tapes available to sixteen carefully chosen libraries, which represented several different types. With the tapes went computer programs that would print out such basic products as individual cards or book catalogs. Once the pilot program was shaken down, a refined MARC II was produced, and it is now the basic format at LC. Tapes are made available to any library, and in 1980, there were sixty-eight institutional subscribers, each buying a weekly 300-foot reel containing some 1,000 new records.

So far so good. But from this point on, almost nothing worked out as the computer industry had predicted. Through the 1960s, literally dozens of computer hardware and software manufacturers visited the Library to get a piece of the action in the hope that being in on the automating of the national library would open all other libraries to their product—only to withdraw, shaken by the immensity of what they found. (A team from the second-largest software house in the country told the authors with only half-humorous hyperbole, "We just checked out the central charge file operation; just the electricity it would take to drive the disks for that thing would cost more than the six people you've got doing it by hand!")

The original estimates had concentrated too heavily on how a reader would get information *out* of the computer and too little on what it was going to take to get the information in. They had failed to anticipate the multiplicity of printed characters that would be necessary, not to mention the fact that rather than being a finite size like a bank check, the "document" could run to many hundreds of characters, and thus there could be no uniform lengths or localities established in the finding programs for retrieval. The complex relationships between order files, charge files, accession files, shelflist files, subject files, language files, and scores of others proved far more complex than originally expected. Similarly the whole catalog had to be kept on-line all the time. There was no way any part could be mounted on certain days of the week or that any portion of the cards could be brought up in response to controlled demands. All 18 million cards had to be ready to be searched at any time.

The result was that by the end of the 1960s, the Library had all but dispensed with the services of the contract firms, who time and again failed to understand how the data were actually created or manipulated, and in their place built an in-house Automated Systems Office of approximately 300 people. The staff is a mixture of librarians who have been trained as computer specialists and computer technicians whom the Library has trained as librarians.

The new system is working very well. The idea of a great computerized system of bibliographic cradle-to-grave information has been pushed back on the shelf, and LC is now automating specific chunks, one procedure or product at a time. Let's examine some of them.

Locked Rooms with Computer Keys

We should remember that the activity we are watching here is slightly different than that of a typical local library. Generally, a library stores vast quantities of knowledge without trying to guess how it will be used, but in most of the applications we will note below, blocks of knowledge have been identified and put aside for intensive manipulation by a specific audience for a recognized purpose. A valid metaphor might easily be a long corridor with rooms on either side. Each room is filled with different kinds of facts, and not only has the Library of Congress devised different keys to get into each room, but within each room, it has devised a single "skeleton key" to get into the files, cabinets, and closets within that room—but only that room. Twenty-five years of experience have proved that instead of designing a master key that would make the entire 80 million pieces accessible, it is better to make different keys to do different things. The rooms and the keys are as follows.

SCORPIO

The first room is filled with legislative data. It was designed first to help the Congressional Research Service answer requests from the Congress and then was expanded so that the legislators and their staffs could go in as well. The computer key or retrieval program is called SCORPIO, and with a single set of retrieval terms, a user can go into the following files:

> The legislative record: the user can retrieve congressional activity for many Congresses by bill number, date, the introducing congressman's or senator's name, public law number, or the general subject of the legislation
> CRS Issue Briefs: the complete text of the hundreds of Issue Briefs, retrievable by subject, title, and number
> Bibliographic citations on legislative topics: magazine articles, documents, and reports found throughout the Library (in excess of 1,000 a month) on congressional topics; retrievable by author, subject, and title
> General Accounting Office program evaluations: the GAO analyses of ongoing government programs retrievable by agency, program name, and subject
> General Accounting Office "recurring reports required by Congress": retrievable by agency, mandating legislation, subject, and title
> National Referral Center Master File: a file of 13,000 organizations of "who knows what" in the United States, retrievable by name, subject, and location
> LCCC: the Library of Congress computerized catalog of books in English and Western languages published since 1969; the equivalent of going to the card catalog and seeing if the Library of Congress has a book by a particular author or about a particular subject; retrievable by author, title, or subject

All of the above files are continuously on-line and updated daily.

MUMS

SCORPIO was designed as a retrieval program, a simple computer language that nonspecialized users can learn quickly so they can get text data up on the screen with ease. MUMS, a different room and a different key, was designed so Processing Services could build data, quickly, on-line. It too contains the complete recent LC monographic

The Library has three large central computers with a total disk storage of 40 billion characters, and numerous minicomputers distributed among its various departments.

The computer service supports nearly two dozen on-line programs, and those files are updated daily. Its customers retrieve data from these programs via 2,040 CRT terminals.

catalog, but it was designed so that thousands of catalogers can be putting data into the system from hundreds of points at any hour of the day. Although it was primarily intended to be used as a catalogers' input tool, it has one characteristic that makes it a convenient retrieval device—component word search. If a reference librarian is trying to recover the books that talk about some topic that either has no subject term covering it (or the subject term would bring up thousands of volumes to be searched), he or she can say, "Show me any book you can find that has the following words anywhere in its title: _____." This rifle approach frequently is more efficient than descriptive subject terms for finding the specific target sought. Similarly, if a user is seeking a specific government report, but cannot recall what the (often ad hoc) unit that issued it was called, MUMS will look for the words that the user thinks must have been in the title somewhere.

MARC

This room/file has in it the carefully structured bibliographic data that goes out each week to the sixty-three computer facilities and national bibliographic centers around the world. The tapes must be so tagged and organized that they can be burst into dozens of different computer programs and there become an integral part of accumulating data, fitting output and retrieval programs in endless applications. The MARC cataloging file keeps tab on 1.5 million book and document records, 120,000 serials, more thousands of films, maps—and a continually updated authority file of some 520,000 names.

COPICS and COINS

COPICS and COINS are the Copyright Office programs. COPICS is a constantly growing, endlessly updated, on-line record of copyrighted books and serials published since 1978, plus tens of thousands of "documents" that keep track of properties transferred from owner to owner. According to the revised copyright law, the Copyright Office is required to keep track of all coin-operated phonorecord players (jukeboxes) in the United States. Thus, since 1978, not only is there a record of ownership and location for 150,000 of these machines, but the licenses must be renewed every year. COINS is somewhat similar to MUMS in that it is made up of the "in-process," on-line, updating programs that keep track of the copyright data as it is polished and made perfect on the way to the "forever" record of COPICS.

ISIS

The next three rooms are filled with working data, and they are devices dedicated to running the Library of Congress. ISIS is the administrative control system of the CRS. The service receives about 1,500 congressional inquiries a day. Some of them will be answered within an hour, others may take as long as a year or more. ISIS keeps track of each inquiry and can tell the CRS who asked what and when, which of the seven research divisions is handling it, when the answer is due, and—once the reply is completed—how much time was spent on it at what salary grade. Through ISIS, the CRS not only can keep track of where each of the 340,000 annual projects is, but it can compare productivity between sections, divisions, previous years, et cetera.

PAGING

The PAGING program is used by the Research Services Department to transfer book requests received in any of the specialized or general reading rooms to the proper decks so that books may be drawn from the shelves and placed in the inquiring readers' hands. This is as far as the system has been developed at the present, but in its next stage, the program will keep track of the location of all books and form the base of both a charge/loan system and a special assignment system throughout the Library.

BUSINESS

As might be expected, the earliest program written for the Library was its check-writing and budgetary program. Being the oldest in the Library, the BUSINESS program is also the most primitive. The next area of LC computer development will be a complete beginning-again of the fiscal management portion of the automated system. The clumsiness and general limitations of this application remind us that not all portions of the computer plan have triumphed. It is to the Library's credit that when it saw that certain applications were in fact counterproductive— costing more to load in data than retrieval would ever justify, rising error rates doing more damage than functioning portions compensated for, endless complications that presaged endless hemorrhaging of pro- gramming resources—the Library had the fortitude to cut its losses and abandon the programs (or at least put them on indefinite back burners).

What Has the Library Learned?

The Library of Congress is now one of the largest computerized storage centers in the world. Although some systems, like those con- taining social security and stock market data, have as many or more "documents," very few installations anywhere contain the variety of data and can retrieve it with the variety or speed of LC. The Library has been automating for more than twenty-five years and, because of this extended experience, can look back with (often painful) knowledge.

LC has learned that it was vastly overoptimistic about the possible delivery dates of systems and about the end costs. It was sold fancy and complicated possibilities along the way that have not only proved to be unrealistic in terms of the present state of the art, but probably will not be seen in our lifetime, anywhere.

As almost everyone working in the computer field has learned, the most unexpected knowledge has been how many resources must be invested to simply keep the systems and the programs running. In the beginning, it was assumed that programs would be developed and made routine and then the programmers could go on and develop new programs. Not so. Well over 70 percent of all manpower that develops a program must be "left behind" to keep the program working and respond to user experience. One of the results of this syndrome is reflected in staff morale. Computerization becomes more bureaucratic, more people do mundane things, there are fewer challenges and fewer things to show off, while more people spend their whole careers "just keeping the system reliable."

Some Statistics

Finally, people are always asking for information about the hardware, so we conclude our hasty look at LC computers with a simple statement of what they are. At the time of this writing, the Library operates three very large "mainframes"—an Amdahl 470/V6, an IBM 3033, and an IBM 370/158—with a total disk storage of 40 billion characters. It also has eight Data Central minicomputers. The central computer is accessed by 1,033 terminals distributed around the various Library of Congress buildings, and the minicomputers are tied to another 113 terminals. In addition to the 1,033 terminals in LC buildings, members of the Senate and the House have slightly more than 1,000 terminals in their offices, and they access the Library of Congress disks by telephone wires. The combined 2,000-plus CRTs result in well over 100,000 transactions each working day.

Leadership in the Library Profession

In this portion of the book, we have been attempting to examine how the Library is serving the various clients it supports, and in particular, to note the areas of stress or disappointment. Thus far, in the Library's relations with the library world, we have found that LC is expected to produce what is, in effect, the national bibliography and it is doing this task well (at least to the satisfaction of the college and research libraries). But the vehicles it has used to provide the service have either stumbled or have been overtaken by time. Cards are failing, book catalogs are failing, but the MARC tapes flourish.

In using the computer, everyone expected LC to lead the profession in automation and to provide a model that could be copied in various sizes from Harvard to the Eureka Springs bookmobile, but it proved to be all LC could do to get its own systems working, much less produce a cloneable copy. There are many reasons for this failure to create a wider universe. Probably paramount was the fact that the Congress did not want its data base accessed by everybody and expressly forbade LC to provide computer services to nongovernment facilities. In addition, while LC was struggling to get started, OCLC designed a truly inspired facility that served an ever-growing audience (at the time of this writing, it supports some 4,000 members and a reported 20,000 additional organizations have access to its files), which took most of the usual pressure off the Library ("Why doesn't LC . . . ?") to provide the service.

Once MARC was well established and the recent collections of the Library were digitalized and on-line, many people expected the Library to build a computer network throughout the country. Congress's reluctance impeded this idea, but even more, "the country" was increasingly less eager for the development of a nationwide network since "the country" had built a variety of regional, responsive, and effective facilities themselves. Any overall network would threaten or erode their own worlds, and a subtle resistance began to build, not only to hold LC at arm's length, but even to joining or linking with each other. This is about where things stand at this writing. The idea of the Library of Congress's heading a great network of bibliographic computers is seldom discussed by anyone any more. The idea of LC providing the professional, high-quality, authority-based bibliographic information for many networks and facilities is accepted and progressing.

15

THE LIBRARY OF CONGRESS
AND THE SCHOLARLY WORLD:
THE SITUATION BEFORE BOORSTIN

We have said that libraries stand on a base of three activities: getting the materials, organizing them for use, and using them. Acquisitions, processing, and reference. For the past forty years, the Library has had leaders who leaned on the first two legs of this tripod. Indeed, not since Herbert Putnam retired in 1939 has a Librarian of Congress felt any particular identification with the user of the Library's great collections. Getting the material took great effort; processing it required high professionalism. The assumption was that once the materials were on the shelves, they would take care of themselves. The result of this bibliothecal laissez-faire was that by the time Daniel J. Boorstin became Librarian, the reference-and-research leg of the institution was in far worse shape than the other two supports. Boorstin, himself a renowned scholar and museum director, related at once to the plight of the patron walking through the Library's doors. (In fact one of the earliest elements to draw the new Librarian's ire was the discovery that of the eight doors that give access to the building, only three had been opened for nearly twenty years. He found the symbolism irresistible and ordered every entrance cleaned, polished, and opened to welcome the daily visitors.)

We are talking here, of course, about *using* the Library of Congress, and by the time Boorstin arrived in 1975, use of the collections, the reading rooms, the indexes and retrieval tools had become difficult in the extreme. Some of these problems came from administrative neglect,

Immediately upon passing through the bronze doors of the Jefferson Building, visitors find themselves in the Library's Great Hall, one of the most beautiful interior spaces in the city of Washington.

but more came from sheer size—problems inherent in any very large research institution. Before we note what Boorstin has done about the problems, let us detail a few of them to get a feel for the kinds of concerns he faced.

It Is Very Difficult to Use the Library of Congress

The first problem comes with a simple frustration: It is not easy to get a book at LC. If a scholar is using either of the great reading rooms (usually in the manner of a public library or college media center), he meets one set of problems; if he is using one of the smaller, specialized reading rooms (like maps, manuscripts, or Chinese materials), he meets another.

Start with the first. In the Library of Congress general reading rooms, a reader goes to the great card catalog or queries the computer; he locates the books he wants and makes out a call slip for each title. He passes in the slips at a receiving desk; they are shot to the appropriate decks by pneumatic tubes; and in a reasonably short time, he gets a few books back along with a majority of his slips, marked curtly, "Not on Shelf." This problem is not news to anyone. The Library even knows what the odds are of a reader's finding the books he wants or of the deck attendant's being able to give them to him. For example, if a reader requests a book on fine arts, the odds of having the book put in his hands are roughly seven out of ten; if he asks for a book on economics, his chances drop to five out of ten; if he wants an economics book published during the past fifteen years, his chances of success drop to two out of ten. Thus, if a reader hands in ten call slips for recent economics volumes, he can expect to receive two books and eight call slips marked "Not on Shelf"—and therefore canceled. The last odds hold true for volumes in political science, international affairs, urban problems, race relations, education, et cetera.

This condition is obviously shocking, and the staff in the early 1970s were well aware of it, but its cause was very difficult to untangle. Take the general area of recent social science publications. Here the reader ran an overall average of 50 percent—out of every ten requests, the reader would get five books delivered and five slips marked unavailable. Why only 50 percent? Where were half of the books that people wanted?

First, some of the absent books were simply being used—the collections of the Library of Congress are worked to exhaustion. Although the Library will usually have two copies of any English language book, the potential number of readers zeroing in on those two volumes is astronomical. On a routine day, 7,000 volumes will be off the shelves in transit to or from the scholars in the public reading rooms. The Congressional Research Service, with nearly 900 staff members, will be drawing on the volumes to answer 1,500 congressional inquiries a day. The 20,000 congressional staff members with borrowing privileges will be borrowing the books directly. The hundreds of federal bureaus and agencies in Washington, D.C., will be borrowing materials on precisely the same topics the Congress is interested in. Such agencies as the Central Intelligence Agency, the National Academy of Sciences, the National Agricultural Library, the National Gallery of Art, the National Security Agency, the Smithsonian Institution, and the Army Topographical Command rely so heavily on LC's collections that they maintain permanent desks and stations in the building, which are continually manned by agency personnel.

In 1980, completely aside from in-house use, 151,000 volumes were loaned out of the building—mostly to scholarly libraries around the country. Thus, all this circulation is occurring even before the visiting scholar enters one of the reading rooms. Once there, he must compete against his fellows who are looking for many of the same books he is.

The first reaction of the frustrated visitor is always, How can LC have 18 million volumes and it be so hard to get one? The problem, of course, is that the overwhelming majority of the 18 million are in a foreign language and/or printed before World War I. If the reader is seeking something on highways in Mali or Pakistan or on the construction of the Appian Way, he finds himself in a bibliographic paradise. But if he wants something on the interstate highway system in California, he finds himself in competition with a dozen users who got there first. Unfortuatately, most of the readers in the general reading rooms are concerned with contemporary U.S. social problems.

Public Reading Room Problem II

The two public reading rooms are visually deceptive. Each contains tens of thousands of reference works around the walls, each has great banks of card catalog trays, and each has rows of computer catalogs. The eye quickly assures the mind that here, indeed, are the keys to all knowledge. Unfortunately, the catalogs and the computers index less than one-fourth of the materials in the Library of Congress! If you are interested in the Civil War, the public catalogs will inform you about the books and some of the government documents on the Civil War, but they will not tell you about the doctoral dissertations the Library owns, the diaries, the maps, the field journals, the photographs, the battle drawings, the contemporary music, the broadsides, the intelligence reports, or even the publications the Government Printing Office issued about the Civil War last year! (U.S. Government Printing Office materials are increasingly being issued on microfiche, and the central catalog of the Library does not index microfilm, microfiche, microcard, word-processing disks, television documentaries, etc.—although the Library owns all of these things in greater quantity than any other library in the world. The Library catalogs only about 20 percent of the U.S. government documents it receives, although it keeps 100 percent of them.) The difference is kept by format in a variety of places, and "before Boorstin," little attempt was made to lead the researcher through this labyrinth.

Without laboring the point, the scholar faces the same problem in dozens of ways, and any scholar in pursuit of ethnic materials is particularly blinded. Materials about Scandinavian immigrants, African slaves, Russian Mennonites, and indentured Chinese abound at the Library of Congress, but countless readers are so awed by the great book catalogs that the far richer folklife, religious, genealogical, and social materials are never discovered because the thousands of books imply, "this must be everything in the world!"

Specialized Reading Room Problem I

The problems of the specialized rooms are those of the general reading rooms in reverse. All of the specialized materials are kept in the special reading rooms and their adjacent stacks—not in the "general collections" at the core—but instead of there being no indexes or catalogs, there are too many. In the Rare Book Reading Room, there are catalogs of children's materials, personal collections, individual authors, cookbooks, broadsides, eighteenth-century newspapers. In the Local History Reading Room, there is a family-name index to the genealogies in the Library, a catalog of the heraldry books, indexes of surnames appearing in U.S. county histories, a coat-of-arms index, a catalog of land grants, a catalog of wills, and registers of birth through the Civil War. In the Prints and Photographs Division, one finds catalogs by donor, by photographer, by city, by format—circus posters, theatrical posters, railroad posters, recruiting posters, propaganda posters—all in different places, some bound, some on cards, some in filing cabinets. Nothing explains itself. The researcher has to know all about it before he can even ask if there is such a thing as ——————.

How Good Are the Collections Themselves?

Again, great masses are deceptive. There is so much, everything *must* be there. But we are dependent on librarians going back as far

Many of the Library's unique and fascinating treasures can be found in its Rare Book and Special Collections Division. Its reading room and collections can be used by any scholar with a serious research purpose.

as ten generations, and the question must be asked, How good a job did they do collecting for our needs today?

There is no question but that the collections are in general the finest of any library in the Western world. No other single institution even approaches them in comprehensiveness, in quantity, in variety. And some parts of the collections are the finest in the world in detail as well. Scholars who have spent their lives researching on five continents underscore the excellence of the special collections. The manuscripts, music, law, and many of the foreign specializations exceed any individual collection anywhere.

But the researcher should remember that the Library has never claimed totality. Primacy in medicine and agriculture was given up once federal libraries were founded in those areas. Putnam refused some government records, saying that there must be a clear distinction between "archives" and "library materials." And according to the Farmington Plan of the 1940s and 1950s LC not only deliberately withdrew from many subject areas, but even assisted in strengthening specialized collections in other libraries throughout the nation by declaring certain new receipts surplus and making them available to the designated institutions.

The collections are relatively better the further back you go. For example, from 1640 to 1940, the materials relating to Americana are superb. If you are seeking European humanities in this period, they too are strong—but Oriental and Hispanic materials are not. People in the know refer to the non-European holdings as "adequate or less." The post-1940 foreign collections have become "excellent," exceeding the hopes of the most optimistic scholar, but the U.S. holdings become *less* comprehensive after 1940. This reversal involves two elements: currency and totality.

The improvement of the collections because of age is the easier to explain, so let's look at it first—and start with a trivial element that is really a footnote but one that frustrates the daily user of the Library because it is unexpected.

Item. The user's batting average improves the longer he waits to do his research simply because of binding practices. LC thinks in terms of the long pull, a fact that is easiest to see when you compare LC's procedures with those of a local public library. When the latter gets a magazine, a document, or a pamphlet, it hurriedly puts it out for use and keeps it unbound, but available, for as long as it is in demand. Once the pressure is off, it goes to the bindery to ensure its preservation for the future.

In LC the preservation process begins immediately on receipt. The moment an item is cataloged or accessioned (in the case of documents and pamphlets) and just as soon as a bound-volume's worth has accumulated (in the case of journals or magazines), the pieces go to the bindery before anything gets lost or worn. Because of this practice, the Congressional Research Service must operate a complete, independent, 5,000-title serial library so the congressmen have access to current material, but the public is left facing a frustrating hiatus of some two years' worth of material until the bound volumes get back on the shelves.

Does this make sense? Yes. LC is more interested in the scholar a decade or a century from now, who must have complete sets to use, than in today's user, who can rely on the local public library for today's news. Can't LC satisfy both? No. To do so would raise the cost of all its acquisition and processing techniques so astronomically it would jeopardize the whole operation.

Item. More significantly, the collections become richer as they age because of the method used to acquire the material. Again, a comparison between LC's approach and a public library's points up the contrast. A public library builds its collection a piece at a time, selecting each

item so it contributes to a planned, controlled, balanced collection—
the brick-and-cinderblock approach. LC does it by accumulating great
mounds of material and then picking out what it wants—the blast-the-
face-off-the-mountain approach. The result is that the average library
misses material because it failed to ask for it; LC misses material because
it is simply impossible to take the face off of *every* hillside.

LC tries to get its masses of materials by establishing automatic
flows of material—hence the automatic copyright deposit of Anglo-
American books, the automatic receipt of government documents, and
the automatic receipt of foreign materials through blanket-order contracts.

This approach is cheaper, but it leaves gaps, and to fill the gaps,
Research Services takes over and methodically, year after year, searches
the collections for lacunae. Its subject specialists travel, visit auctions,
comb book dealers' catalogs, and identify scholars' demands that the
collections were unable to satisfy. The Research Services staff orders
as many as 100,000 pieces a year just to plug the gaps. Obviously, the
longer you refine a subject area, the better it gets; thus, older is better.

Totality

The Library of Congress has never claimed it would keep every
shred of print known. It has said it would keep the materials needed
by the government, it would endeavor to record the history of the
American people, and it would support American scholarship. It did
all these things reasonably well in the days when these goals were
possible. But after World War II, several elements of the picture changed.
The federal agencies began to build their own departmental libraries,
and LC shared government support with them. The state libraries and
the state historical societies began to share the responsibility for Americana, and it soon became evident that local institutions could do a
more efficient job collecting regional materials, town by town, county
by county, than the distant LC. Finally, the great universities began to
build huge, well-supported library systems so that serious research could
be supported through decentralized campus and regional research collections.

Thus, as LC recognized the impossibility of acquiring "everything,"
pure pragmatism suggested that it ease off in areas where others could
do as well or better. Conversely, it should retain those areas of strength
either where it was already preeminent or where it could support
scholarship more efficiently than any other single institution.

The current emphasis on foreign acquisitions reflects the last point.
Remember, the present annual mix is one part U.S. materials to three
parts foreign. This ratio is reinforced by the aforementioned division

by subject, which appears in the medical/agricultural move to the national libraries, and the subject assignments of such agreements as the Farmington Plan.

In the early 1950s, the National Archives declared the logic and efficiency of its taking over LC's traditional role of keeper of the presidential papers. The Congress agreed, and thus LC custody of the great manuscript series from Washington to Coolidge was terminated. Since Hoover, each successive presidential collection has been housed in a hometown memorial library under the supervision of the executive branch. Although the shock of this decision was hard on the LC staff (to add insult to injury, the engrossed copies of the Declaration of Independence and the Constitution were moved from LC to the Archives), the result of the decision has had an even greater impact on manuscript deposits ever since. Traditionally, when a President's papers were given to the Library of Congress, the papers of his cabinet officers, generals, political advisers, and the leading national figures of the time followed along, so the totality of the collections gave a detailed history of each individual period. With the presidential nuclei gone and the Archives actively soliciting peripheral political and social papers, the emphasis in LC's manuscript collection has shifted to American culture and the arts. This shift has caused a fundamental change in the character of the holdings and has altered LC's traditional role in the preservation of the nation's heritage.

But who can say where the proper division of labor falls in any corner of the collections? At the present time, if we are to believe National Union Catalog figures, the Library of Congress is funding, acquiring, processing, and adding to its collections one-half of the significant monographic production of the entire world! Should it try to specialize more and achieve absolute totality in a limited universe of specific areas? Or should it attempt all-encompassing control, embrace ultraphotoreduction techniques and the computer, set up a depository in the Antarctic where space is cheap and deterioration (like the temperature) is zero? Both such extremes have been seriously considered, and there are proponents for all the steps in between.

One LC manager maintains that the best LC can hope for in the way of preeminence is the following: LC has the best collection of Hebraica outside of Israel, the best collection of Chinese literature outside of China, the best collection of Africana outside of Africa—it also has the best collection of Massachusettsiana outside of Massachusetts, the best collection of Oregoniana outside of Oregon—and the best collection of maps, music, and motion pictures anywhere!

The Prints and Photographs Division is a rich resource for scholars doing research in almost any area, from the history of cartoons to architectural design to life in the early western United States.

The Library's Audience

Can anybody use the Library of Congress? Tricky question. Anybody who is decently covered, does not bother his neighbor, and is older than a high school student can enter and use the Library, but how much attention they will get *from* the Library varies wildly—and deliberately.

There is a caste treatment, a pecking order to the attention that is granted by the staff, and although it does not appear anywhere in print, it somehow gets communicated from generation to generation of the people in LC who work with the public. If fifty phone calls came in simultaneously or fifty people surrounded a single reference librarian or fifty people applied for a single study carrel, the odds are they would be served in the following order:

1. Members of Congress and their staffs pursuing public or private research
2. Federal employees engaged in official studies for their agencies

3. The press—representatives of newspapers, television and radio facilities, and the wire services
4. Established individual scholars writing books and scholarly papers
5. Ph.D. candidates writing doctoral dissertations
6. Adult citizens pursuing personal interests
7. College students doing undergraduate or Master's degree work
8. Local high school students bearing a letter from their principal saying that their school does not have information on a given topic and that the student is engaged in serious research

We are looking for problem areas here, and the problem in Library access is that the Library simply cannot make up its mind about what kind of a public institution it is. On certain days of the week or during certain managers' careers, it believes that as a great democratic institution accumulated with the taxpayers' money or the gifts of generous donors, it should make its collections available to any citizen who enters its doors. If this is so, then LC is the public's greatest public library. Having more of the world's wisdom in one place than any other institution, it is the most efficient place to seek answers—one-stop research—and the Library therefore is obligated to tell the world of its wonders, stay open longer (never close?), and be the local public library for the nation.

But on another day with another manager, LC is described as the greatest treasure house of the nation and, as such, should be the court of last resort. Each public library in every town or country should do the best it can to serve its community with information. When its resources are exhausted, the citizen should be directed to the state library and the state university. When these resources fail, the researcher should go on to the regional networks and storehouses like the Midwest Center, the New England Center, and the Southern Net—and when these in turn are exhausted, come at last to the Library of Congress. There highly trained (and highly paid) specialists will work with the (by now senior) researcher, and the taxpayers will get the biggest bang for their buck. Undistracted by every schoolchild, the specialists can make the rarities of the national library return the richest dividend to the nation through the leading writers, major scientists, most creative artists, et cetera.

On a clear day, with a rising barometer and low humidity, either of those cases can be presented with passion and total conviction. Since the decisions of what to keep and whom to serve have to be made every hour of every day, the continuity of the Library has swung briskly from one side to the other for nearly 200 years now. Enough said.

16

THE LIBRARY OF CONGRESS
AND THE SCHOLARLY WORLD:
THE SITUATION SINCE BOORSTIN

Boorstin and the Scholarly User

We have tried to give a sense of the problems Daniel J. Boorstin met when he arrived at the Library in 1975. Let us now examine some of the steps he has taken to ameliorate these concerns and get an idea of what is still left to be done.

Philosophy

The first shift in policy began with Boorstin's refusal to accept the Library's "low profile." In his initial briefings, he was introduced to the belief that the Library of Congress was solely Congress's library and that any public hint that it might also be the national library was suicidal. Such an assertion would bring down the wrath of the legislature upon the institution, and not only he but the Library's staff would suffer. Boorstin refused to accept this premise. He was convinced that the members of Congress whom he knew personally were as proud of the national treasure house as they were of the congressional support aspect, and he was sure that they would join with him in saluting the institution.

Symbolizing the National Library

Boorstin started with a symbolic swearing-in ceremony held in the Great Hall of the Library, which was attended by the President and Vice-President, the chairman of the Joint Committee on the Library, and the Speaker of the House. The occasion was extensively covered

A computer catalog center for the public is located in the Jefferson Building behind the Main Reading Room and the traditional card catalogs. Reference librarians are always on hand to help those who need assistance in using the terminals.

by the Washington media, and the Great Hall appeared on television for the first time in the history of the Library.

Boorstin then proceeded with his physical opening of the Library, redecorating the public areas to look like they had when the institution opened in 1897. The guards' office was displaced by a small orientation theater, which gave hourly slide shows explaining what the Library of Congress did, what kinds of materials it held, and something of its philosophical purpose. Boorstin expanded the sales and publications desk to make the Library's recordings and facsimile copies of its treasures available and to publicize its concerts, poetry readings, and cultural seminars. He placed tables on the Neptune Plaza between the Library and the Capitol, and sponsored American folklife dances and concerts on the piazza during noon hours for visitors and staff. In this way, the building was drawn into the Capitol Hill community. In the reading rooms, he brought the reference staff forward so it was the first element of the Library encountered by visitors and flooded the public areas with signs so that the research materials kept there were made visible.

Boorstin then drew on his own personal ties to the nation's cultural

A free lunchtime concert by the Bluegrass Cardinals attracts a large crowd to the Library's Neptune Plaza.

world and brought the creative elite into the Library first as guests, then as advisers, and ultimately as ambassadors. Across luncheon tables in his own office and small dining tables in the Whittall Pavilion, he introduced the Library to such personal guests as

Barbara Tuchman	Henry Kissinger
Herman Wouk	Bruno Bettelheim
Clare Boothe Luce	Abe Fortas
Howard K. Smith	David McCullough
Yehudi Menuhin	Ray Bradbury
Warren Burger	Eli Wallach
James Michener	John Gardner
Alexander Haig	Mortimer Adler
Danny Kaye	Paul Theroux
Charles Eames	Oscar Handlin
Gerard Piel	Stanley Marcus
Eric Sevareid	George Steiner
Lessing Rosenwald	William Safire
Jaroslav Pelikan	Jack Valenti

Joseph Kraft   Joshua Logan
Lili Palmer   Edmund Morris

The luncheons were only the beginning of many relationships between those people and the Library. The violinist Yehudi Menuhin went
on to write the text for the Library's book on the Brahms Violin Concerto
and to assist in various public seminars staged by the Library. Ray
Bradbury, Joshua Logan, Henry Kissinger, Alexander Haig, and Charles
Eames gave the Library their personal papers; Gerard Piel, publisher
of *Scientific American*, became a continuing member of several of the
Library's boards, as did Jaroslav Pelikan, dean of the Graduate School
at Yale; Dan Lacy, vice-president of McGraw-Hill; et cetera. Lessing
Rosenwald and Clare Boothe Luce were, of course, already longtime
benefactors of the institution.

A series of formal dinners were staged in the Great Hall to link
new library exhibits with themes under active development throughout
the institution. Their titles suggest the targets of attention: "Beginnings,"
"Circle of Knowledge," "The World Encompassed," and "Treasures."

The activities were all designed to bring the creative elite into the
Library and to draw on them for advice on how to make the Library
more useful in their particular fields of expertise. As a corollary to this
activity, Boorstin began filling retirement vacancies among his managerial
staff with eminent leaders in a variety of fields of expertise. Erik
Barnouw, the distinguished media historian and social philosopher, was
persuaded to join the Library as chief of the Motion Picture, Broadcasting,
and Recorded Sound Division. David Ladd, previously Commissioner
of Patents of the United States, agreed to take over the Copyright Office
as Register of Copyrights. Oliver Jensen, founder and editor of *American
Heritage* magazine, became the chief of the Prints and Photographs
Division, and Gilbert Gude, five-term Congressman from Maryland
(bearing with him a record of drawing more votes from *both* parties
than any predecessor in his district's history), left a distinguished career
in the House to take over the directorship of the Congressional Research
Service.

The Council of Scholars

Boorstin's experience with the various activities described above
convinced him that such links with the creative and academic worlds
should be institutionalized into a formal body. As he talked about the
idea with his guests and library managers, the concept of a continuing
entity that would do a number of things for the nation and the Library
began to form. Who would make up such an entity? "Those who collect,
arrange, and preserve the raw materials of scholarship and the literary

The Library's Great Hall makes an elegant setting for a formal dinner.

arts and those who reinterpret and vivify them anew for each generation."
What would they do? Advise the Librarian about the relationship
between the Library and the scholarly world; explore the extent to
which the Library's collections support active scholarship; "participate
in the preparation of an inventory of knowledge in the world today";
and finally, sponsor (and participate in) programs that would "examine
large intellectual questions affecting scholarship and public policy."

All those bannered phrases really added up to a growing conviction
that a maturing, sophisticated country like the United States could use
a body of senior minds (a sort of wide-band Académie Française) which
would be a center of wisdom for the nation. The more Boorstin thought
about the idea, the surer he became of its validity and the more certain
he became that the Library of Congress was the perfect location for
such a group of minds. His enthusiasm was infectious, and by the time
he had decided whom he wanted and had made his plea for their
involvement, he had convinced two dozen outstanding Americans to
become members of the Library's Council of Scholars. The council meets
at regular intervals (each time drawing the Washington media like gulls
around a trawler), and at the time of this writing, the council members
are:

Meyer E. Abrams
  English literature, Cornell
James S. Ackerman,
  Fine arts, Harvard
Paul Berg
  Biochemistry, Stanford
Subrahmanyan Chandrasekhar
  Astrophysics, Chicago
Philip D. Curtin
  History, Johns Hopkins
Elizabeth Eisenstein
  History, Michigan
Jacob W. Getzels
  Education and behavioral
  sciences, Chicago
Nathan Glazer
  Education and social
  structure, Harvard
Chauncy D. Harris
  Geography, Chicago
Gerald Holton
  Physics, Harvard

Maxine Kumin
  Poetry, Library of Congress
Myres S. McDougal
  Law, Yale
Archibald MacLeish
  Literature
Yehudi Menuhin
  Musicology
William Meredith
  Poetry, Library of Congress
Jaroslav J. Pelikan
  History and religious
  studies, Yale
Ernest Samuels
  Humanities, Northwestern
Arthur Schlesinger, Jr.
  Humanities, City University
  of New York
Carl Schorske
  History, Princeton
Theodore W. Schultz
  Economics, Chicago

Henry Kissinger
  Government and international
affairs

Edward G. Seidensticker
  Japanese studies, Columbia

The Center for the Book

In the midst of today's galloping technology development and America's current love affair with the video screen, Librarian Boorstin realized that someone, somewhere, should be concentrating on "the book" as an intellectual device. This was the beginning of the Center for the Book, formally established by Congress in October 1977 by Public Law 95-129 to help organize, focus, and dramatize the nation's interest in books, reading, and the printed word. And what better place to house it than the Library of Congress?

As the Librarian explained shortly after the legislation was approved:

> As the national library of a great free republic, we have a special interest to see that books do not go unread, that they are read by people of all ages and conditions, that books are not buried in their own dross, not lost from neglect or obscured from us by specious alternatives and synthetic substitutes. As the national library of the most technologically advanced nation on earth, we have a special duty, too, to see that the book is the useful, illuminating servant of all other technologies, and that all other technologies become the effective, illuminating acolytes of the book.

The Center for the Book lives off of private, not public funds. The Library of Congress provides only intellectual and administrative support: a full-time staff of two people. A large National Advisory Board, which includes representatives from the book, educational, and business communities (currently headed by George C. McGhee, former U.S. ambassador to Turkey and the Federal Republic of Germany), shapes the Center's programs and gives it direction. Tax-deductible contributions from corporations and private citizens provide the center with the wherewithal to keep going.

By any measure, the Center for the Book has been a great success, convincing even its skeptics at the Library that there is, indeed, a role for such an organization to play. It serves as a catalyst among authors, booksellers, librarians, educators, business leaders, scholars, and especially readers—everyone who has or should have an interest in books and reading. As a catalyst, the Center for the Book works with other organizations and individuals to heighten the general public's "book awareness"; to use new technologies and other media to enhance books and reading; to promote the study of books, reading, and the printed word; to encourage the international flow of books and printed materials; and to improve the quality of book production.

The Center for the Book has held a number of symposia and programs at the Library of Congress to explore the role of the book in our society. Its 1978 symposium on "Television, the Book, and the Classroom," co-sponsored by the U.S. Office of Education, helped to inspire the Office of Education's research program on critical television viewing skills and led directly to the LC/CBS Television "Read More About It" project. This project, mentioned in an earlier chapter, provides information about books related to certain CBS network presentations. Immediately following the telecast, a performer from the program makes a 30-second spot announcement to encourage viewers to look for books on the subject of the program at their local libraries and bookstores. The lists (prepared by the Library's bibliographers) are published in advance in the American Library Association's *Booklist*, the American Booksellers Association's *Newswire*, and in other library and trade publications. In October 1980 the "Read More About It" project received an achievement award from the American Council for Better Broadcasts.

Another reading promotion effort by the Center is "Books Make A Difference." As part of an oral history project, 1,400 individuals across the country were interviewed about how a book—and reading in general—helped to shape and influence their lives. Excerpts from the interviews are being used to support reading promotion projects in local communities.

The Center for the Book strives to stimulate interest in the family-school partnership in reading development, typography and book design, and the international role of the book. Under the auspices of the Center for the Book (made possible by the generous contributions of Mrs. Charles W. Engelhard) the Engelhard Lecture on the Book brings prominent scholars to the Library of Congress on a regular basis to give public lectures on book-related topics. The center has also pursued an active publishing program, compiling the results of some of its own symposia and studies as well as supporting some of the book-related exhibits and events at the Library of Congress.

A Multimedia Encyclopedia

The steps sketched out thus far have been related to Boorstin's "opening" of the Library—linking it to the world of scholarship, raising its profile as a national library, and reminding the creative elites of its presence and potential to serve them. A second area of change has been in the way he has addressed the collections themselves.

As a social historian and a museum director, Boorstin was acutely conscious of the multiple places in which "the answer" might be found. Librarians turn to the book as a natural reflex, and Boorstin believes the book is still the most efficient form of intellectual storage, but he also believes that the photograph, the map, the tape, the newsreel, and the documentary television record must not be ignored. Unfortunately, thanks to the dominance of the traditional card catalog, the book is frequently the single source pursued by the serious scholar. The question was, How to link the Library visitor with the formats and collections outside his or her normal research pattern?

Boorstin introduced his concept of the multimedia encyclopedia. He pictured a scholar visiting the Library for the first time and being confronted by the multiple buildings and hidden collections. Boorstin wants to get that scholar into the hands of a human library specialist as quickly as possible—someone who could enumerate the various ways data the scholar was seeking are stored in the Library and suggest the fastest, most efficient way of finding it. The problem, of course, was that staff was limited, and to provide such personalized service for one million visitors each year was not only hopeless, it would indeed have been overkill in many instances—cases where simply "looking it up in a book" were all that was necessary, no matter what exotic alternatives the Library might be able to offer. How to sort out the various levels of appropriate service?

Boorstin decided to go with three levels of research response. The first was the great central reading room, which would provide the traditional library approach, and would be peopled with reference librarians literally as you entered the door, with more at the central desk, more located in the catalogs, and more circulating in the computer rooms. The Main Reading Room was to be the point of initial interview and assistance.

A second line of service would surround the first. For those instances where the specialized tools of a subject expertise would be called for, the special indexes, the special catalogs scattered throughout the Library, and the special reference books and language facilities would be located here. The central reading room staff would identify scholars who needed these sophisticated tools and would pass them on to a science reading room, a performing arts reading room, a local history and genealogy reading room, a social science reading room, or the geographical and language reading rooms (a European group, an African group, a Hispanic group, and an Asian unit).

These individual reading rooms would have all the proper reference works and indexes lining the walls, with desks and furniture provided for anticipated long-term projects. The reference staffs would be skilled in their subject areas, but most important, they would know which of the unusual formats should be searched. This second line of assistance would tell its users which of the maps, manuscripts, films, or microforms should be pursued to get maximum response to the question at hand.

The third line, then, would be the specialized reading rooms themselves, the traditional Manuscripts, Motion Pictures, Music, Microforms, Government Documents, Newspapers, and Rare Books rooms that had existed all along. The new system would protect these specialized facilities from routine traffic that could be better served by a "public library" approach, reserving them for the advanced or more sophisticated researcher.

Such layering of skills was never possible when all the staff was squeezed into a limited space, but with the near doubling of public areas created by the opening of the Madison Building, the shifting of reference service is now starting as this book is being written. But to underline the point: The purpose is to get the use of the nonbook material up to the level of the traditional catalog–call slip approach to finding answers in a bound volume. Although the great book collections are vastly valuable, the nonbook holdings of the Library of Congress are like nothing else in the world of scholarship.

Thinking the Unthinkable

As a social historian, Boorstin is strongly committed to the idea that without innovation there can be no progress. He applies the thought, "There must be a better way of doing this," to endless library activities, and is highly skilled at thinking the unthinkable. He is constantly testing "new ways," probing to see which are valid and genuinely useful, and which are merely different without satisfying the user's needs. A few examples may be of interest.

Moving the Library to the Users

Boorstin's most spectacular success in this area has been the creation of the Kennedy Center Performing Arts Library. The Kennedy Center not only produces entertainments at matinees and evenings in its auditoriums but also encompasses dozens of workshops, seminars, classes in scene design, and general education in the performing arts. Without trying to detail the successive steps, Boorstin reasoned that the Library's great collections in this area would be most effectively used on the site. He did not wish to denude the Library of Congress of its theatrical materials, but he did want to make them easily available to people using this federal center of the theater.

The solution is the present Performing Arts Library located on the top floor of the Kennedy Center (the room is a beautifully designed architectural gem in itself), which contains a basic, working collection of performing arts reference books and, more important, computer links to the Library. The terminals access all of the multiple LC programs, and by simple telephone ties, factual data can be passed back and forth; through frequent LC truck deliveries, Library materials can be placed in the inquirers' hands within an hour or two at most. Obviously, the Performing Arts Library is staffed with library specialists in drama, dance, theatrical history, and the motion picture. This new library proved to be so rewarding that managerial plans were drawn and tested to create a similar architecture and building library at the new Museum for the Building Arts. Although the Library's collections are unusually strong in this area, the Museum and its clientele did not seem sufficiently developed to warrant further elaboration of the plan at the time.

Another innovation to be tested in taking the Library to the user was Boorstin's idea of moving the Library's foreign language materials to various ethnic centers around the country. Boorstin was distressed by the fact that the foreign materials were used only a fraction as much as the English-language holdings, and he asked the staff to explore the validity of, for example, placing the Chinese and Japanese publications in major research centers on the West Coast, the Scandinavian materials in Minnesota, and the Hispanic materials in Texas or Florida, where they might strengthen regional research and take advantage of local language skills. He postulated that the materials could be kept in tightly controlled units that would maintain their integrity as belonging to the Library of Congress while being closer to departments of Hispanic studies or Oriental language facilities.

Ultimately, the idea was rejected on the grounds that the Library of Congress's great strength is having all the tools and formats physically together, forming a "critical mass." This togetherness, it was concluded, makes everything more valuable and more useful. However, the concept has not been abandoned, but rather held in abeyance until certain technological innovations (to be discussed in Chapter 17) can develop and become generally available.

Another of Boorstin's ideas that was ahead of its time came from procedures he had seen work both at the Smithsonian and at LC. The CRS, he noted, puts its reports in microprocessing storage and holds them in digital form until they are needed; it then assembles bits and pieces into tailor-made replies to congressional inquiries. The CRS also puts its briefings on tape cassettes so Members can listen while driving to work. Linking such storage and use-as-needed devices, Boorstin asked his staff to look into the idea of combining the great information stores of the Smithsonian Institution and the Library of Congress in some electronic form that would allow them to be made available to the public library system, and ultimately, to the scholarly and research institutions.

For example, if a public library in Tucson had a question about some Indian lore or if an ornithologist in Maine was pursuing a rare bird, the local library would send the query to the Smithsonian-LC link via their computer/telephones. Smithsonian would bring the artifact or the bird call to the transmitter, the Library would produce the best words or photographs it could find from its 80 million pieces, all the parts would be placed on the facsimile machine or character scanner, and the combined data would be sped down the wire to the inquirer. The result would be an assemblage of the world's best information sent directly to the person who wanted to have it. Unfortunately, this concept was, as we noted, a bit ahead of the technology available at the time, but with videodisc and interactive cable TV coming along, the gap is closing fast.

The Glass Box

A similar idea that intrigued Boorstin was the thought of using the CRS's techniques for fast factual transfer to three audiences instead of to the single congressional one. The idea involved putting the CRS's clipping files, its rented computer data bases, and the extensive CRS loose-leaf library into a single room or confined deck area. The public Research Services department could then contribute its specialized reference materials and the LC data banks, and the whole mass could be enclosed in what would be known as "the glass box." The CRS could then continue to serve Congress through the "CRS door," while the Library set up a Hot Line telephone answering service for the "national library door." The Hot Line would first be made available to newspapers, wire services, and radio and television stations (who would pay a charge for each question answered). The service could later be made available to any library participating in the American Library Association or Special Libraries Association networks.

The idea was based on the thought that the materials were already bought and paid for with tax dollars, and if a few telephone reference librarians were attached, the riches of the largest reference collection in America could be made available on a "while-you-wait" basis throughout the country. Like the other explorations mentioned here, this development was judged infeasible until various electronic devices could be better developed and become more common in distant communities.

Traveling Exhibitions and Publications

To return to the world of the present, as a former museum director, Boorstin was distressed by the short life and restricted audience of the Library's rather spectacular revolving exhibitions. They were given extensive coverage by the Washington media but seldom could be seen outside the capital. He therefore changed the exhibition program from being based only in Washington to one that would move out to a wider audience. As quickly as word spread that the exhibitions were available, the Library was swamped with requests for them, and it is now expected that any exhibit will be "on the road" for at least two or three years after the close of its Washington, D.C., run. The point, of course, is not only to let the country see the Library's treasures first hand, but to remind scholars throughout the country of the kinds of materials that are available at LC.

A similar purpose lay behind Boorstin's expansion of the Library's publications program. Here the idea was not only to remind the scholars of what was available, but to move as much of the information itself "out there" and save the researchers the ever-increasing cost of travel to Washington.

Long ago, the Library began to convert blocks of its holdings to microfilm and to make them available at cost. At the present time, you can buy all the papers of twenty-three presidents (3,000 reels plus indexes), or you can buy them separately: 97 reels of Lincoln materials, $1,940; 485 reels of Theodore Roosevelt's papers, $9,390; 124 reels of George Washington's, $2,585. Over forty libraries distributed throughout the country now have all 3,000 reels available for their patrons. The range of microfilms for sale covers some unlikely collections: You can get the complete works of Johann Sebastian Bach, forty-seven volumes on 11 reels; forty-four volumes of Beethoven on 9. You can buy twenty-eight African newspapers from their founding to the present, and you can buy dozens of complete manuscript collections: Henry Clay manuscripts on 22 reels, Samuel Gompers's AFL letterbooks on 340 reels, all of LC's holdings of Alexander Hamilton on 46 reels.

The Library is expanding the publication of its own treasures with multicolored facsimiles of its rarest maps and manuscripts. The facsimile of the Brahms Violin Concerto is unusually exact: Inks were specially formulated for each of the six colors, so the reader can easily distinguish the emendations made by Brahms, by Josef Joachim (the violinist for whom it was written), and subsequent editors. LC's most popular form of photoduplication is now its microfiche of complete photographic collections. This program began with an LC publication that reproduced the 301 personal photographs taken by the Wright brothers between 1900 and 1915, covering all their glider and powered flight experiments (plus personal pictures of friends and the family dog, Scorpio). Since fiche can be reproduced for pennies, this format makes the material easily available to individuals or libraries. Some 3,000 sets of the Wright brothers pictures were sold, one set at a time, the first year they were offered.

The Library publishes guides to its collections to make what is there known to scholars, and it publishes indexes to blocks of materials to make their use more efficient. Such publications as *Special Collections in the Library of Congress* (464 pp.), *A Guide to the Study of the United States of America* (1,720 pp.), *Manuscript Sources in the Library of Congress for Research on the American Revolution* (88 pp.), *The United States in Africa: Guide to U.S. Official Documents and Government-Sponsored Publications on Africa, 1785–1975* (949 pp.) are self-explanatory—and expected. More surprising are such publications as *Procedures for Salvage of Water-Damaged Library Materials* (30 pp.), *Polyester Film Encapsulation* (29 pp.), and *A Descriptive List of Treasure Maps and Charts in the Library of Congress* (30 pp.). Under Boorstin, both the quantity and the quality of the Library's publications have steadily improved with a new emphasis on literary style and attractive design.

Difficulties

We have been trying to note some of the problems the Library faces in trying to serve its different audiences, and we sketched out a number of the problems relating to the scholarly world in the previous chapter. Boorstin has been attempting to ameliorate many of them, but the Library is still in the woods with those concerns as well as with problems that relate to its other audiences.

One of the difficulties is one that faces all libraries these days (the national libraries of Europe report the same problem). The simple fact is that the use of all library materials in research centers is going down everywhere. The number of people using the reading rooms throughout the Library of Congress has been declining at a steady rate. The use of the science collections is the least affected, but such areas as manuscript research and Asian studies are sagging annually. Part of the reason for this decline seems to be the way modern research is conducted. Topics of study have become narrower and narrower in contrast to the old "everything about a topic" approach, which served to prove the writer's knowledge of his field. But research techniques have changed and will mean smaller numbers of scholars in the reading rooms because of two factors.

First, the many location tools now available tell a researcher, easily, where the nearest copy of a work is located—and the nearest copy increasingly turns out to be at a nearby college or research center. Not too many years ago, the printed book catalog of the Library, which was housed in literally thousands of libraries throughout the United States, served not only to let the research world know that a book existed, but to pinpoint a copy within the Library of Congress. And the LC copy was the only copy so precisely revealed. Now the *National Union Catalog* and computer files of such computer networks as OCLC and the Research Libraries Information Network locate copies of the cited items throughout their regional areas. The result is that more and more of the research that used to rely on the Library of Congress's collections is being conducted nearer to home.

Even the Library's interlibrary loans have decreased sharply in the past ten years. An optimist looks at this trend and says, "Splendid, the Library of Congress's resources are being saved for what only it can do and do best!"; the pessimist says, "Distress, the Library of Congress is becoming irrelevant, and scholarship is becoming superficial, for if they had not found the one title near home, they would have come here and used our copy and then discovered all the other riches we have sitting on either side of it."

Second, statistical use of the collections and study rooms has gone down because of a new research tool: the photocopy machine. In the past, a researcher would laboriously take notes and frequently work at the Library for months—living in rooms on Capitol Hill even as the British Museum drew its communities around Bloomsbury. Now a modern researcher does much of his bibliographic homework before coming to LC by using LC publications in his home library. Once he arrives in Washington, he efficiently searches his materials, photocopies individual passages, and departs, leaving an order for mass photoduplication to be done by the Library's Photoduplication Service. Like shorter hospital stays, shorter research frees up readers' space and study carrels.

When we queried specialized-subject staff members about the differences between research twenty years ago and now, two interesting footnotes appeared. First, photocopying seems to have improved the accuracy of direct quotes in books, but by reducing the time spent hand copying the words, photocopying has eroded the reflective, "What does it all mean?" aspect. Second, the *kinds* of readers in the specialized collections have shifted away from being the traditional Ph.D. scholars and the authors writing ten-volume biographies of the great. Currently, more and more of the patrons are in the mode of the Barbara Tuchmans, Edmund Morrises, and David McCulloughs, who are writing shorter and more popular, if equally scholarly, studies for more general audiences.

Fugacity: The Destruction of the Library of Congress

And so we end our list of LC's problems in serving the scholarly world with the most paralyzing problem of them all: The collections

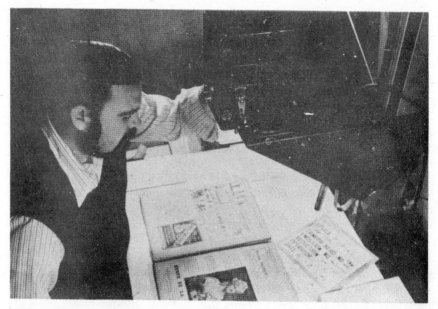

The preservation of its materials is a serious problem for the Library of Congress—and for libraries everywhere. In 1980 almost 3.5 million microfilm exposures were made of pages in brittle books in order to preserve their contents before they crumbled to dust.

the scholars are using, the very pieces that make up the Library of Congress, are crumbling to dust even as they sit on the shelves.

Unfortunately, this is not a philosophical or metaphorical concern. The materials are literally rotting away. Up to about 1860, paper was made of rags, and it has lasted reasonably well—it is readable and flexible and can still be handled today. But the fumes from modern traffic and institutional heating have penetrated even those volumes' pages, moisture has combined with the gas, and the antebellum books are filling with sulphuric acid, while the pages are turning brown and becoming brittle.

For books printed since 1860, the problem is many times worse. At that point, rags became too expensive for mass commercial publishing, so the papermakers turned to wood pulp. Wood pulp contains lignin glue, which holds the fibers together and produces a brown paper like package wrapping. Alum is added to make the brown paper white, and the alum and the lignin combine to make sulphuric acid—moving us quickly to the aforementioned problem of brown and brittle destruction. The problem was bad when it started, and it is much worse now. At

An experimental deacidification chamber used by the Library's Preservation Laboratory to try and prolong the life of the paper in the Library's books.

the present time, the Library's hardbound books are lasting about fifty years, and what few paperbacks it keeps are lasting about thirty years (if nobody uses them).

Sample checks of the Library's collections suggest that as many as one quarter of the 18 million volumes on the shelves have deteriorated severely, and the publications of the underdeveloped countries are in particularly shocking condition. Note: These are not cosmetic troubles— when a user opens a volume, twenty-five browning pages may split into his hands and drop as fragments to the desk before he realizes the book is beyond use. Obviously, this problem is not something new. The Library has been struggling with it for decades, and the library profession as a whole has spent hundreds of thousands of dollars researching a solution—reaping an ever-lengthening series of disappointments.

Twenty years ago, it looked like microfilming was the answer, and the Library of Congress has carried on a massive program of photocopying its deteriorating volumes one page at a time. It is now microfilming over 3 million pages of brittle books a year, trying to capture the volumes before they dissolve, but this is not nearly enough. Further, the library profession is losing confidence in the stability of microfilm.

Restoration of the Library's rare and unique materials is done painstakingly by hand, often a leaf at a time.

Even in spite of extensive washing, deacidification, and stabilization, some of the Library's microfilms have decomposed after thirty years, while others are cracking, splitting, and bubbling after forty or fifty years.

The struggle to deacidify the pages themselves has been going on since World War II. For a while it looked like soaking the books in base solutions was the answer, but this procedure required removing the covers, impregnating the pages, drying them, and finally reassembling the volumes. Each book took about a month to complete at a cost of about $300 per volume—obviously appropriate only for rare or unique materials.

Recently, a Library of Congress chemist invented a gaseous de-acidification process using diethyl-zinc, which permits the treating of some 400 books at a time, and for the moment, this method is exciting the Library's preservationists. Theoretically, the process could be expanded so some 5,000 books could be treated simultaneously, but the process still takes about a week and would cost about $5 a book at present prices.

It is possible to make acid-free paper at the mill, and the library profession has been pleading with the publishers to use such a product for thirty years. At the present time, however, barely 250,000 tons of acid-free paper are made annually throughout the country, and it is used almost exclusively by university presses and such fine arts publishers as Harry N. Abrams. Even the encyclopedia manufacturers refuse to be bothered with it. And while the books are eating themselves up through the decades, similar things are happening to the posters, the photographs, the sheet music, the maps, et cetera.

What Is the Solution?

As this book is being written, a solution appears in sight for the first time since the Chinese invented paper almost 2,000 years ago. If it proves to be as great a breakthrough as the profession now believes, we will finally have succeeded in arresting the destruction of the contents of our libraries—but we will probably also have destroyed libraries as the institutions we now know. The solution is the combination of laser technology and digital storage, and the revolution it presages does not fall into the "Ah, something for the next generation to worry about" category, but instead could result in an explosion that would change the entire way of life at the Library of Congress in the next three to five years. This potential upheaval deserves a whole discussion of its own, which follows—"Question for the Year 2000."

Part Four

QUESTION FOR THE YEAR 2000

17

DO WE NEED
A NATIONAL LIBRARY—
FOR WHOM TO DO WHAT?

We come, then, to the conclusion of our story, and we find that the tale is rather dramatically schizophrenic. In one direction, everything is going very well—the good news. In the opposite direction, there is an ominous amount of bad news accumulating. What happens next? Where will the Library be, *what* will the Library be in the year 2000?

What Was the National Library Here for
in the First Place?

We can start by asking, what was/is the Library supposed to do for the nation? The answer has been fairly firmly stated: three things— help Congress govern; keep the record of the nation's experience; gather facts and knowledge to help the nation make decisions, innovate, and solve the problems that face our society.

How well has the Library done these things? Very well for many decades. It has become extraordinarily skilled at gathering facts from all over the world so American thinkers can know as much as is known anywhere as quickly as possible. Within the limits of traditional technology, the Library has been extremely skillful in **organizing** the knowledge it has gathered so that material can be found and used very quickly. The Library has done a good job telling the users what it has and what knowledge is known. It has done a good job of attaching skilled specialists to this knowledge to help the users use the materials efficiently. It has housed the knowledge with care and (again within the traditional technology) has preserved it as well as anyone. It has satisfied its obligations to the legislature by giving it the fastest, most responsible information transfer system in the country.

The interior dome of the Main Reading Room, showing the collar mural.

But if we look in the other direction, we find the beginning of some problems. The superlatives have slipped away in several areas.

Acquisition: Specialized libraries throughout the nation have better collections on their specialty, and they are better organized for retrieval. Books? No, the sharper targets of reports and studies—what the Library of Congress calls "ephemera," but what the specialists call the daily "nitty-gritty" data for their work. Even such soft and undersupported targets as community public libraries have better collections about their local industries, their local history, and their local resources.

Control of the collections: OCLC computerized for the *users'* needs faster than the Library of Congress, which computerized for the institution's needs. The greater flexibility of the OCLC approach has made it more appealing to local libraries, who have taken Library of Congress data but have organized it in modified models of the OCLC approach. After a hundred years of LC cataloging leadership, applied computerized cataloging and working networks have been developed with the Library of Congress watching helplessly from across the valley.

Private industry has been far more innovative in exploiting the computer's analytical and retrieval potential. Such electronic systems as Lockheed, SDC, the Times Infobank, and NEXIS have placed windows in their data banks and threaded passageways through their stored materials with far greater imagination and precision than the very limited number of access points LC has given to its rich holdings. Thanks to inventive devices from NASA, DDC, and *Chemical Abstracts,* key words in and out of context, analyzed abstracts, and multiple subject headings are taken for granted in the commercial systems.

Telling the world what was in the Library's collections: For seventy-five years, the Library sprayed its printed cards around the Western intellectual world and distributed its book catalogs (with the help of such private publishers as Ursell, University Microfilms, Carrollton Press, et cetera) so everyone knew what was in LC. But with the great overseas acquisition programs, the Library of Congress became so distracted processing books printed in far-off, little-read languages that card preparation for U.S. commercial publishing got slower and slower. U.S. libraries gave up waiting for the ever more expensive bibliographic data to arrive from LC and turned to the private sector. Today, private industry prints catalogs faster, with more flexible formats than LC has ever attained, and the computer networks gush tailored cards and inventory records like a mountain stream.

Specialized curators are getting harder and harder to draw to Washington: Government salaries are no longer as attractive as they once were, regional appeal is now stronger than the traditional "go to New York or Washington and make your mark" lure, and the chance to work in small, innovative units looks ever more tempting to the recognized leaders in subject and format specialties. Each year, it becomes harder to convince "the names" to pull up roots and go to their nation's capital.

Preserving the great collections: Like a stock science fiction plot, "the inexorable enemy" is eating up the stored knowledge. The severest decay started with the materials of the 1890s, and it has now crept straight through to the receipts of the 1930s. From this point on, deterioration will explode through the greatly increased postwar acquisitions at an exponential rate.

A Choice of Directions

From all this we come to a crossroads. From what we have really learned from everything above, one path is decentralization. Smaller units "back home" seem to work better than vast edifices in Washington. Networks are more responsive to their local clienteles. Local libraries know what their users want and can give it to them. Postage rates are going sky-high, and interlibrary loans may soon cost more than the books themselves. Senior scholars who wish to work at the Library of Congress are losing grants and travel money, the cost of air tickets is breathtaking, and hotel rooms in Washington cost more for one night than a week's rent in Amarillo. It is time either to create regional "national libraries" or to start building specialized units that are total— every known book on geology, everything on social security, everything on music regardless of format, source, or application. These specialized pods would be linked by telecommunication in the present manner of the research nets, and we would concentrate on transshipping the material via facsimiles, satellites, even American Library Association couriers in the manner of parcel service companies driving ALA trucks.

The other path is the electronic library, and since the Library of Congress is exploring this option in minute detail as this book is being written, we will look at it in considerable detail. What we are talking about here is embracing the technology of digital storage and *immediately* shifting the entire Library into the world of television screens/videodiscs/ high-speed printers/computer tapes and disk packs. And note, this is not some futuristic fantasy. The Library has already started with portions of the sequence in the Congressional Research Service and the Catalog Distribution Service. If the word is given, the full shift can be in train by 1985. Let's look first at what we're talking about and then at the impact it could have.

The idea hangs on the videodisc, which is presently being sold to show movies on home television screens. The videodisc is "read" by

Videodisc technology may soon radically alter the way the Library of Congress acquires and stores its materials.

a laser beam examining smooth and rough dots in tracks in a manner distantly analogous to the way a phonograph needle tracks a groove and reproduces the original sound of an orchestra. What is news about the device is that for the first time, we can capture and hold not sound but digital "yeses or noes" or "ons or offs" that give us letters and figures, and for the first time, we have a reasonable chance of preserving them. Up to now, these "bytes" have been magnetic on metal, and as anyone who has been frustrated by a computer program that suddenly ceased to work knows, these bytes can be erased and lost by cosmic rays, sun spots, clumsy operators, faulty recording heads, floods, and vengeful employees. The videodisc drills the data into metal, glass, fiber, or ceramic, and (as the sponsors are quick to tell you) you can bury it in sea sand for 100 years, and when you dredge it up from the ocean, all you have to do is rinse it off under the faucet, and it will play as well as the day it was made.

When the videodisc technology is applied to the home movie and television world, it is done crudely so that copies can be produced by the hundreds of thousands yet sell for no more than a ticket to a movie house. The disc that is produced is, in fact, a spiral string of pits that when scanned by a laser beam in the home unit, duplicate the individual frames of a motion picture film. The videodisc holds 54,000 frames per side, and these are re-created on your television screen at 30 frames per second to give the illusion of moving figures. But any single frame can be frozen and displayed endlessly. One of the first applications of the device was to put slides of painting on the discs, one at a time, and thus create an inventory or a catalog of the paintings in museums. In this case, one simply slides the inventory disc into the scanner and punches in a number; the scanner locates that particular frame and projects the painting digitalized in that frame, in color, instantaneously on the TV screen. As startling and effective as the result may be, this is simply the primitive, home version of the invention. The industrial application that will be used by libraries is a much larger, more precise and flexible version of the idea, and this is known as the digital optical disk.

The Digital Optical Disk

The digital optical disk can store library materials in two different ways that are of great importance to the Library of Congress. The first form is an extension of the television videodisc noted above. Instead of capturing frames of motion picture scenes, a library will capture pages—pages of foreign ideographs; pages of historical, handwritten correspondence; pages of photographs or copyright forms. The page will be swept with a laser beam, and in the minutest divisions of space the beam will ask, Is this space dark or light? What gradation of dark or light? It will then store the answer on the disk. The laser can sweep and store typewritten memos with only 200 lines of scan per inch (in the general manner of wirephoto technology). It will require 300 lines to the inch to pick up the four- and six-point subscripts and footnotes of scientific text, 480 lines to the inch to duplicate Japanese and Chinese brush writing, and 1,200 lines to the inch to do fine art facsimiles.

All of these resolutions are now used and are easily acquired, but obviously, the more lines per page that have to be preserved on the disk, the fewer total pages the disk will carry. The book you hold in your hand can be stored and then duplicated with great precision— the serifs on each letter properly captured and redisplayed—and it can be scanned with about 2,700 lines per page. In this mode, a typical optical disk will carry 20,576 pages of a book this size on one side of a disk. This book has approximately 350 pages, and therefore a single, thin optical disk can carry 116 volumes of this size, or more than 10 feet of shelving of books this thick. One foot of optical disks standing side by side will thus store over 10,000 volumes and eliminate the need for nearly 1,000 feet of shelving.

Store 10,000 volumes of *what* books? At this point in the development of the idea, it is essential to ask the question, What books would you put on optical disks? and the answer is, Not the ones most people want! Recall, in a large research library, it is estimated that less than one-fifth of the collection will be used in any twenty-year period. The curse has always been to guess what fifth that will be. But we discovered earlier that in the Library of Congress, the copyrighted, commercial volumes are the most heavily used, even though in any one year, the copyrighted pieces represent only 5 percent of the total volumes acquired. So you need not put the copyrighted volumes on optical disks. The book format is still the most efficient means of storage for these working words, and since only 350,000 copyrighted books are added to the collections in any year, they could be easily deacidified by the diethyl-zinc process before they were put on the shelves.

If you don't put the commercial books on optical disks, what do you capture? Books in nonroman characters, indeed possibly all non-English volumes; all government documents and unbound scientific papers; probably all modern manuscripts. How would you get these materials onto the disks? Simply by substituting the optical disk production line for the present microfilming procedures. Remember, the Library is presently photographing nearly 7 million pages of books and serials each year, one page at a time, with microfilming cameras. Using the new technology, instead of making photographic negatives of each preserved page, the pages would be swept by digital scanners, and the laser would burn the necessary pits and burrs into the disk surfaces.

Thus, the first application of digital optical technology is that of scanning a page, reducing what the laser sees to lines of black and white, storing this data until it is needed, and then duplicating the scans back on a CRT screen or printing it out on paper. The data is indestructible and vastly compressed.

The second application is equally permanent and even more compressed, but it can be used only for Western-language type. It is based on the fact that a page has a great deal of white, wasted space on it. If you didn't have to store the margins, the space between the lines, and the wasted spaces at the beginning and ends of paragraphs, you could "crush" the actual letters into an even smaller storage space. To do this, the inventors abandoned the idea of storing a *picture* of a page and instead store only the digital bytes representing the letters plus instructions telling the printer how much and where to leave white space when the material is printed or projected back. This method permits even greater compression. Something approaching the text content of 3,200 books will go on the same disk that will store only 116 volumes when the facsimile method is used. Using this mode, twelve inches of disks carrying digital text will hold the contents of over 300,000 volumes—half the holdings of most college libraries!

The question, of course, becomes, How do you take a book page and digitalize each character without key-stroking all the letters in (at vast personnel cost)? The answer is twofold. If the printing type is reasonably standard, it can be scanned by the optical scanner used by the post office or book clubs, and the print will be converted to digital text "untouched by human hand." But even better would be to *receive* the text in digitalized form. Nowadays, most books and newspapers are printed from digital text, most government documents are created on digital word processors, and most magazines are sent over the wire to distant printing houses. It would be simple to request the deposit of digital text in return for some service—or indeed, even for payment of a fee by the Library in return for the saving of the present costs of binding and storage.

The Library, surprisingly, has had experience with both of the major choices—facsimile and direct digital text—for several years. In the Cataloging Distribution Service, Japanese and Chinese catalog card copy has routinely been sent to Japan where individual cards are created with all the delicate complexities of oriental ideographs. A single, master copy of each is returned to the Library of Congress where it is scanned by an optical disk recorder, and its delicate characters are stored in optical disk pits. If a U.S. library asks for a set of any specific card, the optical disk is read, and the data are sent to a printer that re-creates it in eight copies (both scanning the disk by laser and then printing it with another laser tied to a xerographic copier). The final product is a complete author-title-subject set of cards for the requesting library.

The Word-Processing World

The basic elements of the digital text storage technique have also been tried in the Congressional Research Service. In 1970, the CRS took away the typewriters (and paper) from a hundred of its researchers and substituted television terminals instead, each with a screen and a silent typewriter keyboard. Thereafter, all their reports, Issue Briefs, and white papers have been typed and displayed on the CRT screens. For the sake of this explanation, let's get out of the multiple formats and trace the development of an Issue Brief—traditionally, a short pamphlet explaining a current congressional issue and the options possible for ameliorating it.

The researcher creates the brief directly on the word processor. The CRT can be manipulated to insert text, create statistical tables, shift footnotes, and generally massage the report until it satisfies the author.

Once the report is finished, a plastic "floppy disk" is pulled out of the side of the machine and sent to the reviewer. The reviewer puts the disk in his machine, displays the text on his CRT, makes whatever changes he thinks are required, and "bursts" the text into the Library's central computer.

The last is the key step. The text of that Issue Brief now sits in the computer indefinitely as digital blips. In the old days, it would have been run off as a mimeographed or multilithed report and 4,000 copies would have been stockpiled. But no longer. If the author wants to keep a copy for his files, he tells his CRT terminal to print one off on the printer by his desk. Otherwise, the text sits in the CRS computer until a congressman or a congressional staff member wants to read it. (For those researchers not yet using the word-processing equipment, secretarial typists key-stroke the approved product into the computer so, at the present time, *all* CRS Issue Briefs are on-line and *only* in the Library's main frame.)

If a congressman wants to read an Issue Brief in his office (let's say he wants one on social security financing), he will ask his CRT terminal for a list of issue subjects, and the CRT will display the number of the proper brief to request. The member can then ask that this Issue Brief be displayed on his CRT, and he can read it instantaneously. If he wants a copy to take home with him, he can have it printed out. If he wants 500 copies made to distribute at a meeting, he calls the CRS, the CRS instructs the computer to make a microfiche of the Issue Brief, the microfiche is put on a high-speed copier, and the "pamphlet" is produced on paper for less than a penny a page.

But the point is, the text of the pamphlet is preserved solely as digital blips in the computer until someone has some use for it. There is no paper "original" anywhere, and the digital blips were created by the author as he wrote the piece, not by a computer person or a typesetter.

But enough about the technology. No matter which of the above choices are embraced, their effect on libraries will be revolutionary. Let's note some of the obvious impacts the invention will have—and note how many of the problems we found building in the Library of Congress that would suddenly be almost miraculously solved!

The Impact of the Invention

The first two solutions the disks make possible leap out at you. The endless construction of new buildings can finally slow down and possibly even stop for a generation or two. Even if only the foreign-language volumes were on disks, any *one* of the present three major buildings of the Library of Congress could hold everything the Library now owns with room for expansion for many years to come. Bulk and size shrink in our concern.

The deterioration of paper, film, and tape can be ignored at last. What the optical disk will be made of is still being debated, but at the present time, the different materials used appear to be stable for at least 100 years. Librarians, of course, have been assured of perpetual permanency before. Their microfilm and their microfiche were supposed to last longer than man, but they have proved to last only thirty to fifty years before serious trouble sets in. It should have been simple enough to rephotograph the microforms, but experience has proved that in microforming from the original, 20 percent of the definition is lost at the outset. When, in turn, duplicates are made of microform, they inherit a second 20 percent loss. In no time at all, the sequential process closes up all open letters, blurs the type, fills in shadows on pictures, and in general, degrades the microforms. In the case of digital storage, on the other hand, if monitoring detects deterioration in the storage material, the conservators can simply reload the same blips onto a new base with zero loss in the duplication.

The most awesome advantage of the technology is the thought of a library without "Not-on-Shelf" reports. The reader, sitting before a CRT, will have the sublime bibliographic experience of knowing that every book is in place and deliverable at his command. It cannot be stolen, misshelved, waiting to be replaced, defaced, or in use. A book will be scanned by the reading head instantaneously, and the digital data moved to the reader's CRT to be held until the reader calls it up for display, thus freeing the prime data on the parent disk for instant scanning and delivery to another reader.

There will be a sobering impact on cataloging. It might be appropriate to go back to Melvil Dewey's catechism from the beginning of nineteenth-century librarianship: Why are we keeping all this material in the first place? Answer: To use it. To educate ourselves with, to preserve our memory, to answer our questions. Then what must we do so we can find it when we need it? Answer: We must know what we have in our libraries, we must know what book (disk) has the answer in it, and where we placed that book (disk) in storage. (We will have to add, we must know where on that disk the particular piece of writing we want is.)

But it is easy to see that the traditional answers to the traditional questions fall apart with videodisc technology—or at least traditional cataloging techniques do. If every disk has some 3,000 books on it, we can no longer shelve "books" by call number and keep inserting the latest volume in among its subject peers. Subject classification by class number on open shelves for browsing can be forgotten. The present guess is that the disks will be loaded in the manner of a bookstore: all fiction on one "wall," political science on another, cookbooks, history by country, psychology, children's books, biology, et cetera. Within each broad category, it is assumed that the books will be stored sequentially by an acquisition number (probably the LC card number or the International Standard Book Number), and they will probably be sorted first by language and then by order of receipt.

A great deal of time is now spent selecting one or two subject headings to describe a book and then to tell the computer what subjects have been assigned each volume. Since the books will no longer be shelved by class number and there will no longer be cards filed by alphabetical subject heading, we can use many more subjects to describe the books; we can search by key words in the titles; and we can consider going on to key words in abstracts, chapter headings, or indexes, et cetera. The computerized catalog, which seemed to be the best of a bad bargain, suddenly makes the compression of many documents on a single storage element both possible and desirable.

And so on. The ramifications of the possible change enlarge geometrically, but for our present purposes the following assertions are sufficient. Everyone in the Library presently studying optical disk technology is convinced that it is real. One or both of the storage techniques *is* the way research materials (as distinct from literary and aesthetic records) will be stored in the future. One or the other of the techniques will work as well for photographic prints, motion pictures, handwritten colonial letters, pen-and-ink musical staffs, underground newspapers, copyrighted soap operas, provincial Pakistani tax records, and Jet Propulsion Lab scans of Io as they do for preserving the current *World Almanac.*

But Do We Need A National Library to Do It?

This brings us to the two bedrock questions of the Library's future: One, What will the Library be in the twenty-first century, now barely years away; and two, What *should* the Library be in the year 2000? Leaving the technology aside (never mind how it is to be done), let us see what the people involved with the Library think it should be doing.

For one and a half years, the authors of this book have been posing those questions both to people working for the Library and to those people across the country who use it and have to deal with it in their own work. We have received an astonishingly broad spectrum of response. On only three aspects is there anything approaching a

As a national library, the Library of Congress reaches out to other like institutions around the world. Here Soviet Culture Minister Petr Demichev and others discuss mutual concerns with Librarian Daniel Boorstin.

consensus regarding the Library's proper role in American life—but the people with whom we spoke have had very clear and definite ideas about what its roles should be. We found we could rarely complete the querying sentence before the responder told us firmly what the proper answer was!

The people we talked with can be rather easily divided into the optimists and the pessimists, and we will deal with their thoughts in like arrangement. The most despairing response of all came from one of the most powerful and professionally important of the respondents, and we would like to state his position at once and then somewhat hastily move on to the more creative projections of the future. His reply: "What will the Library be in the 2000s? Just what it is now. It will go on and on, getting less and less responsive and less and less useful to its audiences. It will get bigger and bigger and grayer and grayer and nothing much will change anywhere." But won't the patrons demand improvements? "No. They'll just go someplace else for what they need, and no one will have the nerve to turn it off. It's like a glacier. A glacier just goes on and on. Sometimes it moves a little faster and sometimes a little slower, but nobody says, 'Hey, that thing is taking up a lot of space, let's get rid of it.' No, the only thing that will really change is the way the materials will be kept. What the librarians will do with them. You can come back in twenty years, and they'll still be holding the same committee meetings they are now."

Fortunately, we heard that view only once, so having fulfilled our promise to put it in the record, let us move on to the perceptions of the year and a half's interviewees.

Consensus

The guesses veered toward two poles. The first involved the belief that efficiency calls for a single great center of data collection and storage, and comments from this group were directed toward how to make this great center one of maximum usefulness to the nation. The opposite pole was the belief that regional centers could place the riches of the national library within reach of a far greater number of users and thus the holdings could enter the intellectual bloodstream of the nation more quickly, through more disciplines and use by more people, if there were Library of Congress outposts in a dozen parts of the country.

Although the two opposing camps were both clear-cut and vehement, there were three roles for the Library on which there was almost total agreement from all the respondents. Let's state these first.

Acquisitions

Everyone agreed that the Library of Congress should be the prime acquirer of research materials for the nation. Acquiring broad sweeps of foreign materials was considered to be of greatest importance, with securing the fragments of the American memory—the totality of the history of the American experience—a close second.

At first glance, both of those two areas of acquisition would appear to be obvious and self-evident. But not so. Of the 100 identifiable national libraries functioning in the world today, only two beside LC make any effort at all to secure materials originating outside their own borders. In the remaining 97 countries, the universities and the specialized institutes are responsible for acquiring the extranational material; the national library in each is limited to domestic output. In a few countries, the national library publishes a central bibliography, which includes some of the university holdings (primarily as a location device), but the national library's role is solely bibliographic. It is not expected to retain or make available the nonnational materials it cites.

And that fact directs attention to one of the most frequent points of issue among the people with whom the authors spoke. A substantial number believe that the Library of Congress should acquire foreign materials in great quantity on the ground that through its single acquisition points in over 200 countries, it can acquire the world's publishing in the most efficient manner. But once it gets the material to this country, it should catalog it ("get it under bibliographic control," "make and publish citations") and then unload the material on to other institutions. The Library of Congress should be the acquisition and bibliographic center (which, of course, could be located in a surplus military base and need not take up Capitol Hill space), and the materials it secures should then be sent free to specialized research centers, universities, professional associations—out where the greatest number of people related to each form of expertise are actually located. This group felt that the Library of Congress should retain books needed by Congress to help it govern the country but that belle lettres from abroad, highly specialized scientific material, and foreign-language publications in general should be transferred directly to representative institutions of the various disciplines.

Congressional Data

Congressional data represent the second area of agreement between the two camps. Everyone agrees that the Library of Congress must remain the world's finest legislative library, which would mean that in the coming century, the Library would greatly enhance its receipts from state and local governments. It also means that the kinds of materials secured for Congress's use would include daily, weekly, and monthly statistical receipts and there would be a greatly expanded program of acquiring in-process studies, agency interim reports, and reports of ongoing governmental activities, in contrast to LC's present practice of waiting for everything to appear in books (usually several years after the resolution of the social issue under inquiry). In the process of serving Congress, every new data bank and computer service should be examined, and if any open any windows of knowledge on the nation's problems, they should be acquired and made available to the legislature through the Library.

Professionwide Standards

The third area of general consensus is that the Library of Congress should remain the center of bibliographic standards. This role means not only that the Library should be the primary point of creation of national and international cataloging rules, but it should also be the primary source of digital bibliographic formats, microfilming standards, uniformity of digital optical formats and materials, standards of photographic preservation techniques, paper treatment studies, interlibrary loan protocols, uniform subject classifications, uniform subject headings for all English-speaking libraries, and (full circle) uniform rules for author entries—the national author authority file.

When asked if the various scientific and social disciplines could not produce more sensitive retrieval tools and more useful classification schedules than could LC's distant librarians, everyone declared a firm no. Scientists at the AAAS convention, historians at the AHA, political scientists at the APSA all agreed that the Library of Congress can fulfill those functions better—"if you leave it up to us, we will argue endlessly, and no subject would ever be resolved."

The library world has become increasingly involved in cooperative cataloging and shared acquisitions, and we posed the question, How would it work if the first institution to receive a volume would catalog it and then feed the cataloging into library nets for everyone else to use? (Since the most specialized libraries tend to be the first to receive books in their specialties, the processing by their own specialized catalogers might be expected to be more suited to how the newly received materials would actually be used.) Couldn't the working specialists do it better? Sometimes, we were told, but not often enough to make it worth changing the system. No, in the year 2000, the Library of Congress should still be the first to catalog all research materials and set the formats for capturing the data. LC should continue to load the tapes for the other nets and facilities, and the only difference between what is and what ought to be is that the Library should do more of it. Indeed much more. The Library should process paperbacks and microforms and more in-process technical reports. It should do more material from local governments and industries and labor unions. But most important overall, LC must set the standards. Realistically, no other institution can do that job as well.

And thus the sympathetic consensus. Now let's hear from the revisionists.

The Pessimistic Point of View

There are some who think the day of the enormous central library is past. They believe that future Librarians of Congress must no longer assume that a comprehensive collection of all subjects and formats, all reinforcing each other, is automatically good. Rather, each element of the traditional activities must be examined to see if the resources invested in it might not be better kept at the local level. Example: If the technology of optical digital storage (or even the simple home videodisc) does come to pass, should not the Library of Congress package its foreign materials by language and distribute "all" French materials, "all" Russian materials, et cetera, to each of the state universities, the land grant colleges, or possibly even the U.S. government document depositories? With motion pictures appearing routinely on commercial videodiscs, does the great central motion picture collection need to be in Washington? Can it not be assumed that most research institutions will have the visual materials as part of their routine collections? (Motion pictures at the Library of Congress are now stored off-site in a huge, multistoried, refrigerated warehouse.) Since any manuscript collection the Library of Congress owns can easily rest on a single optical disk, can't they be sold or loaned to any university when and where appropriate research is going forward? Should not the Manuscript Division be considered a lending library in the future rather than a service area? And so on.

In short, these people believe that the Library in the twenty-first century should shift from bringing all information together in a single, one-stop, highly efficient research environment and change into an institution that is dedicated to getting its informational treasures into as many local research scenes as possible. It should spend its current resources less on perpetual preservation and more on dissemination. If the material the Library holds is so valuable to the thinking leaders of the United States, it should be made as convenient as possible to as many of them as possible.

The "it will never be the same again" school believes that the Library of Congress has grown too large to be governed in the traditional manner. There are too many programs doing different things to try to keep it all together. Although General Motors is enormous, most of it is dedicated to a single product—making moving vehicles. The Library of Congress is dedicated to a hundred different ends and suffers from all the resultant ills. How do you recruit your managers? The Map Division should have a nationally known geographer; the Music Division, a nationally known musicologist; the Congressional Research Service, a nationally known political scientist. But, traditionally, the managerial pyramid has lifted each of these highly specialized leaders higher and higher into supervision of areas worlds apart from their training and personal interests. The Smithsonian Institution, Harvard University, et cetera, have faced the same problem but have solved it by letting each specialized area stand as an entity, headed by a leader in that field. The Library of Congress has never "let go" from the Librarian's Office and has always insisted that the Copyright Office be a *library*-centered activity, the CRS a *library*-kind of division, the activities for the blind a *library*-type program, while each of the specialists who would normally relate to a different world (law, Congress, work with the handicapped, and so on) have felt themselves strangers in a foreign camp. Worse, according to the interviewees expressing this thought, the situation has left the non-library-world staff of the Library convinced that not only can they never get the managerial support and understanding they deserve, but the Library management is forced to discipline them— keep them in their place—in order to keep the institution as a whole coherent, controlled, and working as the *Library* of Congress.

This perception leads people in this group to project a twenty-first-century Library of Congress as a much looser, much more flexible (they would say much more innovative) federalized structure. It would be composed of people with many different kinds of skills "doing their thing" to the best of their ability, more responsive to their own differing clienteles rather than to the least common denominator of the patrons of the general reading rooms.

The criticism that the Library has gotten too big appeared in many complaints about its insensitivity to its clienteles. Some people said that if the Congressional Research Service is to flourish in the year 2000 (and keep the Congressional Budget Office from skimming off the CRS's most significant services), it will have to intensify its querying Congress, "What do you want us to do?" The CRS is perceived as having gone through three stages: (1) its early years of doing *any* service requested by members of Congress in order to assure its survival; (2) being overwhelmed with work and having to choose those products it could do best with the resources it had; and (3) telling Congress in the best bureaucratic manner what the CRS would accept and what it wouldn't and that what was left over was not of its concern. The Copyright Office is perceived as having gotten so large and so tradition-bound that its record keeping and its requirements for protection are unnecessarily complex; European methods of author protection are just as effective with less than half the time, effort, and cost expended by this country. The century-old complaint by the library profession that the Library of Congress is too interested in its own needs and too little concerned with the needs of the public and research libraries could be entered under this category of complaint. Each of these complaints ended with the admonition that if the Library doesn't improve its techniques for finding out what its clients want and then responding to those requests, the clients will simply go somewhere else to satisfy their needs.

Finally, we heard from a few who in effect were challenging the assumption of progress. They noted that the Library of Congress was built on the given that more knowledge results in better solutions. More data spurs innovation. Once people know everything about everything, there is nothing that cannot be made better for man. These commentators worried that there is not enough proof that all the knowledge and experience stored in the Library of Congress has made enough difference to the American society to justify the resources it has absorbed. When pressed as to what device is likely to be better or what damage has been done by the solution thus far tried, they were unwilling to abandon the concept or the institution but fretted that such a massive investment of time and treasure does not seem to have had a comparable impact. People expressing this concern offered little advice on what could be done about their distress, but the frustration was expressed often enough that it appeared to deserve mention.

The Optimists

The people interviewed who held the opposing view defended a large, centralized, comprehensive national library and brushed off the pessimists' concerns with casual disdain. The criticisms expressed by the pessimists, they held, were simply the result of the normal wear and tear of any large institution trying to do many different things for many different people. The optimists believe that the Library of Congress has done an astonishingly effective job of satisfying a broad spectrum of demands and that it makes a major contribution to the nation on many levels.

Symbolism

The Library's mere presence, supported by generations of dedicated professionals, justifies its existence. It states the nation's belief in progress and its dedication to knowledge, to creative culture, to the worth of the American experience. Its role as a keeper of the nation's memory in itself would justify its cost. The symbolic aspect of LC appears at various levels. It symbolizes the profession of librarianship and dignifies each local institution; as a Colorado librarian stated, it helps us in our communities simply by making us important. It makes every library larger than itself because of the knowledge that the Library of Congress is available for the difficult materials, it provides the highest quality of bibliographic data, and it provides a unity of product that permits efficient information control and retrieval from the smallest bookmobile to the largest university library.

Improvements

This group holds that there are many ways of making the Library of Congress more useful in the twenty-first century and that there is no evidence that these improvements will not be embraced. The supporters of an extension of the present LC mode requested (and confidently expected to receive) the following.

1. More innovative leadership at the Library of Congress, so technical advances can be converted to prompt application in all libraries.

Marble pillars and curving arches combine with mosaics, murals, and sculpted figures to create a spectacular effect in the Library's Great Hall.

2. A recognition that the world of electronics and telecommunications can link every library by wire or satellite, making everything larger than any single element. They expect the Library of Congress to head up such elaborations of the present system.

3. They expect the Library of Congress to act as the local libraries' friend at court, presenting the case for the importance of knowledge and information to the Congress and the federal government.

4. Because of strong funding and institutional momentum, they expect the Library of Congress to "take some of the risks"—to be more innovative than the local libraries can be, to move more resources more effectively than smaller libraries can. (The defenders of the decentralized position say that this perception is completely reversed: A small, intensely motivated institution can always innovate faster and more effectively than a large one can. The others argue that the large institution has more resources to manipulate and often can "cover" experimentation more effectively.)

5. They expect the Library to abandon its (to them) arrogance and to quit playing the we-versus-they role. They expect the Library to work much more closely with the formal organizations of its clienteles—the American Historical Association, the Association for the Advancement of Science, the American Bar Association, et cetera—and certainly to

work more closely with the out-of-Washington working librarians. There should be more LC programs with the words "cooperative" and "shared" in them. The leadership role need not be as Olympian as the Library of Congress has traditionally played it.

Comprehensiveness

The supporters of a centralized, national library come down hard on the advantages of having all the world's knowledge in one place. They say that rather than technology making a large central collection irrelevant, it only strengthens the traditional case. Before, the book was preeminent, supported and reinforced by the photograph, the manuscript, the map, the microform. Now, they believe, the book will not become rarer but that the supportive formats will grow enormously. With the computer to index the manuscripts, the contents of the photographs, and the microforms, the varied substance of these added kinds of information will be infinitely easier to find and will relate to research that was previously supported by the book alone. The laser, the xerographic duplicator, and the optical disk will simply make it easier to store and copy and use the other formats. They will not supplant the other options, and being able to work in an environment where comprehensive collections all rest side by side will still be the most efficient way of acquiring, comparing, and analyzing knowledge.

The value of having skilled curators, service librarians, caring for each kind of material makes each piece of knowledge many times more valuable than the simple storage of the content. This broad knowledge would be hard to duplicate if every research institution had to provide its local equivalent. The optimists hold that the multiplicity of collections cultivated by career-trained specialists will continue to make the Library of Congress a unique knowledge center in the twenty-first century.

Conclusion

So where does all this bring us out? This is not the place to recapitulate the last sixteen chapters. If we have achieved our purpose, we have been suggesting choices—it can be done this way or that— all the way through the book, but the perceptions of the participants in the current library story seem to converge on the following points.

First, there is nothing in Holy Writ that decrees there shall be a Library of Congress. It does not appear in the Constitution or the Decalogue or the Code of Hammurabi. Its existence is justified only if it *works*—if it does indeed provide the services for which it has been created through nearly two centuries. Does the Library of Congress really help Congress govern? Does it provide the information Congress needs to make its decisions? Is the information that is selected and transferred accurate, is it appropriate, is it in time to be of any use to anyone? Can any other institution do a better job? Are there any devices that would make the Library of Congress more efficient and more useful in fulfilling its tasks? These are the first tests to be met, and they must be pressed within the congressional users, the library community, the information industry, and the public.

Second, the questions must be raised, Is the Library of Congress doing an adequate job of capturing and preserving the nation's history? Does it in fact cover the complete span of the American experience? Can the task be done better? Is any other institution challenging its role? Are there any devices or techniques that are being overlooked? Is LC carrying its charge aggressively and imaginatively or is it pursuing it passively and from habit?

Finally, there is the broadest of the Library's responsibilities: accumulating the knowledge needed for today's decisions and tomorrow's action. Is the Library really collecting what is known about what matters? Is it organizing that knowledge so it can be used? *Is* it being used? Has the Library told the working and intellectual disciplines what is available to them? Is the public getting its money's worth?

The answer to all these challenges, surprisingly enough, is currently positive. The Library is doing remarkably well for a large, governmental, somewhat remote public institution. But there are just enough criticisms nibbling at the edges, just enough hairline cracks appearing on the periphery to suggest that the next generation of managers must be very careful the Library does not run on inertial momentum but instead that they test every device, every technique, every end purpose to see that the nation is getting what it deserves. It's a fascinating future in a marvelous cause.

LIBRARIANS OF CONGRESS

John James Beckley, 1802–1807; appointed by Thomas Jefferson

Patrick Magruder, 1807–1815; appointed by Thomas Jefferson

George Watterston, 1815–1829; appointed by James Madison

John Silva Meehan, 1829–1861; appointed by Andrew Jackson

John G. Stephenson, 1861–1864; appointed by Abraham Lincoln

Ainsworth Rand Spofford, 1864–1897; appointed by Abraham Lincoln

John Russell Young, 1897–1899; appointed by William McKinley

Herbert Putnam, 1899–1939; appointed by William McKinley (Librarian of Congress Emeritus, by Act of Congress, 1939–1955)

Archibald MacLeish, 1939–1944; appointed by Franklin D. Roosevelt

Luther Harris Evans, 1945–1953; appointed by Harry S. Truman

L. Quincy Mumford, 1954–1974; appointed by Dwight D. Eisenhower

Daniel J. Boorstin, 1975–   ; appointed by Gerald R. Ford

BIBLIOGRAPHY

General

For detailed information on the Library of Congress, two continuing series are available in most of the nation's U.S. Government Document Depository Libraries:

U.S. Library of Congress. Annual report of the Librarian. Washington: The Library, 1866–
U.S. Library of Congress. Quarterly journal of the Library of Congress. Washington: The Library, 1943–

Individual studies follow:

Goodrum, Charles A. Treasures of the Library of Congress. New York: Abrams, 1980. 318 p.
Gurney, Gene and Nick Apple. The Library of Congress: a picture story of the world's largest library. New York: Crown, 1981.
Hamer, Elizabeth E. Everybody's library. Library journal, v. 90, Jan. 1, 1965: 49–55.
Kline, Fred. The Library of Congress: the nation's bookcase. National geographic magazine, v. 148, Nov. 1975: 671–87.
Lethbridge, Mary C. and James W. McClung. The Library of Congress. In Encyclopedia of library and information science, vol. 15. New York: Marcel Dekker, 1975. Pp. 19–93.
U.S. Library of Congress. Guide to the Library of Congress. Washington: The Library, 1982. 128 p.
Williams, Richard L. The Library of Congress can't hold all man's knowledge—but it tries. Smithsonian, v. 11, Apr. 1980: 38–48.

History

Benco, Nancy L. Archibald MacLeish: the poet Librarian. Quarterly journal of the Library of Congress, v. 33, July 1976: 237–55.

Berkeley, Edmund and Dorothy Smith Berkeley. The first Librarian of Congress, John Beckley. *Quarterly journal of the Library of Congress*, v. 32, Apr. 1975: 83–117.

Broderick, John C. John Russell Young: the internationalist as Librarian. *Quarterly journal of the Library of Congress*, v. 33, Apr. 1976: 117–149.

Carter, Constance. John Gould Stephenson: largely known and much liked. *Quarterly journal of the Library of Congress*, v. 33, Apr. 1976: 77–91.

Clapp, Verner W. and William J. Welsh, eds. The age of Cronin: aspect of the accomplishments of John W. Cronin, Library of Congress, 1925–1968. *Library resources & technical services*, v. 12, fall 1968: 385–405.

Cole, John Y. Ainsworth Rand Spofford: the valiant and persistent Librarian of Congress. *Quarterly journal of the Library of Congress*, v. 33, Apr. 1976: 93–115.

Cole, John Y. For Congress and the nation: a chronological history of the Library of Congress through 1975. Washington: U.S. Govt. Print. Off., 1979. 196 p.

Cole, John Y. Of copyright, men, and a national library. *Quarterly journal of the Library of Congress*, v. 28, Apr. 1971: 114–36.

Cole, John Y. A national monument for a national library: Ainsworth Rand Spofford and the new Library of Congress, 1871–1897. *Records of the Columbia Historical Societey of Washington, D.C.*, 1973: 468–507.

Gordon, Martin K. Patrick Magruder: citizen, Congressman, Librarian of Congress. *Quarterly journal of the Library of Congress*, v. 32, July 1975: 155–171.

Hilker, Helen-Anne. Ten First Street, Southeast: Congress builds a library, 1886–1897: an exhibition in the Great Hall and on the second floor of the Thomas Jefferson Building, Library of Congress. Washington: Library of Congress, 1980. 102 p.

Johnston, William D. History of the Library of Congress, Vol. 1, 1800–1864. Washington: U.S. Govt. Print. Off., 1904. 535 p.

Lacy, Dan. The Library of Congress: a sesquicentennial review. *Library quarterly*, v. 20, July 1950: 157–79; Oct. 1950: 235–58.

Ladenson, Alex. "I cannot live without books": Thomas Jefferson, bibliophile. *Wilson library bulletin*, v. 52, Apr. 1978: 624–631.

Malone, Dumas. Thomas Jefferson and the Library of Congress. Washington: Library of Congress, 1978. 31 p.

Matheson, William. George Watterston: advocate of the national library. *Quarterly journal of the Library of Congress*, v. 32, Oct. 1975: 370–388.

McDonough, John. John Silva Meehan: a gentleman of amiable manners. *Quarterly journal of the Library of Congress*, v. 33, Jan. 1976: 3–28.

Mearns, David C. Herbert Putnam, 1861–1955, a memorial tribute. Washington: Library of Congress, 1956. 52 p.

Mearns, David C. The story up to now: the Library of Congress, 1800–1946. Washington: U.S. Govt. Print. Off., 1947. 226 p. (Also in the Library's 1946 annual report, pp. 13–227.)

Milum, Betty. Choosing MacLeish's successor: the recurring debate. *Journal of library history*, v. 12, spring 1977: 92–98, 103–109.

Mumford, L. Quincy. Two decisive decades: the Library of Congress—twice as fast. *American libraries*, v. 3, July-Aug. 1972: 769–73.

Powell, Benjamin E. Lawrence Quincy Mumford: twenty years of progress. *Quarterly journal of the Library of Congress*, v. 33, July 1976: 275–304.

Radice, Anne-Imelda. The original Library of Congress: the history (1800–1814) of the Library of Congress in the United States Capitol. Washington: U.S. Govt. Print. Off., 1981. 110 p.

Sanford, Charles B. Thomas Jefferson and his library: a study of his literary interests and of the religious attitudes revealed by relevant titles in his library. Hamden, Conn.: Archon Books, 1977. 211 p.

Sittig, William J. Luther Evans: man for a new age. *Quarterly journal of the Library of Congress,* v. 33, July 1976: 250–267.

U.S. Congress. Joint Committee on the Library. Condition of the Library of Congress, 54th Cong., 2d sess., 1897. Washington: U.S. Govt. Print. Off., 1897. 302 p.

U.S. Congress. Senate. Committee on the Library. Hearings on various bills proposing the establishment of a Congressional Reference Bureau, 62d Cong., 3d sess. Washington: U.S. Govt. Print. Off., 1912.

U.S. Congress. Senate. Committee on Rules and Administration. Nomination of Daniel J. Boorstin of the District of Columbia to be Librarian of Congress. Washington: U.S. Govt. Print. Off., 1975. 435 p.

U.S. Copyright Office. Copyright in Congress, 1789–1904: a bibliography and chronological record of all proceedings in Congress in relation to copyright form April 15, 1789, to April 28, 1904, First Congress, 1st session, to Fifty-eighth Congress, 2d session, prepared by Thorvald Solberg. Washington: U.S. Govt. Print. Off., 1905. 468 p.

U.S. Library of Congress. The 1812 catalogue of the Library of Congress: a facsimile. Washington: Library of Congress, 1981. 167 p.

Library of Congress Programs and Services

Bestsellers, a selected list of books that have appeared in *Talking Book Topics* and *Braille Book Review.* Washington: National Library Service for the Blind and Physically Handicapped, 1979. 64 p.

A century of photographs, 1846–1946, selected from the collections of the Library of Congress; compiled by Renata V. Shaw. Washington: The Library, 1980. 211 p. (Consists of articles originally published in the *Quarterly journal of the Library of Congress* that explore the collections of the Prints and Photographs Division.)

Clapp, Verner W. The greatest invention since the title page? Auto-bibliography from incipit to cataloging-in-publication. *Wilson library bulletin,* v. 46, Dec. 1971: 348–59.

Cole, John Y. The Center for the Book in the Library of Congress. Washington: Library of Congress, 1979. 18 p.

Documenting a legacy: 40 years of the Historic American Buildings Survey. *Quarterly journal of the Library of Congress,* v. 30, Oct. 1973. 28 p.

Edlund, Paul. A monster and a miracle: the Cataloging Distribution Service of the Library of Congress, 1901–1976. Washington: Library of Congress, 1978. 40 p.

Goff, Frederick R. Uncle Sam has a book. *Quarterly journal of the Library of Congress,* v. 38, summer 1981: 122–133. (In re the Gutenberg Bible.)

Goodrum, Charles A. The reference factory revisited. *Library journal,* v. 93, Apr. 15, 1968: 1577–80.

Gwinn, Nancy E. Capitol Hill's hot line. *Library journal,* v. 100, Apr. 1, 1975: 640–643.

Hamer, Elizabeth E. The Library of Congress and enchanced bibliographical services to history. In Bibliography and the historian, ed. by Dagman H. Perman. Santa Barbara: ABC-Clio Press, 1968. Pp. 57–67.

Hilker, Helen-Anne. The quiet ferment. Library journal, v. 90, May 1, 1965: 2094–2103.

Hu, Shu Chao. The development of the Chinese collection in the Library of Congress. Boulder, Colo.: Westview Press, 1979. 259. p.

Kuiper, John B. Opportunities for film study at the Library of Congress. Film library quarterly, winter 1967-68: 30–32.

The Law Library of the Library of Congress: its history, collections, and services, edited and compiled by Kimberly W. Dobbs and Kathryn A. Haun. Washington: Library of Congress, 1978. 47 p.

Leavitt, Donald L. Recorded sound in the Library of Congress. Library trends, v. 21, July 1972: 53–59.

Liebaers, Herman. Shared cataloging. UNESCO bulletin for libraries, v. 24, March-Apr. 1970: 62–72; May-June 1970: 126–38.

Loo, Shirley and Bruce E. Langdon. Selective dissemination of information to Congress: the Congressional Research Service SDI service. Library resources & technical services, v. 19, fall 1975: 380–388.

Lorenz, John G., and others. The Library of Congress abroad. Library trends, v. 20, Jan. 1972: 548–76.

Malbin, Michael J. CRS—the congressional agency that just can't say "no." National journal, v. 9, Feb. 19, 1977: 284–289.

Mearns, David C. A fog-laden panorama of LC's collections. Library journal, v. 90, Apr. 1, 1965: 1600–07; and Apr. 15, 1965: 1834–40.

Melville, Annette. Special collections in the Library of Congress: a selective guide. Washington: Library of Congress, 1980. 464 p.

Orcutt, William Dana. The Stradivari memorial at Washington, the national capital. New York: Da Capo Press, 1977. 49 p.

Performing Arts Library. The Performing Arts Library of the Library of Congress and the Kennedy Center. Washington: The Library, 1981. 15 p.

That all may read: library services for blind and physically handicapped people, edited by Jane Poel. Washington: National Library Service for the Blind and Physically Handicapped, 1981.

U.S. Library of Congress. Archive of Folk Song. The Archive of Folk Song: a 50th anniversary celebration, November 16, 1978. Washington: Archive of Folk Song, American Folklife Center, Library of Congress, 1978. 16 p.

U.S. Library of Congress. Congressional Research Service. Library of Congress information resources and services for the U.S. House of Representatives: a report prepared for the Ad Hoc Subcommittee on Computers of the Committee on House Administration, written and compiled by CRS Task Force—Robert L. Chartrand et al. Washington: U.S. Govt. Print. Off., 1976. 110 p.

U.S. Library of Congress. Geography and Map Division. The Geography and Map Division: a guide to its collections and services. Washington: The Library, 1975. 42 p.

U.S. Library of Congress. Information resources and services available from the Library of Congress and the Congressional Research Service; communication from the Chairman, House Commission on Information and Facilities. Washington: U.S. Govt. Print. Off., 1976. 100 p. (94dth Cong., 2d sess. House. Document no. 94-527)

U.S. Library of Congress. Music Division. The Coolidge Auditorium and Whittall Pavilion in the Library of Congress. Washington: The Library, 1979. 12 p.

U.S. Library of Congress. Prints and Photographs Division. The poster collection in the Library of Congress. Washington: The Library, 1979. 16 p.

U.S. Library of Congress. Prints and Photographs Division. Viewpoints: a selection from the pictorial collections of the Library of Congress. Washington: The Library, 1975. 223 p.

U.S. Library of Congress. Processing Department. Processing Department of the Library of Congress: organization and functions. Washington: The Library, 1977. 35 p.

U.S. Library of Congress. Rare Book Division. The Rare Book Division: a guide to its collections and services. Rev. ed. Washington: The Library, 1965. 51 p.

U.S. Library of Congress. Science Policy Research Division. Information support for the U.S. Senate: a survey of computerized CRS resources and services, prepared for the Subcommittee on Computer Services of the Committee on Rules and Administration, U.S. Senate. Washington: U.S. Govt. Print. Off., 1977. 88 p.

U.S. Library of Congress. Subject Cataloging Division. Library of Congress subject headings. Washington: Library of Congress, 1980. 2 v. 2591 p.

Witherell, Julian W. Africana in the Library of Congress: the role of the African section. *Quarterly journal of the Library of Congress,* v. 27, July 1970: 184–96.

Administration and Philosophy

Benderly, Beryl Lieff. The world's greatest library: it's not such a good place to read a book. *Washingtonian,* v. 13, Mar. 1978: 136–139, 164–171.

Bowker, Richard R. The American national Library. *Library journal,* v. 21, Aug. 1896: 357–358.

The Bryant Memorandum on "The Library of Congress" and the Report of the Librarian of Congress on the Bryant Memorandum. In the Annual report of the Librarian of Congress for 1962. Washington: U.S. Govt. Print. Off., 1963. Pp. 89–111.

Buckland, Lawrence F. The role of the Library of Congress in the evolving national network: a study commissioned by the Library of Congress Network Development Office and funded by the National Commission on Libraries and Information Science. Washington: Library of Congress, 1978. 141 p.

Butterfield, Lyman H. An African game preserve: a scholar's view of LC. *Library journal,* v. 90, Dec. 15, 1965: 5333–40.

Chartrand, Robert Lee. Congressional management and use of information technology. *Journal of systems management,* v. 29, Aug. 1978: 10–15.

Clarke, Edith E. A Congressional Library or a national Library? *Library journal,* v. 22, Jan. 1897: 7–9.

Cohen, Richard E. The watchdogs for Congress often bark the same tune. *National journal,* v. 11, Sept. 8, 1979: 1484–1488.

Cole, John Y. For Congress and the nation: the dual nature of the Library of Congress. *Quarterly journal of the Library of Congress,* v. 32, Apr. 1975: 118–138.

Congress automates its information. *Government executive,* v. 9, Nov. 1977: 46, 48.

Council on Library Resources. A National Periodicals Center: technical development plan. Washington: The Council, 1978. 255 p.

Jones, Charles A. Why Congress can't do policy analysis (or words to that effect). *Policy analysis,* v. 2, spring 1976: 251–264.

The Library of Congress and its influence on law librarianship. *Law library journal*, v. 69, Nov. 1976: 554–575.

The Library of Congress as the national bibliographic center: report of a program sponsored by the Association of Research Libraries, October 16, 1975. Washington: The Association, 1976. 58 p.

The Library of Congress as the national library: potentialities for service. In Libraries at large: tradition, innovation, and the national interest, ed. by Douglas M. Knight and E. Shepley Nourse. New York: Bowker, 1969. Pp. 435–65.

Library of Congress Network Advisory Group. Toward a national library and information service network: the library bibliographic component, ed. by Henriette D. Avram and Lenore S. Maruyama. Washington: Library of Congress, 1977. 54 p.

The Library of Congress in perspective: a volume based on the reports of the 1976 Librarian's Task Force and advisory groups, ed. by John Y. Cole. New York: Bowker, 1978. 281. p.

MacLeish, Archibald. The reorganization of the Library of Congress, 1939–1944. *Library quarterly*, Oct. 1944: 277–315.

Molz, R. Kathleen. The Library of Congress: hydra and dinosaur. *Library journal*, v. 103, Oct. 15, 1978: 2052–2055.

Plotnik, Art. Washington library power: who has it and how it works for you. *American libraries*, v. 6, Dec. 1975: 647–656, 661–674.

Putnam, Herbert. The Library of Congress as a national library. *Library journal*, v. 30, Sept. 1905: C27–C34.

Rogers, Rutherford D. Administering a giant: an intimate view. *Library journal*, v. 90, Oct. 15, 1965: 4303–10.

Schick, Allan. The supply and demand for analysis on Capitol Hill. *Policy analysis*, v. 2, spring 1976: 215–234.

Spofford, Ainsworth R. The function of a national library. In Handbook of the new Library of Congress, comp. by Herbert Small. Boston: Curtis & Cameron, 1899. Pp. 123–28.

U.S. Library of Congress. Recruitment and Placement Office. Careers in the Library of Congress. Washington: The Library, 1981. 9 p.

Wechsler, Jill. Fact factory for Congress. *Nation's business*, v. 66, May 1978: 50–54, 56.

INDEX